Langenscheidt
Verbtabellen

Englisch

Verbformen nachschlagen und trainieren

Von Dr. Lutz Walther

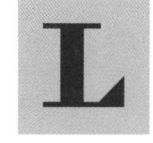

Langenscheidt

München · Wien

Herausgegeben von der Langenscheidt-Redaktion
Layout: Ute Weber
Umschlaggestaltung: KW43 BRANDDESIGN

Laden Sie sich auf **www.langenscheidt.de/verbtabellen** mit dem **Code ve125** kostenlos Ihren Konjugationstrainer herunter.

Systemvoraussetzungen:
Software: Windows 8.1 / 8 / 7 / Vista. Hardware: Pentium PC 1 GHz • 512 MB Arbeitsspeicher • 1,5 GB freier Festplattenspeicher • WSVGA-Grafikkarte (1024 x 600 Bildpunkte bei 96 DPI) • Soundkarte • Kopfhörer/Lautsprecher • Mikrofon (empfohlen).

www.langenscheidt.de

Satz: kaltner verlagsmedien GmbH, Bobingen
Druck und Bindung: Druckerei C. H. Beck, Nördlingen

ISBN 978-3-468-34125-0

17010

Benutzerhinweise

Mit den besonders übersichtlichen und benutzerfreundlichen Langenscheidt Verbtabellen Englisch bekommen Sie einen guten Überblick über die wichtigsten Verben, ihre Grammatik und die unterschiedlichen Konjugationsmuster. Mit dem Konjugationstrainer zum Downloaden (Zugangscode im Impressum auf S. 2) können Sie die Verbformen in den verschiedenen Zeiten und Modi trainieren und so in Ihrem Langzeitgedächtnis verankern.

Konjugationstrainer

Der Konjugationstrainer bietet Ihnen vielfältige Übungsmöglichkeiten, damit Sie sich die Konjugationen der wichtigsten englischen Verben noch besser und schneller einprägen können. Bei sechs verschiedenen Trainingsarten ist für jeden etwas dabei: Sie können die Verbformen entspannt beim Superlearning verinnerlichen, Multiple-Choice-Aufgaben lösen oder sich vom Konjugationstrainer abfragen lassen. Ihr persönlicher Tutor wertet Ihre Erfolge aus und stellt Ihnen ein optimales Programm zusammen. Sie können das Ganze auch spielerisch angehen und die Verbformen mithilfe eines Kreuzworträtsels einüben. Und sollten Sie die Zeit nutzen wollen, die Sie im Zug oder Wartezimmer verbringen, drucken Sie sich einfach Ihre eigenen Karten mit Konjugationen aus.

Konjugationstabellen im Buch

Im Buch werden Ihnen auf 70 Doppelseiten die wichtigsten englischen Verben und ihre Konjugationsmuster vorgestellt. Auf der linken Seite finden Sie das jeweilige Verb in allen relevanten Zeiten und Modi. (1) Hier sehen Sie, ob das Verb regelmäßig oder unregelmäßig konjugiert wird. (2) Über die Konjugationsnummer werden Verben (auch diejenigen im Anhang) einem speziellen Konjugationsmuster zugeordnet. (3) Gelegentlich finden Sie hier eine Kurzbeschreibung der wichtigsten Merkmale eines Verbs. (4) Auf den Musterkonjugationsseiten (z. B. zum Passiv) sind die typischen Formen bzw. Endungen in Schwarz fett hervorgehoben. Ausnahmen werden auf den später folgenden Seiten stets blau hervorgehoben. Abweichende Schreibweisen werden durch fett gesetzte blaue Buchstaben betont.

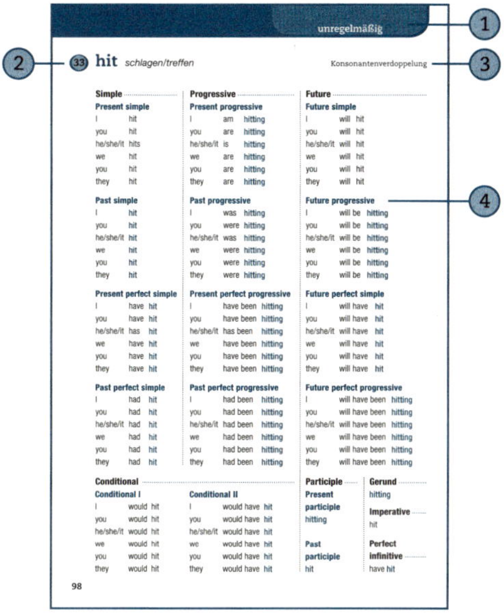

unregelmäßig

(33) **hit** *schlagen/treffen* Konsonantenverdoppelung

Simple			**Progressive**			**Future**		
Present simple			**Present progressive**			**Future simple**		
I	hit		I	am	hitting	I	will	hit
you	hit		you	are	hitting	you	will	hit
he/she/it	hits		he/she/it	is	hitting	he/she/it	will	hit
we	hit		we	are	hitting	we	will	hit
you	hit		you	are	hitting	you	will	hit
they	hit		they	are	hitting	they	will	hit
Past simple			**Past progressive**			**Future progressive**		
I	hit		I	was	hitting	I	will be	hitting
you	hit		you	were	hitting	you	will be	hitting
he/she/it	hit		he/she/it	was	hitting	he/she/it	will be	hitting
we	hit		we	were	hitting	we	will be	hitting
you	hit		you	were	hitting	you	will be	hitting
they	hit		they	were	hitting	they	will be	hitting
Present perfect simple			**Present perfect progressive**			**Future perfect simple**		
I	have	hit	I	have been	hitting	I	will have	hit
you	have	hit	you	have been	hitting	you	will have	hit
he/she/it	has	hit	he/she/it	has been	hitting	he/she/it	will have	hit
we	have	hit	we	have been	hitting	we	will have	hit
you	have	hit	you	have been	hitting	you	will have	hit
they	have	hit	they	have been	hitting	they	will have	hit
Past perfect simple			**Past perfect progressive**			**Future perfect progressive**		
I	had	hit	I	had been	hitting	I	will have been	hitting
you	had	hit	you	had been	hitting	you	will have been	hitting
he/she/it	had	hit	he/she/it	had been	hitting	he/she/it	will have been	hitting
we	had	hit	we	had been	hitting	we	will have been	hitting
you	had	hit	you	had been	hitting	you	will have been	hitting
they	had	hit	they	had been	hitting	they	will have been	hitting

Conditional						**Participle**	**Gerund**
Conditional I			**Conditional II**			**Present participle**	hitting
I	would	hit	I	would have	hit	hitting	**Imperative**
you	would	hit	you	would have	hit		hit
he/she/it	would	hit	he/she/it	would have	hit	**Past participle**	**Perfect infinitive**
we	would	hit	we	would have	hit	hit	have hit
you	would	hit	you	would have	hit		
they	would	hit	they	would have	hit		

98

Infoseiten

Auf der rechten Seite finden Sie zusätzliche Informationen wie Anwendungsbeispiele (5) und feste Redewendungen (6). Alternativ stehen hier manchmal auch Sprichwörter oder Witze. Ferner treffen Sie in der Rubrik Ähnliche bzw. Andere Verben (7) auf Synonyme und/ oder Ableitungen bzw. auf Antonyme. Unter der Rubrik Gebrauch (8) finden Sie besondere Hinweise darauf, wie das Verb verwendet wird. Alternativ zeigen wir Ihnen unter der Rubrik Aufgepasst! Besonderheiten und Stolpersteine auf. Gelegentlich finden Sie die Rubrik Tipps & Tricks (9), die auf Verben mit dem gleichen Konjugationsmuster oder andere praktische Hilfestellungen verweist.

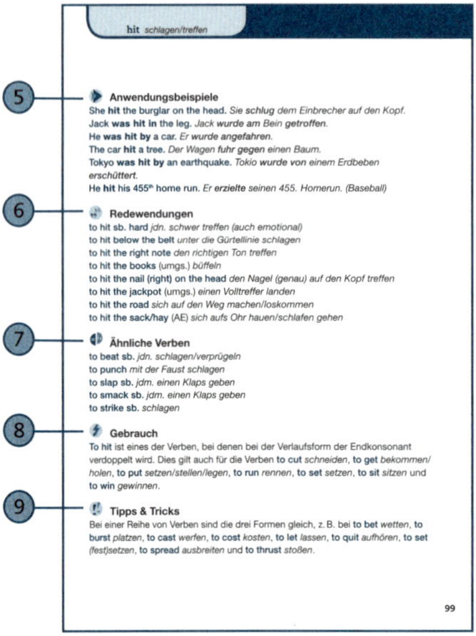

hit *schlagen/treffen*

(5) **Anwendungsbeispiele**
She **hit** the burglar on the head. *Sie* **schlug** *dem Einbrecher auf den Kopf.*
Jack **was hit in** the leg. *Jack* **wurde** *am Bein* **getroffen.**
He **was hit by** a car. *Er* **wurde angefahren.**
The car **hit** a tree. *Der Wagen* **fuhr gegen** *einen Baum.*
Tokyo **was hit by** an earthquake. *Tokio* **wurde von** *einem Erdbeben* **erschüttert.**
He **hit** his 455th home run. *Er* **erzielte** *seinen 455. Homerun.* (Baseball)

(6) **Redewendungen**
to hit sb. hard *jdn. schwer treffen (auch emotional)*
to hit below the belt *unter die Gürtellinie schlagen*
to hit the right note *den richtigen Ton treffen*
to hit the books (umgs.) *büffeln*
to hit the nail (right) on the head *den Nagel (genau) auf den Kopf treffen*
to hit the jackpot (umgs.) *einen Volltreffer landen*
to hit the road *sich auf den Weg machen/loskommen*
to hit the sack/hay (AE) *sich aufs Ohr hauen/schlafen gehen*

(7) **Ähnliche Verben**
to beat sb. *jdn. schlagen/verprügeln*
to punch *mit der Faust schlagen*
to slap sb. *jdm. einen Klaps geben*
to smack sb. *jdm. einen Klaps geben*
to strike sb. *schlagen*

(8) **Gebrauch**
To hit ist eines der Verben, bei denen bei der Verlaufsform der Endkonsonant verdoppelt wird. Dies gilt auch für die Verben **to cut** *schneiden*, **to get** *bekommen/holen*, **to put** *setzen/stellen/legen*, **to run** *rennen*, **to set** *setzen*, **to sit** *sitzen* und **to win** *gewinnen*.

(9) **Tipps & Tricks**
Bei einer Reihe von Verben sind die drei Formen gleich, z. B. bei **to bet** *wetten*, **to burst** *platzen*, **to cast** *werfen*, **to cost** *kosten*, **to let** *lassen*, **to quit** *aufhören*, **to set** *(fest)setzen*, **to spread** *ausbreiten* und **to thrust** *stoßen*.

99

Tipps & Tricks

Damit Ihnen der Einstieg in die verschiedenen Konjugationsmuster der englischen Verben leichterfällt, verraten wir Ihnen vorab in einem Extra-Teil ein paar Tipps & Tricks zum Konjugationstraining.

Grammatik rund ums Verb

In der Grammatik rund ums Verb werden in Kurzfassung alle relevanten Grammatikthemen behandelt, die Sie beherrschen sollten, um die englischen Verben richtig verwenden und konjugieren zu können.

Symbole

Folgende Symbole werden Ihnen in der Grammatik rund ums Verb begegnen:
Unter ⓘ erhalten Sie Informationen zu den speziellen Spracheigenheiten des Englischen sowie zum landestypischen Sprachgebrauch.
Unter 💡 finden Sie einen Merksatz, den Sie sich gut einprägen sollten.
⇄ Hier wird der Sprachgebrauch im britischen dem amerikanischen Englisch gegenübergestellt.
ϟ weist Sie auf Stolpersteine hin, damit Sie diese möglichen Fehlerquellen vermeiden können. Hier handelt es sich zumeist um Unterschiede zwischen dem deutschen und dem englischen Sprachgebrauch.
◐ signalisiert Ihnen, dass es sich hier um eine Ausnahme oder Sonderform handelt, die Sie sich besonders gut merken sollten.
Das Symbol ▷ verweist auf andere Stellen im Buch, die Sie sich bei dieser Gelegenheit ansehen sollten.

Niveaustufenangaben gemäß dem Europäischen Referenzrahmen

In der Grammatik rund ums Verb treffen Sie mitunter auch auf folgende Niveaustufenangaben: A1, A2, B1, B2. Diese verraten Ihnen, welche Grammatikthemen und welche Regeln für Ihr Lernniveau relevant sind. Die Niveaustufen beziehen sich nicht nur auf das jeweilige Grammatikkapitel, sondern auch auf das in den Beispielsätzen verwendete Vokabular. So wissen Sie auch genau, dass Ihnen dieser Wortschatz bekannt sein sollte.
In der Praxis heißt das: Ist ein Grammatikkapitel beispielsweise der Niveaustufe A1 zugeordnet, so sind alle verwendeten Vokabeln A1, es sei denn, sie sind mit einer anderen Niveaustufe, z. B. A2 (direkt vor dem jeweiligen Wort oder Satz), versehen. Alle in diesem Kapitel enthaltenen Grammatikregeln sollten Sie dann beherrschen, es sei denn, eine Niveaustufenangabe am Rand weist Sie darauf hin, dass diese Regel für ein höheres Niveau, z. B. B1, bestimmt ist.

Hier eine kurze Erläuterung, welche Kenntnisse auf die einzelnen Niveaustufen des Europäischen Referenzrahmens zutreffen:

A1/A2: *Elementare Sprachverwendung, d. h.*
A1: Sie können einzelne Wörter und ganz einfache Sätze verstehen und formulieren.
A2: Sie können die Gesprächssituationen des Alltags bewältigen und kurze Texte verstehen oder selbst verfassen.

B1/B2: *Selbstständige Sprachverwendung, d. h.*
B1: Sie können sich in den Bereichen Alltag, Reise und Beruf schriftlich und mündlich gut verständigen.
B2: Sie verfügen aktiv über ein großes Repertoire an grammatikalischen Strukturen und Redewendungen und können im Gespräch mit Muttersprachlern bereits stilistische Nuancen erfassen.

C1/C2: *Kompetente Sprachverwendung, d. h.*
C1: Sie können sich spontan und fließend zu verschiedenen, auch komplexen oder fachspezifischen Sachverhalten äußern und sich schriftlich wie mündlich an die stilistischen Erfordernisse anpassen.
C2: Sie können mühelos jeder Kommunikationsform in der Fremdsprache folgen und sich daran beteiligen. Dabei verfügen Sie über ein umfassendes Repertoire an Grammatik und Wortschatz und beherrschen verschiedene Stilebenen.

Unregelmäßige Verben, Verben mit Präposition und Alphabetische Verblisten

Am Ende des Buches finden Sie eine Übersicht über die wichtigsten unregelmäßigen englischen Verben sowie eine Auflistung einiger Verben, die mit verschiedenen Präpositionen verwendet werden können. Die Alphabetischen Verblisten ermöglichen Ihnen ein schnelles Nachschlagen der Verben sowie eine leichte Zuordnung von über 1000 Verben zu den verschiedenen Konjugationsmustern.

Inhaltsverzeichnis

Grammatik rund ums Verb – Grammar

Konjugationstabellen und Infoseiten – List of Conjugations and Information

Abkürzungen

AE amerikanisches Englisch
BE britisches Englisch
bzw. beziehungsweise
d. h. das heißt
etc. et cetera
etw. etwas
HS Hauptsatz
jd. jemand
jdm. jemandem
jdn. jemanden
jds. jemandes
sb. somebody
Sl. Slang
sth. something
umgs. umgangssprachlich
usw. und so weiter
z. B. zum Beispiel

Tipps & Tricks zum Konjugationstraining

Um Verben richtig konjugieren zu können, muss man nicht zwingend stoisch ganze Verbkonjugationen, Zeitformen und Endungen auswendig lernen oder gar hundertmal das gleiche Konjugationsschema abschreiben. Nein, Verben konjugieren kann Spaß machen und auf unterhaltsame Weise erlernt werden. Um Ihnen den Umgang mit englischen Verben ganz leicht zu machen, verraten wir Ihnen hier einige praktische Tipps & Tricks zum Konjugationstraining.

Pioniergeist ist gefragt

Versuchen Sie, die Andersartigkeit der Fremdsprache und ihrer Konjugationsmuster nachzuvollziehen. Sehen Sie das Erlernen der verschiedenen Zeiten, Formen und Verben einer Fremdsprache als Chance, Ihren eigenen Erfahrungsschatz zu erweitern, als Einblick in Denkweisen, die Ihnen nicht vertraut sind, die für andere Menschen, die diese Sprache täglich sprechen, aber ganz selbstverständlich sind. Zeigen Sie Pioniergeist! Lassen Sie Ihrer Freude am sprachlich Neuen, Fremden und Andersartigen freien Lauf!

Das Gesetz der Regelmäßigkeit

Konjugationstraining ist wie Krafttraining fürs Gehirn. Wer nur einmal alle Jubeljahre trainiert, wird wohl kein Fitnessgenie. Es ist sinnvoller, regelmäßig ein wenig als unregelmäßig viel zu lernen. Setzen Sie einen bestimmten Zeitpunkt fest, zu dem Sie sich ungestört dem Konjugationstraining widmen können, z. B. täglich eine Viertelstunde vor dem Einschlafen oder drei Mal wöchentlich in der Mittagspause. Wie immer Sie sich entscheiden: Lernen Sie kontinuierlich, denn nur so lässt sich auch Ihr Langzeitgedächtnis trainieren.

Aufwärmen lohnt sich

Gelernten Stoff zu wiederholen ist wie leichtes Joggen: Laufen Sie sich warm mit Altbekanntem, bevor Sie sich an Neues wagen. Auch wenn Sie noch nicht alle Konjugationsmuster einer Sprache kennen und noch viel Neues vor sich haben, darf das bereits Erlernte nicht vernachlässigt werden. Wiederholen Sie auch Konjugationen, die Sie schon gut können, das macht Spaß und hält fit.

Das Salz in der Suppe

Versuchen Sie niemals, sich zu viele Konjugationsmuster auf einmal einzuprägen. Man verliert sonst schnell den Überblick und läuft Gefahr, sich etwas Falsches zu merken oder gar die verschiedenen Konjugationen durcheinanderzuwürfeln. Verbkonjugationen sind wie das Salz in der „Fremdsprachen-Suppe“. Ebenso wie man eine Suppe versalzen kann, kann man sich das Erlernen einer Fremdsprache erschweren, indem man versucht, sich zu viele Konjugationsmuster auf einmal zu merken. Lernen Sie langsam, stetig und zielorientiert und verdauen Sie in kleinen Häppchen. Nur Geduld!

Eigenlob stinkt nicht immer

Schauen Sie auf das, was Sie bereits gelernt haben. Loben Sie sich für gemachte Fortschritte oder belohnen Sie sich für gute Leistungen. Lob motiviert und Motivation ist eine grundlegende Voraussetzung fürs Lernen.

L! Schluss mit dem Fachchinesisch
Wenn Sie etwas Neues lernen, kommen immer auch neue Fachbegriffe auf Sie zu, die Sie kennen sollten. Wählen Sie gezielt nach und nach einzelne Grammatikbegriffe aus (▶ Terminologie) und machen Sie sich mit ihrer Bedeutung vertraut. Sie werden sehen, dass es Ihnen im Laufe der Zeit leichterfallen wird, die unterschiedlichen Konjugationsmuster und Zeitformen einer Fremdsprache nachzuvollziehen, wenn für Sie die Fachterminologie nicht mehr Fachchinesisch ist.

L! Hemmungslos werden
Auch wenn die Beschäftigung mit Verbkonjugationen nicht zu Ihren bevorzugten Freizeitaktivitäten gehört, sollten Sie, um Abneigungen, Hemmungen oder Widerwillen abzubauen, die Konjugationsmuster mit anderen, alltäglichen Regeln vergleichen. Straßenverkehrsregeln, mathematische Grundregeln, Regeln von Sportarten etc. sind Ihnen heute völlig vertraut, mussten jedoch erst einmal von Ihnen gelernt werden. Auch die Regeln, die den Verbkonjugationen zugrunde liegen, werden Sie eines Tages verinnerlicht haben und, ohne darüber nachdenken zu müssen, intuitiv anwenden können.

L! Fehleranalyse gegen Fettnäpfchen
Haben Sie keine Angst vor Fehlern! Es ist nicht das Ziel des Lernens, keine Fehler zu machen, sondern gemachte Fehler zu bemerken. Nur wer einen Fehler im Nachhinein erkennt, kann ihn beim nächsten Mal vermeiden. Das Beherrschen der unterschiedlichen Konjugationsmuster einer Fremdsprache und das Verinnerlichen von Musterkonjugationen ist dabei durchaus hilfreich: zum einen, um einen Fehler nachvollziehen zu können, und zum anderen, um nicht ein zweites Mal in dasselbe Fettnäpfchen zu treten.

L! Haben Sie einen Typ?
Finden Sie heraus, welcher Lerntyp Sie sind. Behalten Sie eine Verbform schon im Gedächtnis, wenn Sie sie gehört haben (*Hörtyp*) oder müssen Sie sie gleichzeitig sehen (*Seh-/Lesetyp*) und dann aufschreiben (*Schreibtyp*)? Macht es Ihnen Spaß, verschiedene Konjugationen und Zeitformen in kleinen Rollenspielen auszuprobieren (*Handlungstyp*)? Die meisten Menschen tendieren zum einen oder anderen Lerntyp. Reine Typen kommen nur sehr selten vor. Sie sollten daher sowohl Ihren Typ ermitteln als auch Ihre Lerngewohnheiten Ihren Vorlieben anpassen. Halten Sie also Augen und Ohren offen und lernen Sie ruhig mit Händen und Füßen, wenn Sie der Typ dafür sind.

L! Sag's mit einem Post-it
Auf Post-its wurden schon Heiratsanträge gemacht oder Beziehungen beendet. Also ist es kein Wunder, dass man damit auch Konjugieren lernen kann. Schreiben Sie sich einzelne Verbformen (idealerweise mit Beispielen, s. u.) sepa-

rat auf Blätter oder Post-its und hängen Sie sie dort hin, wo Sie sie täglich sehen können, z. B. ins Bad über den Spiegel, an den Computer, den Kühlschrank oder neben die Kaffeemaschine. So verinnerlichen Sie schwierige Verbformen ganz nebenbei. Denn das Auge lernt mit.

Beispielsätze gegen Trockenfutter

Trockenfutter ist schwer verdaulich. Die verschiedenen Konjugationsmuster trocken aufzunehmen ebenso. Überlegen Sie sich zu jedem Verb einen Beispielsatz und konjugieren Sie diesen durch die verschiedenen Zeiten und Modi.
Fortgeschrittene können in Originaltexten (Zeitungen, Büchern, Filmen, Songtexten) nach konkreten Anwendungsbeispielen suchen. So werden die Konjugationen leicht bekömmlich.

Führen Sie Selbstgespräche

Wählen Sie besonders schwierige Verbformen aus, schreiben Sie dazu einzelne Beispielsätze auf und sprechen Sie diese laut vor sich hin, z. B. unter der Dusche, beim Spazierengehen oder während langer Autofahrten. Reden Sie mit sich selbst in der Fremdsprache, so prägen Sie sich auch komplizierte Verbformen ganz schnell ein.

Grammatik à la Karte

Wie beim Vokabellernen im Allgemeinen lässt sich auch für Verben im Besonderen eine Art Karteikasten mit einzelnen Karten anlegen. Schreiben Sie die Verben – auch in konjugierter Form oder mit Beispielsätzen – auf die eine Seite und die Übersetzungen dazu auf die andere. Schauen Sie sich die Karten regelmäßig an und sortieren Sie die, die Ihnen vertraut sind, allmählich aus.

Gegensätze ziehen sich an

Merken Sie sich Verben paarweise, indem Sie sich immer auch ein Verb, das das Gegenteil bedeutet (Antonym), einprägen oder ein weiteres Verb mit der gleichen Bedeutung (Synonym). Das hilft Ihnen, nicht „sprachlos“ zu sein, wenn Ihnen ein Verb mal nicht gleich einfällt oder Sie sich nicht sicher sind, wie es konjugiert wird. Indem Sie Antonyme und Synonyme mit dazulernen, bauen Sie sich einen breit gefächerten Wortschatz auf und können aus dem Vollen schöpfen.

Vor-/nach-/raus-/rein-/runter-/rüber- …gehen

Manche Verben können durch eine Vorsilbe eine andere Bedeutung annehmen. In der Regel verändert sich dabei jedoch nicht das Konjugationsmuster. Das ist sehr praktisch, denn auf diese Weise müssen Sie nur das Konjugationsmuster eines Verbs lernen und beherrschen so aber gleich automatisch die Konjugation zahlreicher Ableitungen des Verbs.

Haben Sie einen Plan?

Schreiben Sie Verben, die das gleiche Konjugationsmuster haben, auf einem großen Bogen Papier, eventuell mit Zeichnungen, Verweisen oder kurzen Beispielen, überschaubar zusammen und erstellen Sie Ihren persönlichen Lageplan. Mithilfe sogenannter *mind maps* können Sie sich schon durch das bloße Erstellen des Plans ganz schnell einen Gesamtüberblick über die verschiedenen Konjugationsmuster verschaffen. Ob Sie dieses Papier dann auch irgendwo hinhängen oder nicht, ist nicht ausschlaggebend, denn Sie haben dann ja den Plan schon im Kopf.

Denken Sie in Schubladen
Was im wahren Leben nicht unbedingt sinnvoll ist, kann beim Konjugationstraining hilfreich sein. Machen Sie sich gedankliche Schubladen, in die Sie die gelernten Verben einsortieren, und versehen Sie diese mit Etiketten: regelmäßige Verben, unregelmäßige Verben, Hilfsverben etc.

Bleiben Sie in Bewegung
Sie müssen beim Lernen nicht unbedingt am Schreibtisch sitzen. Stehen Sie auf, gehen Sie im Zimmer auf und ab oder wiederholen Sie beim Spazierengehen, beim Joggen, beim Schwimmen in Gedanken die neu gelernten Konjugationen. Ihr Gehirn funktioniert nachweislich besser, wenn Ihr Körper in Bewegung ist. Und Ihr Kreislauf dankt es Ihnen auch.

Beweisen Sie Taktgefühl
Klopfen Sie im Takt dazu (z. B. auf die Tischplatte), wenn Sie sich eine Konjugation einprägen wollen. Takt und Rhythmus fördern Ihr Erinnerungsvermögen. Eventuell hilft auch musikalische Unterstützung in Form von Hintergrundmusik. Und beim Wiederholen der Verbformen können Sie Ihr Taktgefühl und Ihr Gedächtnis zugleich unter Beweis stellen.

Grammatik aus dem Ei
Behelfen Sie sich beim Lernen von Konjugationsmustern oder Verbformen, die eine Ausnahme darstellen, mit Eselsbrücken, Reimen, Merkhilfen und Lernsprüchen. „7-5-3 Rom schlüpft aus dem Ei" – was bei historischen Jahreszahlen funktioniert, klappt auch beim Sprachenlernen.

Machen Sie Witze?
Merken Sie sich Witze, in denen ein bestimmtes Verb, das Sie lernen wollen, vorkommt. Indem Sie sich den Witz in der Fremdsprache einprägen und sich an diesen erinnern, prägen Sie sich auch die Verbform und ihre Bedeutung gut ein. Das funktioniert gleichermaßen mit Sprichwörtern und Redewendungen. Aber denken Sie daran, dass sich feste Wendungen nicht immer wörtlich von einer Sprache in die andere übertragen lassen!

Setzen Sie Ihrer Fantasie keine Grenzen
Machen Sie sich im wahrsten Sinne ein Bild von der Situation, denn auch Bilder, die Sie im Kopf haben, dienen als Gedächtnisstützen. Versuchen Sie also, ein neu gelerntes Verb gedanklich mit einem einfachen Bild zu verknüpfen. Was sagt das Verb aus? Vor allem das Erlernen der Zeiten funktioniert besser, wenn Sie sich das, was die jeweilige Zeitform ausdrückt, visuell vorstellen.

Gretchenfrage: Und wie steht's mit der Muttersprache?

Denken Sie über Ihre eigenen Sprechgewohnheiten nach und schauen Sie sich die Regeln Ihrer Muttersprache an. Die Gesetze der Fremdsprache sind viel einfacher nachvollzieh- und erlernbar, wenn man die Unterschiede zur eigenen Muttersprache kennt. Welche Zeitformen verwenden Sie wann, wie werden sie gebildet etc.? Indem Sie die Fremdsprache mit Ihrer Muttersprache vergleichen, machen Sie sich Parallelen und Unterschiede bewusster und prägen sich diese gleich viel besser ein.

Lieber hin und weg als auf und davon

Lernen Sie die Verben auch gleich in Verbindung mit verschiedenen Präpositionen. Sie werden zum einen merken, dass Sie damit Ihren Wortschatz ganz schnell erweitern können, da die Verben je nach Präposition zumeist auch unterschiedliche Bedeutungen haben. Zum anderen werden Sie feststellen, dass in der Fremdsprache häufig ganz andere Präpositionen mit dem Verb verwendet werden als in Ihrer Muttersprache.

Gebrauchsanweisung

Wenn Sie sich ein Verb und sein Konjugationsmuster einprägen, dann achten Sie auch darauf, den richtigen Gebrauch des Verbs mitzulernen. Denn nur so können Sie das Gelernte auch in der Praxis erfolgreich zur Anwendung bringen.

Wer liest, ist im Vorteil

Wagen Sie sich langsam an fremdsprachige Lektüre heran, sei es in vereinfachter Form mit Übersetzungshilfen, sei es in Form leichter Originaltexte, und schauen Sie sich insbesondere die verwendeten Verbformen immer wieder bewusst an. Es zählt nicht, wie viel Sie lesen, sondern dass Sie einzelne Zeit- und Verbformen im Kontext nachvollziehen und verstehen können, was ausgedrückt werden soll.

Haben Sie O-Töne?

Lernen Sie multimedial. Schauen Sie DVDs oder Kinofilme im Originalton und wenn möglich mit Originaluntertitel an, also z. B. einen englischen Film mit englischem Untertitel. Sie werden sehen, dass Sie durch das Mitlesen das Gesprochene wesentlich besser verstehen als ohne die Texthilfe. Halten Sie die DVD gelegentlich auch mal an und schreiben Sie sich interessante Verben, auch in Verbindung mit verschiedenen Präpositionen oder als ganze Redewendung, auf.

Verben – ab in den Koffer!

Das Spiel „Ich packe in meinen Koffer …" kennt vermutlich jeder. Falls nicht, hier die ultimative Variante zum Konjugationstraining zu zweit: Setzen Sie sich mit Ihrem Mitlerner zusammen und beginnen Sie, indem Sie eine Verbform laut sagen. Ihr Mitlerner muss diese wiederholen und eine andere Verbform hinzufügen. Dann sind wieder Sie an der Reihe mit der nächsten Verbform usw.

Der Vorteil bei dieser Trainingsform ist, dass Sie nicht nur Verbkonjugationen und Vokabeln gleichzeitig lernen, sondern auch Ihr Gedächtnis in Schwung halten und das Ganze auf spielerische und unterhaltsame Art und Weise.

L! Kofferpacken für Fortgeschrittene

Wenn Sie Spaß am spielerischen Lernen gefunden haben, dann gefällt Ihnen sicher auch „Kofferpacken für Fortgeschrittene". Wenn Sie ein Verb „in den Koffer packen", dann muss Ihr Mitspieler ein Verb mit dem in der alphabetischen Reihenfolge folgenden Buchstaben dazupacken usw. Sie sind auf jeden Fall im Vorteil, denn Sie können sich ja mit den Alphabetischen Verblisten am Ende des Buches bestens auf das verbale Duell vorbereiten.
Wenn Ihnen das noch nicht reicht, dann gibt es noch die ultimativ spaßige Verben-in-den-Koffer-pack-Variante: Sie vereinbaren mit Ihrem Mitspieler im Vorfeld zwei Handzeichen. Daumen nach oben heißt, dass die Verben, wie oben beschrieben, in alphabetisch aufsteigender Variante gepackt werden müssen. Daumen nach unten heißt, dass das nächste Verb mit einem Anfangsbuchstaben in alphabetisch absteigender Richtung beginnen muss. Das geht dann so lange so weiter, bis es zum nächsten Richtungswechsel kommt. Sie werden sehen, lachen ist vorprogrammiert und der Lerneffekt auch.

L! Verb-Memo für Einzelkämpfer zur Pärchenbildung

Um Ihrem neu entdeckten Spieltrieb keinen Abbruch zu tun, hier noch ein Spieltipp, den Sie auch alleine umsetzen können. Schreiben Sie sich die gleiche konjugierte Verbform jeweils auf zwei Kärtchen. Insgesamt sollten Sie ca. 20 bis 30 Kärtchen erstellen, die Sie dann umdrehen und mischen. Dann decken Sie ein Kärtchen auf und versuchen unter den umgedrehten Kärtchen das Pendant zu Ihrem Kärtchen zu finden. Werden Sie nicht auf Anhieb fündig, so müssen Sie die Karte wieder umdrehen. Merken Sie sich gut, auf welcher Karte sich welche Verbform befindet, und verwechseln Sie sehr ähnlich aussehende Formen nicht! Wenn Sie ein Pärchen haben, dürfen Sie dieses aus dem Spiel nehmen. Das geht so lange, bis keine Karten mehr im Spiel sind. Auch hier trainieren Sie nicht nur die Konjugationen, sondern Ihr Gedächtnis und manchmal auch Ihre Geduld.

L! Learning by doing in freier Wildbahn

Zu guter Letzt, wenden Sie die gelernten Verben und Konjugationen aktiv an. Reisen Sie in Länder, in denen die Sprache gesprochen wird, genießen Sie es, mit Menschen in der Fremdsprache zu sprechen, die Sie gerade lernen oder dann auch schon können, und freuen Sie sich über die Anerkennung, die Sie dafür bekommen, und die Kontakte, die Sie dabei knüpfen können – weil Sprachen verbinden …

Viel Spaß und Erfolg wünscht Ihnen
Ihre Langenscheidt-Redaktion

Terminologie

Englisch	Deutsch
adjective	*Adjektiv*
adverb	*Adverb*
auxiliary verb	*vollständiges Hilfsverb*
conditional I	*Konditional I*
conditional II	*Konditional II*
conditional sentence	*Konditionalsatz (If-Satz)*
direct object	*direktes Objekt*
future perfect progressive	*Verlaufsform der vollendeten Zukunft*
future perfect simple	*einfache Form der vollendeten Zukunft*
future progressive	*Verlaufsform der Zukunft*
future simple	*einfache Form der Zukunft*
future tense	*Futur (Zukunft)*
gerund	*Gerund (Verbalsubstantiv)*
going to-future	*Going to-Future*
imperative	*Imperativ*
infinitive	*Infinitiv*
ing-form	*Verlaufsform (ing-Form)*
irregular verb	*unregelmäßiges Verb*
linking verb	*Kopulaverb*
modal auxiliary verb	*unvollständiges Hilfsverb*
noun	*Substantiv*
object	*Objekt*
participle	*Partizip*
passive	*Passiv*
passive infinitive	*Infinitiv Passiv*
past participle	*Partizip Perfekt*
past perfect progressive	*Verlaufsform der vollendeten Vergangenheit*
past perfect simple	*einfache Form der vollendeten Vergangenheit*
past progressive	*Verlaufsform der Vergangenheit*
past simple	*einfache Form der Vergangenheit*
past tense	*Vergangenheit*
perfect infinitive	*Infinitiv Perfekt*
personal pronoun	*Personalpronomen*
phrasal verb	*Phrasal verb (Verb in enger Verbindung mit einer oder mehreren Präpositionen)*
plural	*Plural*
preposition	*Präposition*

Englisch	Deutsch
present participle	*Partizip Präsens*
present perfect progressive	*Verlaufsform der vollendeten Gegenwart*
present perfect simple	*einfache Form der vollendeten Gegenwart*
present progressive	*Verlaufsform der Gegenwart*
present simple	*einfache Form der Gegenwart*
present tense	*Präsens (Gegenwart)*
progressive infinitve	*Infinitiv der Verlaufsform*
question tag	*Frageanhängsel*
regular verb	*regelmäßiges Verb*
singular	*Singular*
subject	*Subjekt*
tenses	*Zeiten*
verb	*Verb*
will-future	*Will-Future*

A1
1 Das Verb

A1
1.1 Der Infinitiv

Der Infinitiv ist die Grundform des Verbs: **(to) write** *schreiben*. Allein stehend zeigt er weder Person noch Zeitverhältnis oder Handlung an.

Infinitive können auch in der Verlaufsform (ing-Form), im Perfekt oder im Passiv stehen.
Progressive infinitive: He will still **be working.** *Er wird sicher noch arbeiten.*
A2 Perfect infinitive: It's good **to have finished** it. *Es ist gut, es beendet zu haben.*
B1 Passive infinitive: The car must **be cleaned.** *Das Auto muss gereinigt werden.*

A1
1.2 Der Imperativ

Mit der Befehlsform wird jemand direkt aufgefordert, etwas zu tun. Es gibt nur eine Form, die für Singular und Plural gleich ist. Sie entspricht der Grundform des Verbs (ohne to).
Listen to me. *Hör/Hört/Hören Sie zu!*

Bei negativen Aufforderungen stellt man ein don't vor das Verb. **Don't** do that. *Tu's/Tut's/Tun Sie's nicht!*

A1
2 Die Zeiten

A1
2.1 Die Gegenwart

Formen

Bei der einfachen Gegenwart steht das Verb in der Grundform. In der 3. Person Singular (he, she, it, Name, Person, Ding) wird ein -s angehängt.

Ausnahmen: Das Verb have wird in der 3. Person Singular zu has. Das Verb be wird zu is; go und do werden zu goes und does.

Fragen und Verneinungen

Fragen (mit Ausnahme der Fragen mit who, wenn man nach dem Subjekt – *wer?* – fragt) werden bei Vollverben mit do/does gebildet.

Where **do** you live? Who **do** you like? (*wen?*)	**Does** your brother drink coffee? ⚡ Aber: Who wants to go out tonight? (*wer?*)

Verneinte Sätze werden mit do not (don't) bzw. in der 3. Person Singular mit does not (doesn't) gebildet.

I **don't** speak English.	She **doesn't** live in Ireland.

⚡ Das Verb have wird mit do not/does not verneint; das Verb be nur mit not.

I **don't** have children.	They are**n't** from London.

Gebrauch

- Die einfache Gegenwart beschreibt Handlungen, die wiederholt, regelmäßig, gewohnheitsmäßig oder traditionsgemäß stattfinden.
  I **eat** breakfast **every morning.** *Ich frühstücke jeden Morgen.*
- Auch allgemeine Wahrheiten und natürliche Gesetzmäßigkeiten werden mit ihr ausgedrückt.
  Spring **starts** in March. *Der Frühling beginnt im März.*

2.2 Die Verlaufsform der Gegenwart

A1

Formen

Die Verlaufsform der Gegenwart wird gebildet, indem man eine Form von be (am/are/is oder abgekürzt I'm/you're/he's/we're/they're) vor die Grundform des Vollverbs stellt und -ing anhängt.
I **am** clean**ing** the window. *Ich putze gerade das Fenster.*

Fragen und Verneinungen

Fragen werden durch Umkehrung von Subjekt und be-Form gebildet.

Am I writing a letter?	What **are you** reading?

Die ing-Form wird verneint, indem man die Form von be mit not zu am not, are not (aren't) und is not (isn't) verneint.

I'**m not** reading a book.	You **aren't** dying.

Gebrauch

- Die Verlaufsform der Gegenwart verwendet man für Vorgänge oder Handlungen, die im Moment des Sprechens oder Schreibens ablaufen. Sie wird vor allem bei Verben verwendet, die eine Tätigkeit ausdrücken.
  He's **having** a bath. *Er nimmt gerade ein Bad.*
- Sie bezeichnet auch Beschäftigungen, die nicht abgeschlossen sind und sich über einen längeren Zeitraum erstrecken.
  Mark **is living** with his brother. *Mark wohnt (zurzeit) bei seinem Bruder.*

ⓘ Bestimmte Verben findet man eher selten in der ing-Form, da sie keine aktiven Vorgänge beschreiben, sondern eher statische Zustände darstellen. Dazu gehören Sinneswahrnehmungen, Verben des Glaubens und Meinens und solche, die keine Tätigkeit ausdrücken, wie z. B. to know *wissen*, to need *brauchen*, B1 to seem *scheinen* oder to want *wollen*.

⚡ Ein Verb der Sinneswahrnehmung (B1 smell *riechen*, B1 taste *schmecken* etc.) wird dann in der ing-Form verwendet, wenn es sich um eine Aktivität handelt. Vergleiche:
The dog **smells** bad. *Der Hund riecht schlecht.* (Keine Aktivität des Hundes)
The dog **is smelling** the bone. *Der Hund riecht an dem Knochen.* (Aktivität)

⚡ Das Verb have wird in der ing-Form nicht verwendet, wenn es einen Besitz ausdrückt. In anderen Bedeutungen ist die ing-Form möglich.
We**'re having** breakfast. *Wir frühstücken gerade.*

A2 ⚡ Das Verb be kann nur im Passiv und in Verbindung mit einem Adjektiv, das eine momentane Verhaltensweise ausdrückt, in der ing-Form erscheinen.
My boss **is being** very **nice** today. *Mein Chef ist heute ausgesprochen freundlich.* (Normalerweise ist er schlecht gelaunt.)

A1 2.3 Die Vergangenheit

Formen

Bei der einfachen Vergangenheit unterscheidet man wie im Deutschen zwischen regelmäßigen und unregelmäßigen Verben. Bei den regelmäßigen Verben wird -ed an die Grundform angehängt. Ein nicht gesprochenes -e am Ende entfällt.
I clean**ed** the window. *Ich putzte das Fenster.*

Fragen und Verneinungen

Man bildet Fragen in der Vergangenheit mit did (mit Ausnahme der Fragen mit who, wenn man nach dem Subjekt – *wer?* – fragt).

Did I write a letter? What **did** you read?
Who **did** you see? (*wen?*) Who ate the apple? (*wer?*)

Verneinte Sätze werden in allen Personen gebildet, indem man did not (didn't) vor die Grundform des Vollverbs setzt.
I **didn't** read the book. *Ich habe das Buch **nicht** gelesen.*

Gebrauch
Die einfache Vergangenheit bezeichnet Handlungen, die in der Vergangenheit einmal, mehrmals oder regelmäßig durchgeführt wurden, abgeschlossen sind und keinen Bezug zur Gegenwart haben.
We **called** the police at 4 pm. *Um 16 Uhr riefen wir die Polizei.*

ⓘ Will man betonen, dass man früher etwas regelmäßig getan hat und es heute nicht mehr tut, kann man dafür used to + Grundform verwenden. Das gilt auch bei Zustandsverben. A2
I **used to** smoke 50 cigarettes a day. *Früher rauchte ich 50 Zigaretten am Tag.*

2.4 Die Verlaufsform der Vergangenheit A2

Formen
Die Verlaufsform der Vergangenheit wird gebildet, indem man die Vergangenheitsform von be (was/were) vor die Grundform des Vollverbs stellt und -ing anhängt.
I **was** clean**ing** the window. *Ich putzte gerade das Fenster.*

Gebrauch
Die Verlaufsform der Vergangenheit verwendet man für Vorgänge oder Handlungen, die zu einem bestimmten Zeitpunkt in der Vergangenheit gerade abliefen, also unabgeschlossen waren. Im Deutschen kann man oft das Wort *gerade* hinzufügen.
Last night around ten she **was writing** a letter to a friend. *Gestern Abend gegen zehn Uhr war sie gerade dabei, einen Brief an eine Freundin zu schreiben.*

⚡ Erscheinen beide Vergangenheitsformen in einem Satz, beschreibt die Verlaufsform eine Handlung, die bereits im Gange war, als eine neue (in der einfachen Vergangenheit) eintrat. Die ing-Form bildet also den Hintergrund für eine plötzlich eintretende zweite Handlung.
We **were watching** TV when Jack **phoned**. *Wir schauten gerade fern, als Jack anrief.*

A1
2.5 Die Zukunft

A2
2.5.1 Das Future simple

Formen

Das Future simple (auch Will-Future genannt) wird gebildet, indem man **will ('ll)** vor die Grundform des Vollverbs stellt. Das ist bei allen Personen gleich.
I **will clean** the window tomorrow. *Ich werde das Fenster morgen putzen.*

ℹ Im BE gibt es für die 1. Person Singular und Plural auch die stilistisch gehobenere Form **shall** (ebenfalls abgekürzt zu **'ll**).
I think I **shall** write the letter later. *Ich denke, ich werde den Brief später schreiben.*

Fragen und Verneinungen

Fragen werden gebildet, indem man **will** oder **shall** mit dem Subjekt vertauscht. Fragen mit **shall** benutzt man auch, um jemanden nach seiner Meinung zu fragen. Im Deutschen wird **shall** dann im Sinne von *sollen* verwendet.
Will the weather be nice tomorrow? *Wird das Wetter morgen schön werden?*
Shall I open the window? *Soll ich das Fenster öffnen?*

Bei negativen Sätzen wird **will** zu **will not (won't)** und **shall** zu **shall not (shan't)**.
I **won't** be back tonight. *Ich werde heute Abend nicht zurück sein.*
We **shan't** need the money. *Wir werden das Geld nicht brauchen.*

Gebrauch

Man verwendet das Future simple, um allgemeine zukünftige Informationen mitzuteilen, Voraussagen und Vermutungen zu machen sowie über nicht geplante und nicht unmittelbar vorhersehbare Ereignisse zu sprechen.
I don't think it**'ll** rain tonight. *Ich denke nicht, dass es heute Abend regnen wird.*

Bei spontanen, nicht vorher überlegten Absichtserklärungen verwendet man ebenfalls das Future simple.
I'll have a cup of tea, please. *Ich hätte gern eine Tasse Tee.*

A1
2.5.2 Das Going to-Future

💡 Das Going to-Future ist eine sehr häufig verwendete Form, um etwas Zukünftiges auszudrücken. Man bildet die Verlaufsform des Verbs **go** und hängt **to** + Grundform eines Vollverbs an.
I am **going to clean** the window. *Ich werde das Fenster putzen.*

Diese Form wird auf zweifache Art verwendet: Zum einen, wenn man sich sicher ist, dass etwas in unmittelbarer Zukunft eintreten wird. Oft sieht man es kommen.
I think it **is going to rain.** *Ich glaube, es wird gleich regnen.*

Zum anderen wird sie gebraucht bei geplanten Handlungen, bei denen häufig die Entschlossenheit des Handelnden zum Ausdruck gebracht wird.
We **are going to buy** a new car. *Wir werden uns ein neues Auto kaufen.*

2.5.3 Das Present progressive für zukünftige Handlungen

A1

Die Verlaufsform der Gegenwart wird verwendet, um festgelegte Vereinbarungen und fixierte Pläne auszudrücken. Dabei erscheint oft eine Zeitangabe, um deutlich zu machen, dass es sich um zukünftige und nicht gegenwärtige Aktivitäten handelt.
He**'s having** a party on **Sunday night.** *Sonntagabend gibt er eine Party.*

2.5.4 Das Present simple für zukünftige Handlungen

A1

Die einfache Gegenwart wird für Zukünftiges viel seltener benutzt als im Deutschen. Man gebraucht sie nur im Zusammenhang mit Fahr- und Reiseplänen, Abfahrts- und Ankunftsterminen sowie Veranstaltungs- und Öffnungszeiten. In der Regel wird dabei eine genaue Zeitangabe angegeben.
The train to Brussels **arrives** at **9 pm.** *Der Zug nach Brüssel kommt um 9 Uhr an.*

2.5.5 Die Verlaufsform der Zukunft

B1

Formen

Die Verlaufsform der Zukunft wird gebildet, indem man will be vor die Grundform des Vollverbs stellt und -ing anhängt.
I **will be** clean**ing** the window. *Ich werde (gerade) dabei sein, das Fenster zu putzen.*

Fragen und Verneinungen

Fragen formuliert man, indem man will mit dem Subjekt vertauscht.
Will you be telling her everything? *Wirst du ihr alles erzählen?*

Bei negativen Sätzen wird will zu will not (won't) verneint.
I **won't** be playing golf on Tuesday. *Ich werde am Dienstag nicht Golf spielen.*

Gebrauch

Die Verlaufsform der Zukunft betont eine Handlung, die zu einem bestimmten Zeitpunkt in der Zukunft ablaufen, also unabgeschlossen sein wird.
They'**ll be arriving** in an hour. *Sie kommen in einer Stunde an.*

Man benutzt diese Form auch für Fragen nach Absichten und um eigene Absichten auszudrücken. Die ing-Form klingt hier höflicher und vorsichtiger als das eher sachliche Future simple.
Will you be staying overnight? *Wirst du über Nacht bleiben?*

A1

2.6 Die vollendete Gegenwart

Formen

Das Present perfect bildet eine Art Brücke zwischen der Vergangenheit und der Gegenwart, wobei ein Wirkungszusammenhang zwischen beiden Zeiten vorliegt. Es setzt sich aus **have ('ve)** + Past participle (3. Form) zusammen. In der 3. Person Singular (**he**, **she**, **it**, Name, Person, Ding) steht **has ('s)**.
I **have cleaned** the window. *Ich habe das Fenster geputzt.*

Fragen und Verneinungen

Fragen werden durch Umkehrung von Subjekt und have oder has gebildet.

Have you/Has she been to South Africa?

Die verneinten Formen lauten **have not (haven't)** und **has not (hasn't)**.

No, I **haven't** seen her. She **hasn't** arrived yet.

Gebrauch

Beim Present perfect steht man gedanklich in der Gegenwart und schaut auf Vorgänge in der Vergangenheit zurück. Oftmals sind diese vergangenen Handlungen zwar abgeschlossen, doch der Zeitrahmen reicht bis in die Gegenwart hinein oder das Ergebnis der Handlung ist noch relevant. Im Deutschen werden häufig Wörter wie *bisher*, *bereits*, *bis jetzt*, *schon* oder *bis zu diesem Zeitpunkt* hinzugefügt.
She **has written** 20 e-mails. *Sie hat (bereits) 20 E-Mails geschrieben.*

Auch im Englischen können in Present perfect-Sätzen Zeitangaben stehen, vorausgesetzt sie drücken eine Zeitdauer aus, die noch nicht abgeschlossen ist: this morning *heute Morgen*, this week *diese Woche*, today *heute* etc.

I've read ten books **this year.** *Ich habe bereits zehn Bücher in diesem Jahr gelesen.*

Wenn Handlungen *gerade* (just) beendet wurden und das Ergebnis noch wichtig ist, stehen sie im Present perfect. Wichtig ist hier, dass kein Zeitwort verwendet wird, das eine abgeschlossene Zeitdauer anzeigt, wie yesterday *gestern*, five weeks ago *vor fünf Wochen* etc., da sonst das Past simple benutzt werden müsste.
He**'s just closed** the window. *Er hat gerade das Fenster geschlossen.*

Amerikaner verwenden nach just häufig das Past simple. Sie betonen damit die vergangene Handlung und weniger das gegenwärtige Ergebnis.

Des Weiteren benutzt man das Present perfect, wenn man fragt, ob jemand *jemals* (ever) oder *niemals* (never) etwas getan oder erlebt hat. Hier denkt man sich das ganze Leben als Zeitraum, der bis zur Gegenwart heranreicht.
Have you **ever** been to Canada? *Bist du schon mal in Kanada gewesen?*

Schließlich steht das Present perfect für Handlungen oder Zustände, die in der Vergangenheit angefangen haben und noch anhalten. Im Deutschen stehen diese Sätze meist im Präsens. Im englischen Satz das Present simple zu verwenden, wäre falsch.
Meggie **has lived** in Chicago **for 8 years.** *Meggie* ***wohnt*** *seit 8 Jahren in Chicago.*

Hierbei wird häufig erwähnt, wie lange etwas schon andauert. Das deutsche *seit* wird im Englischen mit since oder for ausgedrückt.

since (Zeitpunkt, Anfangspunkt)	for (Zeitraum bis heute)
since January; since Monday; since 2005; since she moved to Chicago	for an hour; for two days; forever; for ages, for some time; for a while

2.7 Die Verlaufsform der vollendeten Gegenwart

A2

Formen

Die Verlaufsform des Present perfect wird gebildet, indem man have been ('ve been), in der 3. Person Singular has been ('s been) vor die Grundform des Vollverbs stellt und -ing anhängt.
I **have been** clean**ing** the window. *Ich habe (gerade) das Fenster geputzt.*
oder: *Ich putze schon eine Zeit lang das Fenster.*

Fragen und Verneinungen

Fragen werden gebildet, indem man have und has mit dem Subjekt vertauscht.

Have you/Has she been waiting long?

Bei negativen Sätzen wird die Form have zu have not (haven't) und has zu has not (hasn't) verneint.

No, it **hasn't** been raining.

Gebrauch

Die Verlaufsform des Present perfect wird vor allem für Aktivitäten verwendet. Sie müssen in der Vergangenheit angefangen haben und in der Gegenwart noch anhalten oder gerade abgeschlossen worden sein.
We **have been living** in Dallas **since 2002**. *Wir wohnen seit 2002 in Dallas.*

B1 2.8 Die vollendete Vergangenheit

Formen

Das Past perfect funktioniert wie die deutsche Vorvergangenheit (*Ich war gelaufen. Ich hatte gespielt.*). Es bezeichnet eine Handlung, die vor einer anderen in der Vergangenheit stattgefunden hat. Auch das Past perfect fungiert als Brücke zwischen zwei Zeiten: der Vergangenheit und der Vorvergangenheit. Es setzt sich in allen Personen aus had ('d) + Past participle (3. Form) zusammen.
I **had** cleane**d** the window. *Ich hatte das Fenster geputzt.*

Fragen und Verneinungen

Fragen werden durch Umkehrung von Subjekt und had gebildet.

Had the film already begun when you arrived?

Die verneinte Form lautet had not (hadn't).

No, I **hadn't** seen her.

Gebrauch

Man verwendet das Past perfect fast immer im Zusammenhang mit einer zweiten Handlung in der Vergangenheit, wobei die weiter zurückliegende in der Vorvergangenheit stattgefunden hat.
When she came home last night, her mother **had** already **gone** to bed. *Als sie letzte Nacht nach Hause kam, war ihre Mutter bereits zu Bett gegangen.*

Ebenso drückt das Past perfect Handlungen und Zustände aus, die bis zu einem bestimmten Zeitpunkt in der Vergangenheit heranreichten.
We had lived in our house **for 25 years** when we sold it. *Wir hatten 25 Jahre lang in unserem Haus gewohnt, als wir es verkauften.*

2.9 Die Verlaufsform der vollendeten Vergangenheit

B1

Formen

Die Verlaufsform des Past perfect wird gebildet, indem man in allen Personen had been ('d been) vor die Grundform des Vollverbs stellt und -ing anhängt.
I **had been** clean**ing** the window. *Ich war gerade dabei, das Fenster zu putzen.*

Fragen und Verneinungen

Gefragt wird, indem man had mit dem Subjekt vertauscht.

How long **had she** been writing that letter?

Bei negativen Sätzen wird die Form had zu had not (hadn't) verneint.

She **hadn't** read the letter when I met her.

Gebrauch

Die Verlaufsform des Past perfect wird vor allem verwendet, um Handlungen auszudrücken, die in der Vergangenheit angefangen haben und zu einem späteren Zeitpunkt in der Vergangenheit noch anhielten oder gerade abgeschlossen waren.
When we left the theatre we saw that **it had been raining**. *Als wir das Theater verließen, sahen wir, dass es geregnet hatte.*

2.10 Die vollendete Zukunft

B2

Formen

Beim Future perfect steht man gedanklich in der Zukunft und schaut auf eine abgeschlossene Handlung zurück. Es setzt sich in allen Personen aus will have ('ll have) + Past participle (3. Form) zusammen.
I **will have** clean**ed** the window. *Ich werde das Fenster geputzt haben.*

Fragen und Verneinungen
Fragen werden durch Umkehrung von Subjekt und will gebildet.

Will you have done your homework by tomorrow?

Verneinungen werden gebildet, indem man will zu will not (won't) verneint.

I **won't** have read the book by tonight.

Gebrauch
Das Future perfect verwendet man, um auszudrücken, dass eine Handlung oder ein Zustand in der Zukunft abgeschlossen sein wird.
Will he have read it **by Monday**? *Wird er es bis Montag gelesen haben?*

B2

2.11 Die Verlaufsform der vollendeten Zukunft

Das seltene Future perfect progressive (will ('ll) have been + ing-Form) bezeichnet den Verlauf einer bereits vergangenen Handlung in der Zukunft. Fragen werden durch die Umstellung von will und Subjekt, Verneinungen durch die Verneinung von will zu will not (won't) gebildet.
I **will have been living** in Rome for ten years in December. *Im Dezember werde ich zehn Jahre lang in Rom gelebt haben.*

A1

3 Die Hilfsverben

A1

3.1 Die vollständigen Hilfsverben

Die vollständigen Hilfsverben be, have und do werden mit einem Vollverb verwendet, um zusammengesetzte Zeit- und Passivformen zu bilden. Es lassen sich Aussagen, Verneinungen und Fragesätze formulieren.

A1

3.2 Die unvollständigen Hilfsverben

Die unvollständigen Hilfsverben can, could, may, might, must, ought to, shall, should, will, would und need (im BE) haben folgende Merkmale:
- Sie haben kein -s in der 3. Person Singular der einfachen Gegenwart.
- Sie bilden keine Verlaufsform.

- Sie werden immer mit einem Vollverb verbunden; nur bei Frageanhängseln und Kurzantworten können sie allein stehen.
- Sie verlangen bei Fragen und in der Verneinung keine Umschreibung mit do/does/did. Verneint werden sie mit not.
- Folgende Kurzformen sind in der Verneinung gebräuchlich: cannot (can't), could not (couldn't), must not (mustn't), need not (needn't), should not (shouldn't) und would not (wouldn't).
- Hilfsverben werden mit have + Past participle (3. Form) verbunden, um Vergangenes auszudrücken.
- Sie können nur im Präsens verwendet werden (◖ Ausnahme: could und eingeschränkt should). Möchte man andere Zeitformen benutzen, muss man auf eine *Ersatzform* zurückgreifen, z. B. be able to (für can), be allowed to (für may), have to (für must), be supposed to (für shall).

Können – can/could

Mit can werden körperliche und geistige Fähigkeiten wiedergegeben. Bei Fragen geht es oftmals um eine Erlaubnis oder Bitte.

She **can** speak Spanish. *Sie kann Spanisch sprechen.*
Can I watch TV now? *Kann ich jetzt fernsehen?*

Die Vergangenheitsform could *konnte* drückt vergangene Fähigkeiten aus.
He **could** speak French when he was little. *Er konnte Französisch sprechen, als er klein war.*

Die Form could wird auch als Möglichkeitsform (*könnte*) in der Gegenwart verwendet.
She **could** write that e-mail now, but she doesn't want to. *Sie könnte die E-Mail jetzt schreiben, aber sie will nicht.*

In allen Zeiten kann die entsprechende Form von be able to verwendet werden.
I **was**n't **able to** see her. Have you **been able to** invite them?

Müssen – must/have (got) to

Das Hilfsverb must drückt eine innere Verpflichtung, einen Zwang oder eine Notwendigkeit aus. Es sollte nur im Present tense verwendet werden.
I **must** see this film. *Ich muss diesen Film sehen.*

Kommt dieser Zwang von außen, so ist er eine allgemeine oder regelmäßige Verpflichtung und wird meist mit have (got) to ausgedrückt. Ohne got kann diese Form in allen Zeiten verwendet werden.
I **have (got) to** do my homework now. *Ich muss jetzt meine Hausaufgaben machen.*
She **had to** put it back. *Sie musste es zurückstellen.*

Nicht müssen/nicht brauchen – do not have to

Für die Verneinung von *müssen* (*etw. nicht tun müssen*) verwendet man in allen Zeiten do not have to. Häufig wird do not have to im Deutschen mit *etw. nicht zu tun brauchen* wiedergegeben.
You **don't have to** do this. *Sie müssen das nicht tun.*
She **didn't have to** pay for the children. *Sie brauchte für die Kinder nicht zu zahlen.*

Nicht dürfen – must not

Die Verneinung must not (mustn't) ist ein Verbot und heißt *nicht dürfen*.
The doctor said I **mustn't** eat apples. *Der Arzt sagte, ich dürfe keine Äpfel essen.*
You **mustn't** be late. *Du darfst nicht zu spät kommen.*

A2 Könnte/vielleicht – may/might

Wenn *können* eine Möglichkeit ausdrückt, verwendet man in der Gegenwart may. Im Vergleich zu can klingt may höflicher und förmlicher.
May I open the window, please? *Könnte ich bitte das Fenster öffnen?*

Im Deutschen wird may auch häufig mit *vielleicht* übersetzt.
She **may** be right. *Sie könnte recht haben.* Oder: *Vielleicht hat sie recht.*

Die Vergangenheitsform might wird mit *vielleicht*, *möglicherweise* oder ähnlichen Begriffen wiedergegeben.
We **might** come on Sunday. *Wir kommen vielleicht am Sonntag.*

A2 Dürfen – may/may not

Auch höfliche Fragen um Erlaubnis übersetzt man mit may.
May I come too? *Darf ich auch mitkommen?*

Bei Erlaubnis oder Verbot im Allgemeinen kann in allen Zeiten auch (not) be allowed to verwenden werden.
Yes, you **are allowed to** smoke in here. *Ja, Sie dürfen hier drin rauchen.*

Wenn mit *nicht dürfen* ein Ratschlag oder eine Aufforderung ausgedrückt wird, dann verwendet man in der Gegenwart should not oder must not.
You really **shouldn't** go there. *Du solltest da wirklich nicht hingehen.*
You **mustn't** go there. *Du darfst da nicht hingehen.*

A2 Sollen – shall/should (ought to)

Shall im Sinn von *sollen* zu verwenden, ist problematisch, da shall nur in Fragen und Verneinungen (meist biblisch) mit *sollen* übertragen werden kann. In Aussagesätzen heißt shall *werden* (in der 1. Person Singular und Plural).

Shall I open the door? *Soll ich die Tür öffnen?*
You **shall** not steal. *Du sollst nicht stehlen.*
I **shall** spend the holiday in Bath. *Ich werde den Feiertag in Bath verbringen.*

In den Fällen, in denen *sollen* eine Aufforderung oder Vereinbarung ausdrückt, werden die Ersatzformen be supposed to oder be to verwendet. Das gilt auch bei vergangenen Tätigkeiten, die man hätte tun sollen.
I'm supposed to write an essay. *Ich soll einen Aufsatz schreiben.*
You**'re to** be home by six. *Du sollst bis spätestens sechs zu Hause sein.*

Wenn mit *sollen* eine höfliche oder bestimmte Aufforderung, ein Vorschlag oder ein Appell ans Gewissen ausgedrückt wird, sagt man should oder stärker ought to.
We **should** write a thank-you letter. *Wir sollten einen Dankesbrief schreiben.*
Wenn *sollen* ein Gerücht bzw. eine unbestätigte Behauptung wiedergibt, verwendet man die entsprechende Form von be said to.
More than a million people **are said to** be homeless. *Über eine Million Menschen sollen obdachlos sein.*

Werden – will/would

A2

Das Hilfsverb will wird fast ausschließlich für die Bildung der Zukunft verwendet. Gelegentlich hört man es noch in Fragen im Sinne von want oder wish.
Will you have a cup of tea? *Willst du eine Tasse Tee haben?*

Bei Fragen dieser Art ist es meist höflicher, would you like zu verwenden.
Would you like a cup of tea? *Hätten Sie gern eine Tasse Tee?*

Brauchen/müssen – need

A2

Das Verb need kann als Hilfsverb oder als Vollverb verwendet werden. Als Hilfsverb (ohne to) tritt es häufig in negativer Form auf.
Amerikaner verwenden in diesen Fällen eher don't have to.
BE: You **needn't** drive so fast. AE: You **don't have to** drive so fast. *Du brauchst/musst nicht so schnell (zu) fahren.*

Als Vollverb ist need (mit to) wie alle anderen Verben in allen Zeiten verwendbar.
You don't **need to** read that article. *Du brauchst diesen Artikel nicht zu lesen.*

Hilfsverben im Past tense

B1

Verbindet man die Hilfsverben mit have + Past participle (3. Form), wird etwas Vergangenes, das so hätte sein können oder sollen, ausgedrückt. Bei can ist dies eher ungebräuchlich.
I **should have said** something. *Ich hätte etwas sagen sollen.*

Haben – Have/have got

Im modernen Englisch gibt es im Präsens für have im Sinne von *haben/ besitzen* zwei Formen: have und have got. Have benutzt man wie ein Vollverb (Frage und Verneinung mit do/does/did); have got wie ein Hilfsverb (Frage durch Umstellung von Subjekt und Verb, Verneinung mit not). Inhaltlich besteht kein Unterschied zwischen beiden Formen.

A1

4 Die Partizipien

Partizipien sind Mittelwörter der Gegenwart oder Vergangenheit, die als Verben, Verbformen oder Adjektive gebraucht werden. Present und Past participle werden häufig wie Adjektive verwendet und mit Substantiven verbunden:
a **flying** plane *ein fliegendes Flugzeug*, a **closed** window *ein geschlossenes Fenster*.

B1

Falls es nicht möglich ist, das Partizip vor das Substantiv zu stellen, wird es nachgestellt und man erhält häufig einen verkürzten Relativsatz.
I saw a woman **reading.** (= I saw a woman who was reading.) *Ich sah eine lesende Frau./Ich sah eine Frau, die gerade ein Buch las.*

Das Present und das Past participle werden häufig zur Verkürzung von Nebensätzen verwendet. Dies ist jedoch nur möglich, wenn beide Satzteile dasselbe Subjekt haben. Im Deutschen steht dafür ein Nebensatz mit *da*, *weil*, *als*, *indem*, *und* etc.
Looking through the window, I saw my ex-husband. *Als/Da/Weil ich durch das Fenster schaute, sah ich meinen Ex-Mann.*

A1

5 Die Kopulaverben

Kopulaverben, wie be *sein*, B1 seem *scheinen* und B2 remain *bleiben*, sind Verben, die eine besondere Beziehung zum Subjekt eingehen. Sie können direkt von einem Substantiv oder Adjektiv, jedoch nicht von einem Adverb, gefolgt werden:
She is **happy.** *Sie ist glücklich.*

Das Adjektiv bezieht sich hier auf das Subjekt; ein Adverb bezieht sich in der Regel auf ein Tätigkeitsverb.

6 Das Gerund

A2

Das Gerund ist eine substantivierte Verbform (*das Rennen*, *das Schwimmen*). Formal ist es mit der Verlaufsform identisch: running, swimming.

Vielen Verben folgt ein erweiterter Infinitiv mit to:
He wants **to go** home. *Er möchte nach Hause gehen.*

Einige Verben benötigen jedoch eine ing-Form:
He enjoys **playing** baseball. *Er spielt gerne Baseball.*
Leider gibt es keine feste Regel, welches Verb zu welcher Gruppe gehört.

Steht ein Verb unmittelbar nach einer Präposition, erscheint es in der ing-Form.
He talked **about** playing chess. *Er redete davon, dass er Schach spielen wolle.*

Nach einigen Ausdrücken mit to steht kein Infinitiv, sondern die ing-Form, da das to hier als Präposition zum Verb gehört und keine Ergänzung zum Infinitiv ist.
I look forward **to** seeing you. *Ich freue mich darauf, dich zu sehen.*

7 Das Passiv

A2

Das Passiv dient dazu, von einer Handlung zu berichten, ohne den Handelnden zu erwähnen. Im Mittelpunkt steht die Person oder Sache, mit der etwas geschieht. Im Deutschen gebraucht man dazu eine Form von *werden*; im Englischen eine Form von be.

Present tense und Past tense

Das Passiv wird wie folgt gebildet:

Present tense: Passives Subjekt + is/are + Past participle (3. Form)

She **is** always **invited** to parties. *Sie wird dauernd zu Partys eingeladen.*

Past tense: Passives Subjekt + was/were + Past participle (3. Form)

My bicycle **was stolen** yesterday. *Mein Fahrrad wurde gestern gestohlen.*

Möchte man die handelnde Person erwähnen, fügt man ein by sb. an. In Fragen wird es meist nachgestellt.
He was seen **by a neighbour**. *Er wurde von einem Nachbarn gesehen.*

Das persönliche Passiv

Anders als im Deutschen steht bei einer Reihe von Verben das passive Subjekt (meist als Personalpronomen) im Nominativ und nicht im Dativ.

She was given a letter. ***Ihr*** *wurde ein Brief gegeben.*

B2

Die Verlaufsform im Passiv

Die Verlaufsform im Passiv ist nur im Present tense und Past tense geläufig.

Present tense: Passives Subjekt + is being/are being + Past participle (3. Form)

I think we **are being watched.** *Ich glaube, wir werden (gerade) beobachtet.*

Past tense: Passives Subjekt + was being/were being + Past participle (3. Form)

He **was being followed** by the police. *Er wurde von der Polizei verfolgt.*

B2

Das Passiv in anderen Zeitformen

Alle einfachen/„simple"-Zeitformen können Passivsätze bilden. Es muss nur die entsprechende Form von be eingesetzt werden.

Present perfect: Passives Subjekt + have been/has been + Past participle (3. Form)

My car **has** never **been stolen.** *Mein Auto ist noch nie gestohlen worden.*

Past perfect: Passives Subjekt + had been + Past participle (3. Form)

The room **hadn't been cleaned** when I checked in. *Als ich eincheckte, hatte man das Zimmer noch nicht gereinigt.*

Future simple: Passives Subjekt + will be + Past participle (3. Form)

He **will be questioned.** *Er wird befragt werden.*

Future perfect: Passives Subjekt + will have been + Past participle (3. Form)

The construction of the bridge **will have been finished** by next March. *Der Bau der Brücke wird bis zum nächsten März beendet worden sein.*

A2

8 Die Konditionalsätze

Es gibt drei Grundtypen von Konditionalsätzen, sogenannten If-Sätzen. Sie bestehen in der Regel aus zwei Teilen: einem Nebensatz mit einer Bedingung (if *wenn*, *falls*) und einem Hauptsatz (HS), in dem die Folge der Bedingung ausgedrückt wird.

Formen und Gebrauch

- Typ 1: Tatsächliche Ereignisse und Zustände in Gegenwart und Zukunft

If-Satz: Present (simple, progressive)	HS: Future (simple, ing-Form, Going to-Future)
If you **give** it to him	he **will break** it.
Wenn du es ihm gibst,	*wird er es kaputt machen.*

Variante von Typ 1:

If-Satz: Present perfect	HS: Future
If she **has bought** a ticket	she **will fly** to Rome tomorrow.
Wenn sie ein Ticket gekauft hat,	*wird sie morgen nach Rom fliegen.*

- Typ 2: Unrealistische Ereignisse und Zustände in Gegenwart oder Zukunft B1

If-Satz: Past (simple, progressive)	HS: would + Infinitiv ohne to (Konditional I)
If you **gave** it to him	he **would break** it.
Wenn du es ihm geben würdest,	*würde er es kaputt machen.*

Typ 2 mit Hilfsverb:

If I didn't have to work	I **could** go out tonight.
Wenn ich nicht arbeiten müsste,	*könnte ich heute Abend ausgehen.*

- Typ 3: Unrealistische und nicht mehr erfüllbare Ereignisse und Zustände B1

If-Satz: Past perfect (simple, progressive)	HS: would have + Past participle (Konditional II)
If you **had given** it to him	he **would have broken** it.
Wenn du es ihm gegeben hättest,	*hätte er es kaputt gemacht.*

Typ 3 mit Hilfsverb:

If she had read the newspaper	she **could** have seen the article.
Wenn sie die Zeitung gelesen hätte,	*hätte sie den Artikel sehen können.*

1 praise *loben/preisen*

Musterkonjugation; Passiv

Simple

Present simple

I	**am**	praised
you	**are**	praised
he/she/it	**is**	praised
we	**are**	praised
you	**are**	praised
they	**are**	praised

Past simple

I	**was**	praised
you	**were**	praised
he/she/it	**was**	praised
we	**were**	praised
you	**were**	praised
they	**were**	praised

Present perfect simple

I	**have been**	praised
you	**have been**	praised
he/she/it	**has been**	praised
we	**have been**	praised
you	**have been**	praised
they	**have been**	praised

Past perfect simple

I	**had been**	praised
you	**had been**	praised
he/she/it	**had been**	praised
we	**had been**	praised
you	**had been**	praised
they	**had been**	praised

Progressive

Present progressive

I	**am being**	praised
you	**are being**	praised
he/she/it	**is being**	praised
we	**are being**	praised
you	**are being**	praised
they	**are being**	praised

Past progressive

I	**was being**	praised
you	**were being**	praised
he/she/it	**was being**	praised
we	**were being**	praised
you	**were being**	praised
they	**were being**	praised

Present perfect progressive

–
–
–
–
–
–

Past perfect progressive

–
–
–
–
–
–

Future

Future simple

I	**will be**	praised
you	**will be**	praised
he/she/it	**will be**	praised
we	**will be**	praised
you	**will be**	praised
they	**will be**	praised

Future progressive

–
–
–
–
–
–

Future perfect simple

I	**will have been**	praised
you	**will have been**	praised
he/she/it	**will have been**	praised
we	**will have been**	praised
you	**will have been**	praised
they	**will have been**	praised

Future perfect progressive

–
–
–
–
–
–

Conditional

Conditional I

I	**would be**	praised
you	**would be**	praised
he/she/it	**would be**	praised
we	**would be**	praised
you	**would be**	praised
they	**would be**	praised

Conditional II

I	**would have been**	praised
you	**would have been**	praised
he/she/it	**would have been**	praised
we	**would have been**	praised
you	**would have been**	praised
they	**would have been**	praised

Participle

Present participle

being praised

Past participle

praised

Gerund

being praised

Imperative

be praised

Perfect infinitive

have been praised

Anwendungsbeispiele

I **was praised by** my teacher. *Ich **wurde von** meiner Lehrerin **gelobt**.*
Her essay **has been** widely **praised**. *Ihr Essay **ist** weithin **gelobt worden**.*
They **were** all **praised for** their good behaviour. *Sie **wurden** alle **für** ihr gutes Betragen **gelobt**.*
He **was** highly **praised for** helping the poor. *Er **wurde** sehr **dafür gelobt**, dass er den Armen geholfen hat.*
God **was** just **being praised** when the alarm went off. *Gott **wurde** gerade **gepriesen**, als der Alarm losging.*
Heaven **be praised**! *Dem Himmel **sei Dank**!*

Redewendungen

to praise sb. for doing sth. *jdn. loben, etw. zu tun/getan zu haben*
to praise sb./sth. to the skies *jdn./etw. in den Himmel loben*
to praise God/the Lord *Gott/den Herrn loben*

Ähnliche Verben

to admire sb. *jdn. bewundern*
to compliment sb. *jdm. ein Kompliment machen*
to flatter sb. *jdm. schmeicheln*
to honour sb. *jdn. ehren*
to say good things about sb. *Gutes über jdn. sagen*

Aufgepasst!

Nur Verben, die ein Objekt haben, können ins Passiv gesetzt werden. Dennoch gibt es auch einige Verben, die man nicht ins Passiv setzen kann, obwohl ihnen ein Objekt folgt. Dazu gehören u. a. fit *passen*, have *haben*, lack *fehlen* und resemble *ähneln*. Andererseits gibt es das Verb to own *besitzen*, das man im Englischen anders als im Deutschen problemlos ins Passiv setzen kann:
The factory **is owned** by an old women. *Die Fabrik **gehört** einer alten Frau.*
The factory **is privately owned**. *Die Fabrik **ist in Privatbesitz**.*

Tipps & Tricks

Passivformen in den Verlaufsformen der Perfektzeiten sowie im Futur sind unüblich. Man drückt diese aktivisch aus.

2 be *sein*

Musterkonjugation;
Vollverb und vollständiges Hilfsverb; Kopulaverb

Simple

Present simple

I	am
you	are
he/she/it	is
we	are
you	arc
they	are

Past simple

I	was
you	were
he/she/it	was
we	were
you	were
they	were

Present perfect simple

I	have	been
you	have	been
he/she/it	has	been
we	have	been
you	have	been
they	have	been

Past perfect simple

I	had	been
you	had	been
he/she/it	had	been
we	had	been
you	had	been
they	had	been

Progressive

Present progressive

I	am	being
you	are	being
he/she/it	is	being
we	are	being
you	arc	bcing
they	are	being

Past progressive

I	was	being
you	were	being
he/she/it	was	being
we	were	being
you	were	being
they	were	being

Present perfect progressive

I	(have been being)
you	(have been being)
he/she/it	(has been being)
we	(have been being)
you	(have been being)
they	(have been being)

Past perfect progressive

I	(had been being)
you	(had been being)
he/she/it	(had been being)
we	(had been being)
you	(had been being)
they	(had been being)

Future

Future simple

I	will be
you	will be
he/she/it	will be
we	will be
you	will bc
they	will be

Future progressive

I	(will be being)
you	(will be being)
he/she/it	(will be being)
we	(will be being)
you	(will be being)
they	(will be being)

Future perfect simple

I	will have	been
you	will have	been
he/she/it	will have	been
we	will have	been
you	will have	been
they	will have	been

Future perfect progressive

I	(will have been being)
you	(will have been being)
he/she/it	(will have been being)
we	(will have been being)
you	(will have been being)
they	(will have been being)

Conditional

Conditional I

I	would be
you	would be
he/she/it	would be
we	would be
you	would be
they	would be

Conditional II

I	would have	been
you	would have	been
he/she/it	would have	been
we	would have	been
you	would have	been
they	would have	been

Participle

Present participle

being

Past participle

been

Gerund

being

Imperative

be

Perfect infinitive

have been

Anwendungsbeispiele

She **is** a politician. *Sie **ist** Politikerin.*
He **was** reading the paper when the phone rang. *Er las **gerade** die Zeitung, als das Telefon klingelte.*
There **are** three apples on the table. *Drei Äpfel **liegen** auf dem Tisch.*
We **are being** followed. *Wir **werden** verfolgt.*
I **was** informed yesterday. *Ich **wurde** gestern benachrichtigt.*
What **am** I **to** do? *Was **soll** ich tun?*
I **was to** find out later that he had lied. *Später **sollte** ich herausfinden, dass er gelogen hatte.*
If I **were** you, I wouldn't do it. *Wenn ich du **wäre**, würde ich es nicht tun.*

Redewendungen

to be on holiday (BE)/vacation (AE) *im Urlaub sein*
to be into sth. (Sl.) *an etw. interessiert sein/in etw. verwickelt sein*
to be left speechless *sprachlos sein*
to be all ears *ganz Ohr sein*
to be friends with sb. *mit jdm. befreundet sein*

Ähnliche Verben

to live *leben*
to exist *existieren*
to take place *stattfinden*

Gebrauch

To be wird als Hilfsverb für die Verlaufsform, das Passiv und für Konditionalsätze verwendet. Als Kopulaverb kann ihm ein Substantiv oder Adjektiv (kein Adverb!) folgen:
He **is** slow. *Er **ist** langsam.*
Die Verlaufsformen im Futur und in den Perfektzeiten werden in der Regel vermieden, weil sie unschön und umständlich klingen.

Tipps & Tricks

Genauso wie to be *sein* konjugiert man to see *sehen*.

3 do *tun/machen*

Musterkonjugation;
Vollverb und vollständiges Hilfsverb; 3. Person Singular mit **-es**

Simple

Present simple

I	do
you	do
he/she/it	**does**
we	do
you	do
they	do

Past simple

I	**did**
you	**did**
he/she/it	**did**
we	**did**
you	**did**
they	**did**

Present perfect simple

I	have	**done**
you	have	**done**
he/she/it	has	**done**
we	have	**done**
you	have	**done**
they	have	**done**

Past perfect simple

I	had	**done**
you	had	**done**
he/she/it	had	**done**
we	had	**done**
you	had	**done**
they	had	**done**

Progressive

Present progressive

I	am	doing
you	are	doing
he/she/it	is	doing
we	are	doing
you	are	doing
they	are	doing

Past progressive

I	was	doing
you	were	doing
he/she/it	was	doing
we	were	doing
you	were	doing
they	were	doing

Present perfect progressive

I	have been	doing
you	have been	doing
he/she/it	has been	doing
we	have been	doing
you	have been	doing
they	have been	doing

Past perfect progressive

I	had been	doing
you	had been	doing
he/she/it	had been	doing
we	had been	doing
you	had been	doing
they	had been	doing

Future

Future simple

I	will	do
you	will	do
he/she/it	will	do
we	will	do
you	will	do
they	will	do

Future progressive

I	will be	doing
you	will be	doing
he/she/it	will be	doing
we	will be	doing
you	will be	doing
they	will be	doing

Future perfect simple

I	will have	**done**
you	will have	**done**
he/she/it	will have	**done**
we	will have	**done**
you	will have	**done**
they	will have	**done**

Future perfect progressive

I	will have been	doing
you	will have been	doing
he/she/it	will have been	doing
we	will have been	doing
you	will have been	doing
they	will have been	doing

Conditional

Conditional I

I	would	do
you	would	do
he/she/it	would	do
we	would	do
you	would	do
they	would	do

Conditional II

I	would have	**done**
you	would have	**done**
he/she/it	would have	**done**
we	would have	**done**
you	would have	**done**
they	would have	**done**

Participle

Present participle

doing

Past participle

done

Gerund

doing

Imperative

do

Perfect infinitive

have **done**

Anwendungsbeispiele

What **are** your dirty shoes **doing** on my bed? *Was **machen** deine dreckigen Schuhe auf meinem Bett?*

Have you **done** your homework yet? ***Hast** du schon deine Hausaufgaben **gemacht**?*

No, I **didn't** write any e-mails. *Nein, ich **habe keine** E-Mails geschrieben.*

You know Jack, **don't** you? *Du kennst Jack, **nicht wahr**?*

What **do** you **do** (for a living)? *Was **machen** Sie beruflich?*

Redewendungen

to do without sb./sth. *ohne jdn./etw. auskommen*

to do sb./sth. down *jdn./etw. schlechtmachen*

to do the dishes *abwaschen/das Geschirr spülen*

to do the laundry/ironing *die Wäsche waschen/bügeln*

to do the shopping *einkaufen gehen/den Einkauf machen*

to do ... kilometers *... Kilometer schnell fahren*

to do well at school *gut in der Schule sein*

Ähnliche Verben

to accomplish sth. *etw. schaffen/erreichen*

to carry out sth. *etw. durchführen*

to make *machen/tun*

to work *arbeiten*

to redo sth. *etw. nochmals tun*

to overdo sth. *etw. übertreiben*

to undo sth. *etw. rückgängig/zunichte machen*

Gebrauch

Das Verb to do hat eine Doppelfunktion als Hilfsverb (bei Fragen und Verneinungen) und als Vollverb. Ferner benutzt man es als Frageanhängsel, wenn im Hauptsatz ein Vollverb steht:

He **speaks** Spanish, **doesn't** he? ***Nicht wahr**, er spricht doch Spanisch?*

und gelegentlich zur Verstärkung einer Aussage:

He **does** need a bath. *Er braucht **wirklich** ein Bad.*

Tipps & Tricks

Does und Grundform, das steht fest – nach does steht nie ein Verb mit -s.

4 have (got) *haben*

Musterkonjugation; Vollverb und vollständiges Hilfsverb; Verlaufsform ohne -e

Simple

Present simple

I	have (got)
you	have (got)
he/she/it	has (got)
we	have (got)
you	have (got)
they	have (got)

Past simple

I	had
you	had
he/she/it	had
we	had
you	had
they	had

Present perfect simple

I	have	had
you	have	had
he/she/it	has	had
we	have	had
you	have	had
they	have	had

Past perfect simple

I	had	had
you	had	had
he/she/it	had	had
we	had	had
you	had	had
they	had	had

Progressive

Present progressive

I	am	having
you	are	having
he/she/it	is	having
we	are	having
you	are	having
they	are	having

Past progressive

I	was	having
you	were	having
he/she/it	was	having
we	were	having
you	were	having
they	were	having

Present perfect progressive

I	have been	having
you	have been	having
he/she/it	has been	having
we	have been	having
you	have been	having
they	have been	having

Past perfect progressive

I	had been	having
you	had been	having
he/she/it	had been	having
we	had been	having
you	had been	having
they	had been	having

Future

Future simple

I	will	have
you	will	have
he/she/it	will	have
we	will	have
you	will	have
they	will	have

Future progressive

I	will be	having
you	will be	having
he/she/it	will be	having
we	will be	having
you	will be	having
they	will be	having

Future perfect simple

I	will have	had
you	will have	had
he/she/it	will have	had
we	will have	had
you	will have	had
they	will have	had

Future perfect progressive

I	will have been	having
you	will have been	having
he/she/it	will have been	having
we	will have been	having
you	will have been	having
they	will have been	having

Conditional

Conditional I

I	would	have
you	would	have
he/she/it	would	have
we	would	have
you	would	have
they	would	have

Conditional II

I	would have	had
you	would have	had
he/she/it	would have	had
we	would have	had
you	would have	had
they	would have	had

Participle

Present participle

having

Past participle

had

Gerund

having

Imperative

have

Perfect infinitive

have had

Anwendungsbeispiele

I've (got) two brothers. *Ich **habe** zwei Brüder.*
Do you **have** any brothers and sisters? ***Haben** Sie Geschwister?*
I've had this car for 20 years. *Ich **habe** dieses Auto schon seit 20 Jahren.*
We**'ve been having** some difficulties lately. *Wir **haben** in letzter Zeit ein paar Schwierigkeiten.*
Have you **had** your hair cut? ***Hast** du dir die Haare schneiden lassen?*
You **had better** go home now. *Du **solltest** jetzt **lieber** nach Hause gehen.*
Have you **got** the time? ***Wissen** Sie, wie viel Uhr es ist?*

Redewendungen

to have (got) to do some work *etw. arbeiten müssen*
to have (got) the radio on *das Radio anhaben*
to have some friends over *Freunde zu sich einladen*
to have (got) nothing against sb. *nichts gegen jdn. haben*
to have an accident *einen Unfall haben*
to have a child *ein Kind bekommen*

Ähnliche Verben

to acquire sth. *etw. erwerben*
to get sth. *etw. bekommen*
to hold sth. *etw. halten*
to obtain sth. *etw. erhalten*
to own sth. *etw. besitzen*
to possess sth. *etw. besitzen*

Aufgepasst!

Es gibt keinen inhaltlichen Unterschied zwischen to have sth. und have got sth. Grammatikalisch gesehen ist have ein Vollverb und have got wird wie ein Hilfsverb verwendet: d. h. nur im Präsens, es hat keine Verlaufsform und Fragen und Verneinungen werden gebildet durch Umstellung von Subjekt und Verb.

Tipps & Tricks

To have steht nur bei bestimmten Redewendungen in der Verlaufsform:
I'm having a bath *Ich bade **gerade*** oder We**'re having** breakfast *Wir frühstücken **gerade*** usw.

5 ask *fragen/bitten*

Musterkonjugation;
Regelmäßiges Verb

Simple

Present simple

I	ask
you	ask
he/she/it	ask**s**
we	ask
you	ask
they	ask

Past simple

I	ask**ed**
you	ask**ed**
he/she/it	ask**ed**
we	ask**ed**
you	ask**ed**
they	ask**ed**

Present perfect simple

I	have	ask**ed**
you	have	ask**ed**
he/she/it	has	ask**ed**
we	have	ask**ed**
you	have	ask**ed**
they	have	ask**ed**

Past perfect simple

I	had	ask**ed**
you	had	ask**ed**
he/she/it	had	ask**ed**
we	had	ask**ed**
you	had	ask**ed**
they	had	ask**ed**

Progressive

Present progressive

I	am	ask**ing**
you	are	ask**ing**
he/she/it	is	ask**ing**
we	are	ask**ing**
you	are	ask**ing**
they	are	ask**ing**

Past progressive

I	was	ask**ing**
you	were	ask**ing**
he/she/it	was	ask**ing**
we	were	ask**ing**
you	were	ask**ing**
they	were	ask**ing**

Present perfect progressive

I	have been	ask**ing**
you	have been	ask**ing**
he/she/it	has been	ask**ing**
we	have been	ask**ing**
you	have been	ask**ing**
they	have been	ask**ing**

Past perfect progressive

I	had been	ask**ing**
you	had been	ask**ing**
he/she/it	had been	ask**ing**
we	had been	ask**ing**
you	had been	ask**ing**
they	had been	ask**ing**

Future

Future simple

I	will	ask
you	will	ask
he/she/it	will	ask
we	will	ask
you	will	ask
they	will	ask

Future progressive

I	will be	ask**ing**
you	will be	ask**ing**
he/she/it	will be	ask**ing**
we	will be	ask**ing**
you	will be	ask**ing**
they	will be	ask**ing**

Future perfect simple

I	will have	ask**ed**
you	will have	ask**ed**
he/she/it	will have	ask**ed**
we	will have	ask**ed**
you	will have	ask**ed**
they	will have	ask**ed**

Future perfect progressive

I	will have been	ask**ing**
you	will have been	ask**ing**
he/she/it	will have been	ask**ing**
we	will have been	ask**ing**
you	will have been	ask**ing**
they	will have been	ask**ing**

Conditional

Conditional I

I	would	ask
you	would	ask
he/she/it	would	ask
we	would	ask
you	would	ask
they	would	ask

Conditional II

I	would have	ask**ed**
you	would have	ask**ed**
he/she/it	would have	ask**ed**
we	would have	ask**ed**
you	would have	ask**ed**
they	would have	ask**ed**

Participle

Present participle

ask**ing**

Past participle

ask**ed**

Gerund

ask**ing**

Imperative

ask

Perfect infinitive

have ask**ed**

Anwendungsbeispiele

“Where do you live?” he **asked.** *„Wo wohnst du?“, **fragte** er.*
He **asked** a question. *Er **stellte** eine Frage.*
Can I **ask** you something? *Kann ich Sie etwas **fragen**?*
They**’re asking** a high price for the T-shirt. *Sie **verlangen** einen stolzen Preis für das T-Shirt.*
She **asked** him to close the door. *Sie **bat** ihn, die Tür zu schließen.*
He **was asking for** it. *Er **hat** es **verdient**.*
That**’s asking** a lot. *Sie **verlangen** eine ganze Menge.*
How did your date go? – Don’t **ask**. *Wie war dein Date? – **Frag** bloß nicht.*

Redewendungen

to ask sb. for advice *jdn. um Rat fragen*
to ask sb. over *jdn. zu sich nach Hause einladen*
to ask sb. out for dinner *jdn. zum Essen einladen*
to ask sb. a favour *jdn. um einen Gefallen bitten*
to ask for help *um Hilfe bitten*

Ähnliche Verben

to consult sb. *jdn. um Rat fragen*
to demand sth. *etw. fordern*
to enquire/inquire *sich erkundigen*
to interrogate sb. *jdn. verhören/vernehmen*
to question sth. *etw. bezweifeln*
to request sth. *um etw. bitten*

Gebrauch

Das Verb to ask ist sehr vielseitig und nimmt neben seinen Grundbedeutungen *fragen* und *bitten* in Verbindung mit Präpositionen, wie about, around, for, in, out oder over, ganz verschiedene Bedeutungen an. Es empfiehlt sich also immer, die Präposition mitzulernen.

Tipps & Tricks

Es gibt einige Verben, die fast alle Präpositionen nach sich ziehen können, z. B. to come *kommen*, to look *schauen*, to put *setzen/stellen/legen*, to run *rennen* und to set *festsetzen*.

6 become *werden*

Verlaufsform ohne **-e**;
Kopulaverb

Simple

Present simple

I	become
you	become
he/she/it	becomes
we	become
you	become
they	become

Past simple

I	**became**
you	**became**
he/she/it	**became**
we	**became**
you	**became**
they	**became**

Present perfect simple

I	have	**become**
you	have	**become**
he/she/it	has	**become**
we	have	**become**
you	have	**become**
they	have	**become**

Past perfect simple

I	had	**become**
you	had	**become**
he/she/it	had	**become**
we	had	**become**
you	had	**become**
they	had	**become**

Progressive

Present progressive

I	am	becoming
you	are	becoming
he/she/it	is	becoming
we	are	becoming
you	are	becoming
they	are	becoming

Past progressive

I	was	becoming
you	were	becoming
he/she/it	was	becoming
we	were	becoming
you	were	becoming
they	were	becoming

Present perfect progressive

I	have been	becoming
you	have been	becoming
he/she/it	has been	becoming
we	have been	becoming
you	have been	becoming
they	have been	becoming

Past perfect progressive

I	had been	becoming
you	had been	becoming
he/she/it	had been	becoming
we	had been	becoming
you	had been	becoming
they	had been	becoming

Future

Future simple

I	will	become
you	will	become
he/she/it	will	become
we	will	become
you	will	become
they	will	become

Future progressive

I	will be	becoming
you	will be	becoming
he/she/it	will be	becoming
we	will be	becoming
you	will be	becoming
they	will be	becoming

Future perfect simple

I	will have	**become**
you	will have	**become**
he/she/it	will have	**become**
we	will have	**become**
you	will have	**become**
they	will have	**become**

Future perfect progressive

I	will have been	becoming
you	will have been	becoming
he/she/it	will have been	becoming
we	will have been	becoming
you	will have been	becoming
they	will have been	becoming

Conditional

Conditional I

I	would	become
you	would	become
he/she/it	would	become
we	would	become
you	would	become
they	would	become

Conditional II

I	would have	**become**
you	would have	**become**
he/she/it	would have	**become**
we	would have	**become**
you	would have	**become**
they	would have	**become**

Participle

Present participle

becoming

Past participle

become

Gerund

becoming

Imperative

become

Perfect infinitive

have **become**

Anwendungsbeispiele

She **became** head mistress of our school. *Sie **wurde** Rektorin unserer Schule.*
He **became** a father of twins at the age of 80. *Mit 80 **wurde** er Vater von Zwillingen.*
The weather **has become** warmer. *Das Wetter **ist** wärmer **geworden**.*
Global warming **has become** a serious problem. *Die globale Erderwärmung **ist** zu einem ernsten Problem **geworden**.*
Pink **doesn't** really **become** you. *Pink **steht** dir wirklich **nicht**.*
What **has become** of Mrs Norris? *Was **ist** aus Mrs Norris **geworden**?*

Redewendungen

to become friends *Freunde werden*
to become jealous *eifersüchtig werden*
to become angry *böse werden*
to become pregnant *schwanger werden*
to become a rule *zur Regel werden*

Ähnliche Verben

to develop into sth. *sich zu etw. entwickeln*
to grow into sb./sth. *in etw. hineinwachsen*
to get *hier: werden*
to go *hier: werden*
to turn *hier: werden*

Gebrauch

Die beiden Verben to become und to get können, wenn sie im Sinne von *werden* stehen, häufig ausgetauscht werden. Sie beschreiben beide Veränderungen physischer oder emotionaler Natur, wobei become formeller ist als get. Die Verben to go und to turn haben eine ähnliche Funktion: go wird häufig bei negativen Veränderungen (to **go** crazy *verrückt werden*) und turn für Farbwechsel (to **turn** red *rot werden*) verwendet.

Tipps & Tricks

To become wird genauso konjugiert wie to come *kommen*.

7 begin *beginnen/anfangen*

Konsonatenverdoppelung

Simple

Present simple

I	begin
you	begin
he/she/it	begins
we	begin
you	begin
they	begin

Past simple

I	began
you	began
he/she/it	began
we	began
you	began
they	began

Present perfect simple

I	have	begun
you	have	begun
he/she/it	has	begun
we	have	begun
you	have	begun
they	have	begun

Past perfect simple

I	had	begun
you	had	begun
he/she/it	had	begun
we	had	begun
you	had	begun
they	had	begun

Progressive

Present progressive

I	am	beginning
you	are	beginning
he/she/it	is	beginning
we	are	beginning
you	are	beginning
they	are	beginning

Past progressive

I	was	beginning
you	were	beginning
he/she/it	was	beginning
we	were	beginning
you	were	beginning
they	were	beginning

Present perfect progressive

I	have been	beginning
you	have been	beginning
he/she/it	has been	beginning
we	have been	beginning
you	have been	beginning
they	have been	beginning

Past perfect progressive

I	had been	beginning
you	had been	beginning
he/she/it	had been	beginning
we	had been	beginning
you	had been	beginning
they	had been	beginning

Future

Future simple

I	will	begin
you	will	begin
he/she/it	will	begin
we	will	begin
you	will	begin
they	will	begin

Future progressive

I	will be	beginning
you	will be	beginning
he/she/it	will be	beginning
we	will be	beginning
you	will be	beginning
they	will be	beginning

Future perfect simple

I	will have	begun
you	will have	begun
he/she/it	will have	begun
we	will have	begun
you	will have	begun
they	will have	begun

Future perfect progressive

I	will have been	beginning
you	will have been	beginning
he/she/it	will have been	beginning
we	will have been	beginning
you	will have been	beginning
they	will have been	beginning

Conditional

Conditional I

I	would	begin
you	would	begin
he/she/it	would	begin
we	would	begin
you	would	begin
they	would	begin

Conditional II

I	would have	begun
you	would have	begun
he/she/it	would have	begun
we	would have	begun
you	would have	begun
they	would have	begun

Participle

Present participle

beginning

Past participle

begun

Gerund

beginning

Imperative

begin

Perfect infinitive

have begun

Anwendungsbeispiele

When **did** you **begin** to learn Dutch? *Wann **hast** du **angefangen**, Holländisch zu lernen?*
What time **does** the film **begin**? *Um wie viel Uhr **fängt** der Film **an**.*
I don't know where to **begin**. *Ich weiß nicht, wo ich **anfangen** soll.*
Her first name **begins** with an e. *Ihr Vorname **fängt** mit einem e **an**.*
It**'s beginning** to rain. *Es **fängt gerade** an zu regnen.*
He **began by** saying that he liked our town. *Er **begann damit, dass** er sagte, er möge unsere Stadt.*
He **began life** as the son of a blacksmith. *Er **kam** als Sohn eines Schmieds **zur Welt**.*
Let's **begin**. *Lasst uns **anfangen!/Fangen** wir an.*
My Latin class is hard, but **I'm beginning** to see the light. *Mein Lateinunterricht ist schwer, doch ich **fange langsam an**, Licht zu sehen.*

Redewendungen

to begin promisingly *vielversprechend anfangen*
to begin work *mit der Arbeit beginnen*
to begin on a new bottle *eine neue Flasche anbrechen/öffnen*

Andere Verben

to cease sth. *etw. beenden*
to end sth. *etw. beenden*
to finish sth. *etw. beenden*
to quit sth. *mit etw. aufhören*
to stop sth. *etw. beenden*

Gebrauch

Der Unterschied zwischen to begin und to start ist minimal; begin ist etwas förmlicher und nur start kann im Zusammenhang mit Maschinen verwendet werden:
The computer **won't start**. *Der Computer **geht nicht an**.*

Tipps & Tricks

Die Verben to drink *trinken*, to ring *anrufen/klingeln*, to sing *singen*, to sink *sinken*, to spring *springen*, to shrink *schrumpfen*, to stink *stinken* und to swim *schwimmen* konjugiert man genauso wie to begin.

8 believe *glauben*

Verlaufsform eher selten

Simple

Present simple

I	believe
you	believe
he/she/it	believes
we	believe
you	believe
they	believe

Past simple

I	believed
you	believed
he/she/it	believed
we	believed
you	believed
they	believed

Present perfect simple

I	have	believed
you	have	believed
he/she/it	has	believed
we	have	believed
you	have	believed
they	have	believed

Past perfect simple

I	had	believed
you	had	believed
he/she/it	had	believed
we	had	believed
you	had	believed
they	had	believed

Progressive

Present progressive

I	am	believing
you	are	believing
he/she/it	is	believing
we	are	believing
you	are	believing
they	are	believing

Past progressive

I	was	believing
you	were	believing
he/she/it	was	believing
we	were	believing
you	were	believing
they	were	believing

Present perfect progressive

I	have been	believing
you	have been	believing
he/she/it	has been	believing
we	have been	believing
you	have been	believing
they	have been	believing

Past perfect progressive

I	had been	believing
you	had been	believing
he/she/it	had been	believing
we	had been	believing
you	had been	believing
they	had been	believing

Future

Future simple

I	will	believe
you	will	believe
he/she/it	will	believe
we	will	believe
you	will	believe
they	will	believe

Future progressive

I	will be	believing
you	will be	believing
he/she/it	will be	believing
we	will be	believing
you	will be	believing
they	will be	believing

Future perfect simple

I	will have	believed
you	will have	believed
he/she/it	will have	believed
we	will have	believed
you	will have	believed
they	will have	believed

Future perfect progressive

I	will have been	believing
you	will have been	believing
he/she/it	will have been	believing
we	will have been	believing
you	will have been	believing
they	will have been	believing

Conditional

Conditional I

I	would	believe
you	would	believe
he/she/it	would	believe
we	would	believe
you	would	believe
they	would	believe

Conditional II

I	would have	believed
you	would have	believed
he/she/it	would have	believed
we	would have	believed
you	would have	believed
they	would have	believed

Participle

Present participle

believing

Past participle

believed

Gerund

believing

Imperative

believe

Perfect infinitive

have believed

Anwendungsbeispiele

Do you **believe in** God? *Glaubst du **an** Gott?*
She **didn't believe** a word of it. *Sie **glaubte kein** Wort davon.*
He **is believed to be** a Mexican. ***Man hält** ihn **für** einen Mexikaner.*
Would you **believe** it? *Kannst du das **glauben**?*
Believe it or not. *Ob du es **glaubst** oder nicht.*
She could hardly **believe** her eyes/ears. *Sie **traute** ihren Augen/Ohren nicht.*
It **is** widely **believed** that 13 is an unlucky number. *Viele Menschen **glauben**, dass die 13 eine Unglückszahl ist.*

Redewendungen

to not believe in doing sth. *nicht viel/nichts davon halten, etw. zu tun*
to believe sb. to be stupid *jdn. für dumm halten*
to make believe that ... /to be ... *so tun, als ob ...*
to believe in fate *an das Schicksal glauben*

Andere Verben

to be sceptical *skeptisch sein*
to be uncertain *unsicher sein*
to be distrustful *misstrauisch sein*
to disbelieve in sth. *an etw. nicht glauben*
to doubt sth. *etw. bezweifeln*
to have no faith in sth. *kein Vertrauen haben zu/in etw.*
to query sth. *etw. infrage stellen/etw. bezweifeln*

Aufgepasst!

To believe ist ein Verb, dass einen geistig-seelischen Zustand ausdrückt. Es wird nicht als Handlung aufgefasst und von daher nicht in der Verlaufsform verwendet. Ähnliche Verben des Glaubens oder Zweifelns, die man in der Regel nicht in der ing-Form benutzen sollte, sind to doubt *zweifeln*, to suppose *annehmen* und to suspect *vermuten*.

9 bite *beißen*

Simple

Present simple

I	bite
you	bite
he/she/it	bites
we	bite
you	bite
they	bite

Past simple

I	bit
you	bit
he/she/it	bit
we	bit
you	bit
they	bit

Present perfect simple

I	have	bitten
you	have	bitten
he/she/it	has	bitten
we	have	bitten
you	have	bitten
they	have	bitten

Past perfect simple

I	had	bitten
you	had	bitten
he/she/it	had	bitten
we	had	bitten
you	had	bitten
they	had	bitten

Progressive

Present progressive

I	am	biting
you	are	biting
he/she/it	is	biting
we	are	biting
you	are	biting
they	are	biting

Past progressive

I	was	biting
you	were	biting
he/she/it	was	biting
we	were	biting
you	were	biting
they	were	biting

Present perfect progressive

I	have been	biting
you	have been	biting
he/she/it	has been	biting
we	have been	biting
you	have been	biting
they	have been	biting

Past perfect progressive

I	had been	biting
you	had been	biting
he/she/it	had been	biting
we	had been	biting
you	had been	biting
they	had been	biting

Future

Future simple

I	will	bite
you	will	bite
he/she/it	will	bite
we	will	bite
you	will	bite
they	will	bite

Future progressive

I	will be	biting
you	will be	biting
he/she/it	will be	biting
we	will be	biting
you	will be	biting
they	will be	biting

Future perfect simple

I	will have	bitten
you	will have	bitten
he/she/it	will have	bitten
we	will have	bitten
you	will have	bitten
they	will have	bitten

Future perfect progressive

I	will have been	biting
you	will have been	biting
he/she/it	will have been	biting
we	will have been	biting
you	will have been	biting
they	will have been	biting

Conditional

Conditional I

I	would	bite
you	would	bite
he/she/it	would	bite
we	would	bite
you	would	bite
they	would	bite

Conditional II

I	would have	bitten
you	would have	bitten
he/she/it	would have	bitten
we	would have	bitten
you	would have	bitten
they	would have	bitten

Participle

Present participle

biting

Past participle

bitten

Gerund

biting

Imperative

bite

Perfect infinitive

have bitten

Anwendungsbeispiele

She **bit into** an apple. *Sie **biss in** einen Apfel.*

She**'s been bitten by** a mosquito. *Sie **ist von** einer Stechmücke **gebissen** worden.*

Are the fish **biting** today? ***Beißen** die Fische heute?*

Is she still **biting** her nails? ***Kaut** sie immer noch **an** den Nägeln?*

Come on, ask him. He **won't bite**. *Na los, frag ihn. Er **beißt nicht**.*

You don't **bite** the hand that feeds you. *Man soll nicht Gutes mit Schlechtem vergelten.*

He **bit off** more than he can chew. *Er hat sich zu viel zugemutet.*

Witz

A postman walked into a hospital, complaining that a dog **had** just **bitten** him **in** the leg.

"Did you put anything on it?" asked the nurse.

"No," replied the postman. "He liked it just as it was."

Ähnliche Verben

to chew *kauen*

to crunch *knirschend zerkauen*

to nibble *knabbern*

to peck *picken*

to sting *stechen*

Gebrauch

Der Gebrauch von to bite ist im Englischen ganz ähnlich wie im Deutschen. Sogar wenn ein neues Produkt sich schlecht verkauft, weil die Konsumenten nicht „angebissen" haben, lässt sich das mit bite ausdrücken:

We had to withdraw the new mobile phone from the market because consumers failed to **bite**. *Wir mussten das neue Handy wieder vom Markt nehmen, weil die Konsumenten nicht **anbissen**.*

Tipps & Tricks

Genauso wie to bite werden die Verben to hide *(sich) verstecken*, to light *erhellen/beleuchten* und to slide *gleiten/rutschen* konjugiert.

10 break *brechen/kaputt machen/kaputtgehen*

Simple

Present simple

I	break
you	break
he/she/it	breaks
we	break
you	break
they	break

Past simple

I	broke
you	broke
he/she/it	broke
we	broke
you	broke
they	broke

Present perfect simple

I	have	broken
you	have	broken
he/she/it	has	broken
we	have	broken
you	have	broken
they	have	broken

Past perfect simple

I	had	broken
you	had	broken
he/she/it	had	broken
we	had	broken
you	had	broken
they	had	broken

Progressive

Present progressive

I	am	breaking
you	are	breaking
he/she/it	is	breaking
we	are	breaking
you	are	breaking
they	are	breaking

Past progressive

I	was	breaking
you	were	breaking
he/she/it	was	breaking
we	were	breaking
you	were	breaking
they	were	breaking

Present perfect progressive

I	have been	breaking
you	have been	breaking
he/she/it	has been	breaking
we	have been	breaking
you	have been	breaking
they	have been	breaking

Past perfect progressive

I	had been	breaking
you	had been	breaking
he/she/it	had been	breaking
we	had been	breaking
you	had been	breaking
they	had been	breaking

Future

Future simple

I	will	break
you	will	break
he/she/it	will	break
we	will	break
you	will	break
they	will	break

Future progressive

I	will be	breaking
you	will be	breaking
he/she/it	will be	breaking
we	will be	breaking
you	will be	breaking
they	will be	breaking

Future perfect simple

I	will have	broken
you	will have	broken
he/she/it	will have	broken
we	will have	broken
you	will have	broken
they	will have	broken

Future perfect progressive

I	will have been	breaking
you	will have been	breaking
he/she/it	will have been	breaking
we	will have been	breaking
you	will have been	breaking
they	will have been	breaking

Conditional

Conditional I

I	would	break
you	would	break
he/she/it	would	break
we	would	break
you	would	break
they	would	break

Conditional II

I	would have	broken
you	would have	broken
he/she/it	would have	broken
we	would have	broken
you	would have	broken
they	would have	broken

Participle

Present participle

breaking

Past participle

broken

Gerund

breaking

Imperative

break

Perfect infinitive

have broken

Anwendungsbeispiele

The other day he **broke** his arm. *Neulich **brach** er sich den Arm.*
Don't touch the figure. It'**ll break**. *Berühre nicht die Figur. Sie **geht kaputt**.*
My printer **is broken** again. *Mein Drucker **ist** schon wieder **kaputt**.*
Don't break the speed limit. ***Übertritt** nicht die Geschwindigkeitsbegrenzung.*
We had just arrived when a storm **broke**. *Wir waren gerade angekommen, als ein Sturm **losbrach**.*
That was the straw that **broke** the camel's back. *Das war der Tropfen, der das Fass **zum Überlaufen brachte**.*
Break a leg! *Hals und Bein**bruch**!*

Redewendungen

to break sth. in half/two *etw. entzweibrechen*
to break down in tears *in Tränen ausbrechen*
to break down *niederreißen/liegen bleiben (Auto)*
to break an egg *ein Ei aufschlagen*
to break a promise *ein Versprechen brechen*
to break a habit *mit einer Gewohnheit brechen*
to break a record *einen Rekord brechen*
to break sb.'s heart *jdm. das Herz brechen*

Ähnliche Verben

to destroy sth. *etw. zerstören*
to shatter sth. *etw. zerschmettern*
to smash sth. *etw. zerschlagen*

Gebrauch

To break ist eines jener Verben, die mit einer ganzen Reihe von Präpositionen verbunden werden können und dabei die vielfältigsten Bedeutungen annehmen, z. B. to break **in** ***ein**brechen/**unter**brechen*, to break **away** ***ab-/los**brechen*, to break **out** ***aus**brechen* oder to break **up with** sb. ***mit** jdm. Schluss machen*.

Tipps & Tricks

Genauso wie to break konjugiert man die Verben to awake *erwachen* und to wake sb. *jdn. wecken*.

11 bring *mitbringen*

Simple

Present simple

I	bring
you	bring
he/she/it	brings
we	bring
you	bring
they	bring

Past simple

I	brought
you	brought
he/she/it	brought
we	brought
you	brought
they	brought

Present perfect simple

I	have	brought
you	have	brought
he/she/it	has	brought
we	have	brought
you	have	brought
they	have	brought

Past perfect simple

I	had	brought
you	had	brought
he/she/it	had	brought
we	had	brought
you	had	brought
they	had	brought

Progressive

Present progressive

I	am	bringing
you	are	bringing
he/she/it	is	bringing
we	are	bringing
you	are	bringing
they	are	bringing

Past progressive

I	was	bringing
you	were	bringing
he/she/it	was	bringing
we	were	bringing
you	were	bringing
they	were	bringing

Present perfect progressive

I	have been	bringing
you	have been	bringing
he/she/it	has been	bringing
we	have been	bringing
you	have been	bringing
they	have been	bringing

Past perfect progressive

I	had been	bringing
you	had been	bringing
he/she/it	had been	bringing
we	had been	bringing
you	had been	bringing
they	had been	bringing

Future

Future simple

I	will	bring
you	will	bring
he/she/it	will	bring
we	will	bring
you	will	bring
they	will	bring

Future progressive

I	will be	bringing
you	will be	bringing
he/she/it	will be	bringing
we	will be	bringing
you	will be	bringing
they	will be	bringing

Future perfect simple

I	will have	brought
you	will have	brought
he/she/it	will have	brought
we	will have	brought
you	will have	brought
they	will have	brought

Future perfect progressive

I	will have been	bringing
you	will have been	bringing
he/she/it	will have been	bringing
we	will have been	bringing
you	will have been	bringing
they	will have been	bringing

Conditional

Conditional I

I	would	bring
you	would	bring
he/she/it	would	bring
we	would	bring
you	would	bring
they	would	bring

Conditional II

I	would have	brought
you	would have	brought
he/she/it	would have	brought
we	would have	brought
you	would have	brought
they	would have	brought

Participle

Present participle

bringing

Past participle

brought

Gerund

bringing

Imperative

bring

Perfect infinitive

have brought

Anwendungsbeispiele

He **brought** his mother to the party. *Er **hat** seine Mutter zur Feier **mitgebracht**.*
What **brings** you here? *Was **führt** Sie zu uns?*
Did you **bring** something to eat? ***Hast** du was zu essen **mitgebracht**?*
I just **couldn't bring** myself to do it. *Ich **konnte** mich einfach **nicht** dazu **durchringen**, es zu tun.*

Redewendungen

to bring sb. a present *jdm. ein Geschenk (mit)bringen*
to bring problems (up)on oneself *sich Probleme einhandeln*
to bring sb. bad luck *jdm. Unglück bringen*
to bring sth. to mind *sich etw. in Erinnerung rufen*
to bring about a change *einen Wandel bewirken*
to bring sb. to health *jdn. gesund machen*
to bring sb./sth. down *etw./jdn. zu Fall bringen*
to bring out a book *ein Buch herausbringen*
to bring up a child *ein Kind auf-/großziehen*

Ähnliche Verben

to bear sth. *etw. (er)tragen*
to carry sth. *etw. tragen*
to fetch sth. *etw. holen (gehen)*
to take sth. *etw. (mit)nehmen/(weg)bringen*

Gebrauch

Die Verben to bring und to take kann man schnell verwechseln. Vereinfacht gesagt bezeichnet bring die Bewegung zum Sprecher oder Hörer und take die vom Sprecher oder Hörer weg. Wenn man sich in die Sichtweise eines anderen begibt, dann heißt es also auch bring:
Can I **bring** a friend to your party? *Kann ich eine Freundin zu deiner Party **mitbringen**?*

Tipps & Tricks

Genauso wie to bring konjugiert man die Verben to seek *suchen*, to teach *unterrichten* und to think *denken*.

12 buy *kaufen*

Simple

Present simple

I	buy
you	buy
he/she/it	buys
we	buy
you	buy
they	buy

Past simple

I	bought
you	bought
he/she/it	bought
we	bought
you	bought
they	bought

Present perfect simple

I	have	bought
you	have	bought
he/she/it	has	bought
we	have	bought
you	have	bought
they	have	bought

Past perfect simple

I	had	bought
you	had	bought
he/she/it	had	bought
we	had	bought
you	had	bought
they	had	bought

Progressive

Present progressive

I	am	buying
you	are	buying
he/she/it	is	buying
we	are	buying
you	are	buying
they	are	buying

Past progressive

I	was	buying
you	were	buying
he/she/it	was	buying
we	were	buying
you	were	buying
they	were	buying

Present perfect progressive

I	have been	buying
you	have been	buying
he/she/it	has been	buying
we	have been	buying
you	have been	buying
they	have been	buying

Past perfect progressive

I	had been	buying
you	had been	buying
he/she/it	had been	buying
we	had been	buying
you	had been	buying
they	had been	buying

Future

Future simple

I	will	buy
you	will	buy
he/she/it	will	buy
we	will	buy
you	will	buy
they	will	buy

Future progressive

I	will be	buying
you	will be	buying
he/she/it	will be	buying
we	will be	buying
you	will be	buying
they	will be	buying

Future perfect simple

I	will have	bought
you	will have	bought
he/she/it	will have	bought
we	will have	bought
you	will have	bought
they	will have	bought

Future perfect progressive

I	will have been	buying
you	will have been	buying
he/she/it	will have been	buying
we	will have been	buying
you	will have been	buying
they	will have been	buying

Conditional

Conditional I

I	would	buy
you	would	buy
he/she/it	would	buy
we	would	buy
you	would	buy
they	would	buy

Conditional II

I	would have	bought
you	would have	bought
he/she/it	would have	bought
we	would have	bought
you	would have	bought
they	would have	bought

Participle

Present participle

buying

Past participle

bought

Gerund

buying

Imperative

buy

Perfect infinitive

have bought

Anwendungsbeispiele

Where **did** you **buy** that skirt? *Wo **hast** du diesen Rock **gekauft**?*

Can I **buy** you an ice-cream? *Kann ich dir ein Eis **kaufen**?*

Today € 100 **buys** a lot less than it used to. *Für € 100 **bekommt** man heute viel weniger als früher.*

She**'ll** never **buy** that. *Das **wird** sie dir nie **abkaufen**.*

He **bought** some flowers for her birthday. *Er **hat** ihr ein paar Blumen zum Geburtstag **gekauft**.*

Redewendungen

to buy a witness (off) *einen Zeugen bestechen*

to buy into a company *sich in eine Firma einkaufen*

to buy out a company *eine Firma aufkaufen*

to buy sth. at the expense of sth. *etw. auf Kosten von etw. kaufen*

to buy time *Zeit gewinnen*

to buy the pig in a poke *die Katze im Sack kaufen*

Andere Verben

to exchange sth. *etw. umtauschen*

to dispose of sth. *etw veräußern*

to put sth. up for sale *etw. zum Verkauf anbieten*

to sell sth. *etw. verkaufen*

to trade sth. *etw. tauschen*

Gebrauch

Der Unterschied zwischen get, buy und purchase ist stilistischer Natur. Während get vor allem im gesprochenen Englisch verwendet wird, findet man buy in der gesprochenen Sprache ebenso wie in der Schriftsprache. Das Verb purchase *käuflich erwerben* gehört dem formellen Sprachgebrauch an und wird hauptsächlich in der Geschäftssprache verwendet, z. B. **purchasing** power *Kaufkraft*, **purchasing** department *Einkaufsabteilung* etc.

Tipps & Tricks

Genauso konjugiert wie to buy werden folgende Verben: to bring *mitbringen*, to catch *fangen*, to fight *kämpfen*, to seek *suchen*, to teach *lehren* und to think *denken*.

13 can *können*

Unvollständiges Hilfsverb;
Ersatzform: **to be able to do sth.**

Simple

Present simple		Progressive: Present progressive	Future: Future simple		
I	can	–	I	will	be able to
you	can	–	you	will	be able to
he/she/it	can	–	he/she/it	will	be able to
we	can	–	we	will	be able to
you	can	–	you	will	be able to
they	can	–	they	will	be able to

Past simple		Past progressive	Future progressive
I	could	–	–
you	could	–	–
he/she/it	could	–	–
we	could	–	–
you	could	–	–
they	could	–	–

Present perfect simple		Present perfect progressive	Future perfect simple		
I	have been able to	–	I	will have	been able to
you	have been able to	–	you	will have	been able to
he/she/it	has been able to	–	he/she/it	will have	been able to
we	have been able to	–	we	will have	been able to
you	have been able to	–	you	will have	been able to
they	have been able to	–	they	will have	been able to

Past perfect simple		Past perfect progressive	Future perfect progressive
I	had been able to	–	–
you	had been able to	–	–
he/she/it	had been able to	–	–
we	had been able to	–	–
you	had been able to	–	–
they	had been able to	–	–

Conditional

Conditional I		Conditional II	
I	could	I	could have
you	could	you	could have
he/she/it	could	he/she/it	could have
we	could	we	could have
you	could	you	could have
they	could	they	could have

Participle

Present participle
being able to

Past participle
been able to

Gerund
being able to

Imperative
–

Perfect infinitive
have been able to

Anwendungsbeispiele

Can he swim? ***Kann*** *er schwimmen?*
You **can** park over there. *Dort drüben* ***dürfen*** *Sie parken.*
He **could** speak Russian when he was two. *Als er zwei war,* ***konnte*** *er Russisch sprechen.*
She **could** be right. *Sie* ***könnte*** *recht haben.*
You **could have** helped me. *Du* ***hättest*** *mir helfen* ***können.***
You**'ll never be able** to learn Spanish. *Du* ***wirst niemals*** *Spanisch lernen* ***können.***

Witz

Little John is approached by the lifeguard at the public swimming pool:
"You **can't** pee in the pool!" says the lifeguard.
"But everyone pees in the pool," says Little John.
"Maybe," says the lifeguard, "but not from the diving board!"

Ähnliche Verben

to manage to do sth. *schaffen, etw. zu tun*
to succeed in doing sth. *etw. erfolgreich tun*
to be capable of doing sth. *in der Lage sein, etw. zu tun*
to be fit to do sth. *geeignet/fähig sein, etw. zu tun*
to be qualified to do sth. *qualifiziert sein, etw. zu tun*
to be skilled to do sth. *erfahren (genug) sein, etw. zu tun*

Aufgepasst!

Die Past tense-Form could wird verwendet, wenn man von allgemeinen Fähigkeiten in der Vergangenheit spricht:
He **could** speak five languages. *Er* ***konnte*** *fünf Sprachen sprechen.*
Bei besonderen Anlässen verwendet man be able to:
I **was able to** convince him not to leave his wife. *Ich* ***konnte*** *ihn überzeugen, seine Frau nicht zu verlassen.*

Tipps & Tricks

Wie alle Hilfsverben hat auch can kein -s in der dritten Person Singular und keine Verlaufsform. Fragen werden wie im Deutschen gebildet, indem man Subjekt und Hilfsverb vertauscht:
Can I go now. ***Kann*** *ich jetzt gehen?*

14 catch *fangen*

3. Person Singular mit **-es**

Simple

Present simple

I	catch
you	catch
he/she/it	**catches**
we	catch
you	catch
they	catch

Past simple

I	**caught**
you	**caught**
he/she/it	**caught**
we	**caught**
you	**caught**
they	**caught**

Present perfect simple

I	have	**caught**
you	have	**caught**
he/she/it	has	**caught**
we	have	**caught**
you	have	**caught**
they	have	**caught**

Past perfect simple

I	had	**caught**
you	had	**caught**
he/she/it	had	**caught**
we	had	**caught**
you	had	**caught**
they	had	**caught**

Progressive

Present progressive

I	am	catching
you	are	catching
he/she/it	is	catching
we	are	catching
you	are	catching
they	are	catching

Past progressive

I	was	catching
you	were	catching
he/she/it	was	catching
we	were	catching
you	were	catching
they	were	catching

Present perfect progressive

I	have been	catching
you	have been	catching
he/she/it	has been	catching
we	have been	catching
you	have been	catching
they	have been	catching

Past perfect progressive

I	had been	catching
you	had been	catching
he/she/it	had been	catching
we	had been	catching
you	had been	catching
they	had been	catching

Future

Future simple

I	will	catch
you	will	catch
he/she/it	will	catch
we	will	catch
you	will	catch
they	will	catch

Future progressive

I	will be	catching
you	will be	catching
he/she/it	will be	catching
we	will be	catching
you	will be	catching
they	will be	catching

Future perfect simple

I	will have	**caught**
you	will have	**caught**
he/she/it	will have	**caught**
we	will have	**caught**
you	will have	**caught**
they	will have	**caught**

Future perfect progressive

I	will have been	catching
you	will have been	catching
he/she/it	will have been	catching
we	will have been	catching
you	will have been	catching
they	will have been	catching

Conditional

Conditional I

I	would	catch
you	would	catch
he/she/it	would	catch
we	would	catch
you	would	catch
they	would	catch

Conditional II

I	would have	**caught**
you	would have	**caught**
he/she/it	would have	**caught**
we	would have	**caught**
you	would have	**caught**
they	would have	**caught**

Participle

Present participle

catching

Past participle

caught

Gerund

catching

Imperative

catch

Perfect infinitive

have **caught**

Anwendungsbeispiele

He **didn't catch** the ball. *Er **hat** den Ball **nicht gefangen**.*
Jack **didn't catch** her name. *Jack **hat** ihren Namen **nicht verstanden**.*
She **was caught** cheating. *Sie **wurde** beim Mogeln **erwischt**.*
I **caught a cold** last night. *Ich **habe mich** gestern Abend **erkältet**.*
They **got caught** in a storm. *Sie **wurden** von einem Sturm **überrascht**.*
She **caught** his eye. *Ihre Blicke **trafen sich**.*

Redewendungen

to catch it (Sl.) *sein Fett abkriegen*
to catch fire *Feuer fangen*
to catch a train/plane/bus *einen Zug/ein Flugzeug/einen Bus kriegen*
to get caught *erwischt werden*
to catch sb. red-handed *jdn. auf frischer Tat ertappen*
to catch sb. with their trousers/pants down *jdn. in flagranti erwischen*
to catch up with sth. *sich bei etw. verbessern*
to catch on one's sleep *Schlaf nachholen*

Andere Verben

to cast sth. *etw. werfen*
to fling sth. *etw. schleudern/werfen*
to hurl sth. *etw. schleudern*
to pitch sth. *etw. schlagen (Ball)*
to sling sth. *etw. schleudern*
to throw sth. *etw. werfen*

Gebrauch

Das Verb to catch heißt in seiner Grundbedeutung *fangen*. In Verbindung mit Präpositionen, Adjektiven und Substantiven nimmt es jedoch eine Vielzahl von Bedeutungen an, wie z. B. *erwischen*, *begreifen* oder *bekommen*, sodass man am besten die ganze Phrase lernt.

15 choose *wählen*

Verlaufsform ohne **-e**

Simple

Present simple

I	choose
you	choose
he/she/it	chooses
we	choose
you	choose
they	choose

Past simple

I	chose
you	chose
he/she/it	chose
we	chose
you	chose
they	chose

Present perfect simple

I	have	chosen
you	have	chosen
he/she/it	has	chosen
we	have	chosen
you	have	chosen
they	have	chosen

Past perfect simple

I	had	chosen
you	had	chosen
he/she/it	had	chosen
we	had	chosen
you	had	chosen
they	had	chosen

Progressive

Present progressive

I	am	choosing
you	are	choosing
he/she/it	is	choosing
we	are	choosing
you	are	choosing
they	are	choosing

Past progressive

I	was	choosing
you	were	choosing
he/she/it	was	choosing
we	were	choosing
you	were	choosing
they	were	choosing

Present perfect progressive

I	have been	choosing
you	have been	choosing
he/she/it	has been	choosing
we	have been	choosing
you	have been	choosing
they	have been	choosing

Past perfect progressive

I	had been	choosing
you	had been	choosing
he/she/it	had been	choosing
we	had been	choosing
you	had been	choosing
they	had been	choosing

Future

Future simple

I	will	choose
you	will	choose
he/she/it	will	choose
we	will	choose
you	will	choose
they	will	choose

Future progressive

I	will be	choosing
you	will be	choosing
he/she/it	will be	choosing
we	will be	choosing
you	will be	choosing
they	will be	choosing

Future perfect simple

I	will have	chosen
you	will have	chosen
he/she/it	will have	chosen
we	will have	chosen
you	will have	chosen
they	will have	chosen

Future perfect progressive

I	will have been	choosing
you	will have been	choosing
he/she/it	will have been	choosing
we	will have been	choosing
you	will have been	choosing
they	will have been	choosing

Conditional

Conditional I

I	would	choose
you	would	choose
he/she/it	would	choose
we	would	choose
you	would	choose
they	would	choose

Conditional II

I	would have	chosen
you	would have	chosen
he/she/it	would have	chosen
we	would have	chosen
you	would have	chosen
they	would have	chosen

Participle

Present participle

choosing

Past participle

chosen

Gerund

choosing

Imperative

choose

Perfect infinitive

have chosen

Anwendungsbeispiele

You **can't choose** your parents. *Man* ***kann sich*** *seine Eltern* ***nicht aussuchen.***
There were 20 items to **choose from**. *Es gab 20 Sachen* ***zur Auswahl.***
He just **couldn't choose between** red and green. *Er* ***konnte sich*** *einfach* ***nicht zwischen*** *Rot und Grün* ***entscheiden.***
There is **little to choose** between the two of them. *Die beiden* ***sind gleich gut.***
The magazine **chose** her **as** politician of the year. *Das Magazin* ***wählte*** *sie* ***zur*** *Politikerin des Jahres.*
They **chose** to take the bus. *Sie* ***zogen es vor,*** *mit dem Bus zu fahren.*

Redewendungen

to choose a team *ein Team zusammenstellen*
to choose one's words carefully *seine Worte mit Bedacht wählen*
to choose sb. as spokesperson *jdn. zum Sprecher/zur Sprecherin bestimmen*

Ähnliche Verben

to appoint sb. *jdn. ernennen*
to elect sb. *jdn. wählen*
to decide *sich entscheiden*
to go for sb. (umgs.) *jdn. begehren/in jdn. verknallt sein*
to nominate sb. *jdn. berufen/ernennen*
to opt for sth. *sich für etw. entscheiden*
to pick sth. *etw. auswählen*
to prefer sth. *etw. vorziehen*
to select from sth. *aus etw. auswählen*

Aufgepasst!

Den Infinitiv von to choose schreibt man mit -oo, den von to lose hingegen nur mit -o. Merken Sie sich einfach:
Choose to be honest, don't **lose** a friend. *Entscheide dich dafür, ehrlich zu sein; verliere nicht einen Freund.*

Tipps & Tricks

If und would – Satz kaputt!

16 come *kommen*

Verlaufsform ohne -e

Simple

Present simple

I	come
you	come
he/she/it	comes
we	come
you	come
they	come

Past simple

I	came
you	came
he/she/it	came
we	came
you	came
they	came

Present perfect simple

I	have	come
you	have	come
he/she/it	has	come
we	have	come
you	have	come
they	have	come

Past perfect simple

I	had	come
you	had	come
he/she/it	had	come
we	had	come
you	had	come
they	had	come

Progressive

Present progressive

I	am	coming
you	are	coming
he/she/it	is	coming
we	are	coming
you	are	coming
they	are	coming

Past progressive

I	was	coming
you	were	coming
he/she/it	was	coming
we	were	coming
you	were	coming
they	were	coming

Present perfect progressive

I	have been	coming
you	have been	coming
he/she/it	has been	coming
we	have been	coming
you	have been	coming
they	have been	coming

Past perfect progressive

I	had been	coming
you	had been	coming
he/she/it	had been	coming
we	had been	coming
you	had been	coming
they	had been	coming

Future

Future simple

I	will	come
you	will	come
he/she/it	will	come
we	will	come
you	will	come
they	will	come

Future progressive

I	will be	coming
you	will be	coming
he/she/it	will be	coming
we	will be	coming
you	will be	coming
they	will be	coming

Future perfect simple

I	will have	come
you	will have	come
he/she/it	will have	come
we	will have	come
you	will have	come
they	will have	come

Future perfect progressive

I	will have been	coming
you	will have been	coming
he/she/it	will have been	coming
we	will have been	coming
you	will have been	coming
they	will have been	coming

Conditional

Conditional I

I	would	come
you	would	come
he/she/it	would	come
we	would	come
you	would	come
they	would	come

Conditional II

I	would have	come
you	would have	come
he/she/it	would have	come
we	would have	come
you	would have	come
they	would have	come

Participle

Present participle

coming

Past participle

come

Gerund

coming

Imperative

come

Perfect infinitive

have come

Anwendungsbeispiele

I'm coming. *Ich* ***komme****.*
I **come from** Germany. *Ich* ***komme aus*** *Deutschland.*
Did you **come** here **by** train? ***Sind*** *Sie* ***mit*** *dem Zug* ***gekommen****?*
I saw it **coming.** *Ich habe es* ***kommen*** *sehen.*
Her sister **came by** in the afternoon. *Ihre Schwester* ***schaute*** *am Nachmittag* ***vorbei****.*
It **never came to pass**. *Es* ***ist nie geschehen****.*
Coming up next ... ***Als Nächstes*** *sehen Sie (z. B. im Fernsehen) …*
Come what may. ***Komme****, was wolle.*

Redewendungen

to come to know sb. *jdn. kennenlernen*
to come true *in Erfüllung gehen*
to come back from a journey *von einer Reise zurückkommen*
to come down with a cold *sich einen Schnupfen eingefangen haben*
to come into power *an die Macht kommen*
to come to a decision *zu einer Entscheidung gelangen*

Ähnliche Verben

to arrive *ankommen*
to approach *sich nähern*
to happen *sich ereignen*
to occur *sich ereignen/vorkommen*
to reach sb./sth. *jdn./etw. erreichen*
to turn up (umgs.) *auftauchen*

Gebrauch

Bitte beachten Sie den Unterschied zwischen to come und to go: come bezeichnet eine Bewegung zum Sprecher oder Hörer hin; go wird für Bewegungen zu anderen Zielen verwendet.

Tipps & Tricks

Genauso wie to come werden die mit come zusammengesetzten Verben to become *werden* und to overcome *überwinden/bewältigen* konjugiert.

17 cost *kosten*

Simple

Present simple

I	cost
you	cost
he/she/it	costs
we	cost
you	cost
they	cost

Past simple

I	cost
you	cost
he/she/it	cost
we	cost
you	cost
they	cost

Present perfect simple

I	have	cost
you	have	cost
he/she/it	has	cost
we	have	cost
you	have	cost
they	have	cost

Past perfect simple

I	had	cost
you	had	cost
he/she/it	had	cost
we	had	cost
you	had	cost
they	had	cost

Progressive

Present progressive

I	am	costing
you	are	costing
he/she/it	is	costing
we	are	costing
you	are	costing
they	are	costing

Past progressive

I	was	costing
you	were	costing
he/she/it	was	costing
we	were	costing
you	were	costing
they	were	costing

Present perfect progressive

I	have been	costing
you	have been	costing
he/she/it	has been	costing
we	have been	costing
you	have been	costing
they	have been	costing

Past perfect progressive

I	had been	costing
you	had been	costing
he/she/it	had been	costing
we	had been	costing
you	had been	costing
they	had been	costing

Future

Future simple

I	will	cost
you	will	cost
he/she/it	will	cost
we	will	cost
you	will	cost
they	will	cost

Future progressive

I	will be	costing
you	will be	costing
he/she/it	will be	costing
we	will be	costing
you	will be	costing
they	will be	costing

Future perfect simple

I	will have	cost
you	will have	cost
he/she/it	will have	cost
we	will have	cost
you	will have	cost
they	will have	cost

Future perfect progressive

I	will have been	costing
you	will have been	costing
he/she/it	will have been	costing
we	will have been	costing
you	will have been	costing
they	will have been	costing

Conditional

Conditional I

I	would	cost
you	would	cost
he/she/it	would	cost
we	would	cost
you	would	cost
they	would	cost

Conditional II

I	would have	cost
you	would have	cost
he/she/it	would have	cost
we	would have	cost
you	would have	cost
they	would have	cost

Participle

Present participle

costing

Past participle

cost

Gerund

costing

Imperative

cost

Perfect infinitive

have cost

Anwendungsbeispiele

What does the CD **cost**? *Was **kostet** die CD?*
It **costs** € 15. *Sie **kostet** € 15.*
The operation saved his life but **cost** him one leg. *Die Operation rettete ihm zwar das Leben, doch sie **kostete** ihn ein Bein.*
It **doesn't cost** anything to ask. *Fragen **kostet** nichts.*
It almost **cost** him his life. *Es **hat** ihn fast das Leben **gekostet**.*
The new car must **have cost** them a fortune. *Das neue Auto muss sie ein Vermögen **gekostet haben**.*
That'**ll cost** you dearly. *Das **wird** dich teuer **zu stehen kommen**.*
It'**ll cost** you to have that machine fixed. *Die Maschine zu reparieren **wird** dich **ganz schön was kosten**.*
His behaviour **cost** his mother many sleepless nights. *Sein Verhalten **bereitete** seiner Mutter so manch schlaflose Nacht.*
It'**ll cost** them much time and trouble. *Es **wird** sie viel Zeit und Mühe **kosten**.*

Witz

Jack: "This new hearing-aid I've got is so small that nobody notices it."
John: "That's great. How much did it **cost**?"
Jack: "Half past four."

Ähnliche Verben

to be *hier: kosten*
to come to *auf etw. kommen (Preis)*
to sell sth. at € ... *etw. zum Preis von € ... verkaufen*
to be priced at € ... *zum Preis von € ... ausgezeichnet sein*

Gebrauch

Auch wenn es zunächst etwas ungewohnt klingen mag, das Verb to cost ist in allen drei Verbformen gleich. Der Satz It **cost** € 50 kann also *Es **kostete** € 50* oder *Es **hat** € 50 **gekostet*** heißen.

Tipps & Tricks

Bei einer Reihe von Verben sind die drei Verbformen gleich, z. B. bei to bet *wetten*, to burst *platzen*, to cast *werfen*, to cut *schneiden*, to hit *schlagen*, to let *lassen*, to shut *schließen* und to spread *ausbreiten*.

18 cut *schneiden/reduzieren*

Konsonantenverdoppelung

Simple

Present simple

I	cut
you	cut
he/she/it	cuts
we	cut
you	cut
they	cut

Past simple

I	cut
you	cut
he/she/it	cut
we	cut
you	cut
they	cut

Present perfect simple

I	have	cut
you	have	cut
he/she/it	has	cut
we	have	cut
you	have	cut
they	have	cut

Past perfect simple

I	had	cut
you	had	cut
he/she/it	had	cut
we	had	cut
you	had	cut
they	had	cut

Progressive

Present progressive

I	am	cutting
you	are	cutting
he/she/it	is	cutting
we	are	cutting
you	are	cutting
they	are	cutting

Past progressive

I	was	cutting
you	were	cutting
he/she/it	was	cutting
we	were	cutting
you	were	cutting
they	were	cutting

Present perfect progressive

I	have been	cutting
you	have been	cutting
he/she/it	has been	cutting
we	have been	cutting
you	have been	cutting
they	have been	cutting

Past perfect progressive

I	had been	cutting
you	had been	cutting
he/she/it	had been	cutting
we	had been	cutting
you	had been	cutting
they	had been	cutting

Future

Future simple

I	will	cut
you	will	cut
he/she/it	will	cut
we	will	cut
you	will	cut
they	will	cut

Future progressive

I	will be	cutting
you	will be	cutting
he/she/it	will be	cutting
we	will be	cutting
you	will be	cutting
they	will be	cutting

Future perfect simple

I	will have	cut
you	will have	cut
he/she/it	will have	cut
we	will have	cut
you	will have	cut
they	will have	cut

Future perfect progressive

I	will have been	cutting
you	will have been	cutting
he/she/it	will have been	cutting
we	will have been	cutting
you	will have been	cutting
they	will have been	cutting

Conditional

Conditional I

I	would	cut
you	would	cut
he/she/it	would	cut
we	would	cut
you	would	cut
they	would	cut

Conditional II

I	would have	cut
you	would have	cut
he/she/it	would have	cut
we	would have	cut
you	would have	cut
they	would have	cut

Participle

Present participle

cutting

Past participle

cut

Gerund

cutting

Imperative

cut

Perfect infinitive

have cut

Anwendungsbeispiele

Could you **cut** the cake, please? *Könntest du bitte den Kuchen* ***(an)schneiden****?*
I'**ve cut** my finger. *Ich* ***habe*** *mich in den Finger* ***geschnitten****.*
She **cut** herself with a knife. *Sie* ***hat*** *sich mit einem Messer* ***geschnitten****.*
We need to **cut back** on spending. *Wir müssen unsere Ausgaben* ***kürzen****.*

Redewendungen

to cut costs *die Kosten senken*
to cut down smoking *das Rauchen reduzieren*
to cut the lawn *den Rasen mähen*
to cut down a tree *einen Baum fällen*
to get/have one's hair cut *sich die Haare schneiden lassen*
to cut sb. short *jdn. unterbrechen*
to cut into a conversation *sich in ein Gespräch einmischen*
to cut a long story short ... *um es kurz zu machen ...*
to cut sb. down to size *jdn. zurechtstutzen/in seine Schranken weisen*
to cut in line (AE) *sich vordrängeln*
to cut school/class (AE) *die Schule/eine Stunde schwänzen*

Ähnliche Verben

to chop sth. *etw. klein schneiden*
to mow sth. *etw. mähen*
to reduce sth. *etw. verringern*
to separate sth. *etw. trennen*
to slice sth. *etw. in Scheiben schneiden*

Gebrauch

Obwohl bei dem Verb to cut alle drei Verbformen gleich sind, ist es nicht schwer zu erkennen, in welcher Zeit es steht. Entweder man erkennt das Zeitverhältnis an einer Zeitangabe, wie yesterday oder tomorrow, oder man erkennt es daran, dass die Form zusammengesetzt ist: **have** cut, **had** cut, **will** cut usw.

Tipps & Tricks

Bei einer Reihe von Verben sind die drei Verbformen gleich, z. B. bei to bid *bieten*, to cost *kosten*, to hurt *wehtun*, to put *setzen/stellen/legen*, to set *festsetzen*, to slit *aufschlitzen*, to split *spalten* und to thrust *stoßen*.

19 draw *zeichnen/ziehen*

Simple

Present simple

I	draw
you	draw
he/she/it	draws
we	draw
you	draw
they	draw

Past simple

I	drew
you	drew
he/she/it	drew
we	drew
you	drew
they	drew

Present perfect simple

I	have	drawn
you	have	drawn
he/she/it	has	drawn
we	have	drawn
you	have	drawn
they	have	drawn

Past perfect simple

I	had	drawn
you	had	drawn
he/she/it	had	drawn
we	had	drawn
you	had	drawn
they	had	drawn

Progressive

Present progressive

I	am	drawing
you	are	drawing
he/she/it	is	drawing
we	are	drawing
you	are	drawing
they	are	drawing

Past progressive

I	was	drawing
you	were	drawing
he/she/it	was	drawing
we	were	drawing
you	were	drawing
they	were	drawing

Present perfect progressive

I	have been	drawing
you	have been	drawing
he/she/it	has been	drawing
we	have been	drawing
you	have been	drawing
they	have been	drawing

Past perfect progressive

I	had been	drawing
you	had been	drawing
he/she/it	had been	drawing
we	had been	drawing
you	had been	drawing
they	had been	drawing

Future

Future simple

I	will	draw
you	will	draw
he/she/it	will	draw
we	will	draw
you	will	draw
they	will	draw

Future progressive

I	will be	drawing
you	will be	drawing
he/she/it	will be	drawing
we	will be	drawing
you	will be	drawing
they	will be	drawing

Future perfect simple

I	will have	drawn
you	will have	drawn
he/she/it	will have	drawn
we	will have	drawn
you	will have	drawn
they	will have	drawn

Future perfect progressive

I	will have been	drawing
you	will have been	drawing
he/she/it	will have been	drawing
we	will have been	drawing
you	will have been	drawing
they	will have been	drawing

Conditional

Conditional I

I	would	draw
you	would	draw
he/she/it	would	draw
we	would	draw
you	would	draw
they	would	draw

Conditional II

I	would have	drawn
you	would have	drawn
he/she/it	would have	drawn
we	would have	drawn
you	would have	drawn
they	would have	drawn

Participle

Present participle

drawing

Past participle

drawn

Gerund

drawing

Imperative

draw

Perfect infinitive

have drawn

Anwendungsbeispiele

When I was young I used to **draw** a lot. *Als ich klein war,* ***zeichnete*** *ich viel.*
Do you mind if I **draw** the curtains? *Hast du etwas dagegen, wenn ich die Vorhänge* ***zuziehe****?*
The accident **drew** a huge crowd. *Der Unfall* ***zog*** *eine große Menschenmenge an.*
Let me **draw** your attention **to** the following aspects. ***Richten*** *Sie bitte Ihre Aufmerksamkeit* ***auf*** *die folgenden Aspekte.*

Redewendungen

to draw a conclusion *eine Schlussfolgerung ziehen*
to draw a comparison *einen Vergleich ziehen*
to draw a deep breath *tief Luft holen*
to draw lots/straws *Strohalm ziehen/losen*
to draw the short straw *den Kürzeren ziehen*
to draw money from a bank *Geld abheben*
to draw the sword *das Schwert ziehen*
to draw to a close/an end *zu Ende gehen*
to draw up sth. *etw. verfassen/aufsetzen (z. B. ein Schriftstück)*

Ähnliche Verben

to depict sb. *jdn. bildlich darstellen*
to paint sth. *etw. malen*
to portray sb. *jdn. porträtieren*
to pull sth. *etw. ziehen*
to sketch sth. *etw. skizzieren*
to withdraw sth. *etw. abheben (Geld)*

Gebrauch

Das schlichte Verb to draw hat es in sich. In Verbindung mit Präpositionen oder Substantiven kann es vielseitig eingesetzt werden. Es geht kein Weg umhin, jeweils die ganze Phrase zu lernen.

Tipps & Tricks

He, she, it, das -s muss mit. Doch sei klug, ein -s ist genug.

20 drive *fahren/treiben*

Verlaufsform ohne **-e**

Simple

Present simple

I	drive
you	drive
he/she/it	drives
we	drive
you	drive
they	drive

Past simple

I	drove
you	drove
he/she/it	drove
we	drove
you	drove
they	drove

Present perfect simple

I	have	driven
you	have	driven
he/she/it	has	driven
we	have	driven
you	have	driven
they	have	driven

Past perfect simple

I	had	driven
you	had	driven
he/she/it	had	driven
we	had	driven
you	had	driven
they	had	driven

Progressive

Present progressive

I	am	driving
you	are	driving
he/she/it	is	driving
we	are	driving
you	are	driving
they	are	driving

Past progressive

I	was	driving
you	were	driving
he/she/it	was	driving
we	were	driving
you	were	driving
they	were	driving

Present perfect progressive

I	have been	driving
you	have been	driving
he/she/it	has been	driving
we	have been	driving
you	have been	driving
they	have been	driving

Past perfect progressive

I	had been	driving
you	had been	driving
he/she/it	had been	driving
we	had been	driving
you	had been	driving
they	had been	driving

Future

Future simple

I	will	drive
you	will	drive
he/she/it	will	drive
we	will	drive
you	will	drive
they	will	drive

Future progressive

I	will be	driving
you	will be	driving
he/she/it	will be	driving
we	will be	driving
you	will be	driving
they	will be	driving

Future perfect simple

I	will have	driven
you	will have	driven
he/she/it	will have	driven
we	will have	driven
you	will have	driven
they	will have	driven

Future perfect progressive

I	will have been	driving
you	will have been	driving
he/she/it	will have been	driving
we	will have been	driving
you	will have been	driving
they	will have been	driving

Conditional

Conditional I

I	would	drive
you	would	drive
he/she/it	would	drive
we	would	drive
you	would	drive
they	would	drive

Conditional II

I	would have	driven
you	would have	driven
he/she/it	would have	driven
we	would have	driven
you	would have	driven
they	would have	driven

Participle

Present participle

driving

Past participle

driven

Gerund

driving

Imperative

drive

Perfect infinitive

have driven

Anwendungsbeispiele

I **drove to** Berlin last week. *Letzte Woche **bin** ich **nach** Berlin **gefahren**.*
Can you **drive**? *Kannst du Auto **fahren**?*
He **drove** his horse quite hard. *Er **trieb** sein Pferd ziemlich an.*
She **drives** me crazy. *Sie **macht** mich noch wahnsinnig.*
He **drove** the nail **into** the wall. *Er **trieb** den Nagel **in** die Wand.*
What **is** she **driving at**? *Worauf **will** sie **hinaus**?*
Don't drive it **to** the last minute. ***Schiebe** es **nicht auf** die lange Bank.*

Witz

"Harry," said little Betsy to her big brother, "what does that L on the car mean?"
"It means I'm learning to **drive**," said Harry.
A few weeks later Harry had passed the test and was just affixing a GB sticker to the back of his car.
"Harry," said little Betsy, "does GB mean you're getting better?"

Andere Verben

to hike *wandern*
to plod (on/along) *sich dahinschleppen*
to ride (bicycle) *fahren (Fahrrad)*
to run *rennen*
to rush *eilen/hetzen*
to stroll *schlendern*
to trudge *sich schleppen*
to walk/to go on foot *(zu Fuß) gehen*

Gebrauch

Das Verb to drive im Sinne von *fahren* verwendet man nur, wenn man selbst hinter dem Steuer sitzt. Wenn das nicht der Fall ist, benutzt man to go, auch wenn man mit der Bahn fährt oder im Flugzeug fliegt. Das normale Zufußgehen heißt to walk oder to go on foot.

Tipps & Tricks

Die Verben to arise *aufstehen/auftauchen*, to ride *reiten/fahren*, to rise *sich erheben/aufstehen*, to stride *schreiten*, to strive *streben* und to write *schreiben* werden genauso konjugiert wie to drive.

21 eat *essen*

Simple

Present simple

I	eat	
you	eat	
he/she/it	eats	
we	eat	
you	eat	
they	eat	

Past simple

I	ate
you	ate
he/she/it	ate
we	ate
you	ate
they	ate

Present perfect simple

I	have	eaten
you	have	eaten
he/she/it	has	eaten
we	have	eaten
you	have	eaten
they	have	eaten

Past perfect simple

I	had	eaten
you	had	eaten
he/she/it	had	eaten
we	had	eaten
you	had	eaten
they	had	eaten

Progressive

Present progressive

I	am	eating
you	are	eating
he/she/it	is	eating
we	are	eating
you	are	eating
they	are	eating

Past progressive

I	was	eating
you	were	eating
he/she/it	was	eating
we	were	eating
you	were	eating
they	were	eating

Present perfect progressive

I	have been	eating
you	have been	eating
he/she/it	has been	eating
we	have been	eating
you	have been	eating
they	have been	eating

Past perfect progressive

I	had been	eating
you	had been	eating
he/she/it	had been	eating
we	had been	eating
you	had been	eating
they	had been	eating

Future

Future simple

I	will	eat
you	will	eat
he/she/it	will	eat
we	will	eat
you	will	eat
they	will	eat

Future progressive

I	will be	eating
you	will be	eating
he/she/it	will be	eating
we	will be	eating
you	will be	eating
they	will be	eating

Future perfect simple

I	will have	eaten
you	will have	eaten
he/she/it	will have	eaten
we	will have	eaten
you	will have	eaten
they	will have	eaten

Future perfect progressive

I	will have been	eating
you	will have been	eating
he/she/it	will have been	eating
we	will have been	eating
you	will have been	eating
they	will have been	eating

Conditional

Conditional I

I	would	eat
you	would	eat
he/she/it	would	eat
we	would	eat
you	would	eat
they	would	eat

Conditional II

I	would have	eaten
you	would have	eaten
he/she/it	would have	eaten
we	would have	eaten
you	would have	eaten
they	would have	eaten

Participle

Present participle

eating

Past participle

eaten

Gerund

eating

Imperative

eat

Perfect infinitive

have eaten

Anwendungsbeispiele

What **did** you **eat** last night? *Was* ***hast*** *du gestern Abend* ***gegessen****?*
Have you **eaten**? ***Haben*** *Sie schon* ***gegessen****?*
You should **eat** more healthily. *Du solltest dich gesünder* ***ernähren****.*
Have you **had** anything to **eat** today? ***Hast*** *du heute schon etwas* ***gegessen****?*
I'm so hungry; I could **eat** a horse. *Ich bin so hungrig; ich könnte ein ganzes Pferd* ***verdrücken****.*
He**'s eaten up with** pride. *Er* ***ist von*** *Stolz* ***zerfressen****.*
What**'s eating** him? *Was* ***hat*** *er denn?*

Redewendungen

to eat breakfast/lunch/supper *frühstücken/zu Mittag/Abend essen*
to eat in/out *zu Hause/auswärts essen*
to eat up *aufessen*
to eat like a bird *wie ein Spatz essen*
to eat like a horse *wie ein Scheunendrescher fressen*
to be eaten up with envy/pride *vor Neid/Stolz zerfressen sein*
to be eaten by worms *wurmstichig sein*
to eat oneself sick on sth. *sich an etw. überfressen*
to eat one's heart out *sich vor Kummer verzehren*
to eat one's hat *einen Besen fressen*
to eat out of sb.'s hand *jdm. aus der Hand fressen*
to eat one's words *alles, was man gesagt hat, zurücknehmen*

Andere Verben

to be boozing (umgs.) *saufen*
to drink *trinken*
to guzzle sth. (umgs.) *etw. in sich hineinkippen*

Gebrauch

Bitte beachten Sie die unterschiedliche Aussprache der Vergangenheitsform ate.

22 fall *fallen*

Simple

Present simple

I	fall
you	fall
he/she/it	falls
we	fall
you	fall
they	fall

Past simple

I	fell
you	fell
he/she/it	fell
we	fell
you	fell
they	fell

Present perfect simple

I	have	fallen
you	have	fallen
he/she/it	has	fallen
we	have	fallen
you	have	fallen
they	have	fallen

Past perfect simple

I	had	fallen
you	had	fallen
he/she/it	had	fallen
we	had	fallen
you	had	fallen
they	had	fallen

Progressive

Present progressive

I	am	falling
you	are	falling
he/she/it	is	falling
we	are	falling
you	are	falling
they	are	falling

Past progressive

I	was	falling
you	were	falling
he/she/it	was	falling
we	were	falling
you	were	falling
they	were	falling

Present perfect progressive

I	have been	falling
you	have been	falling
he/she/it	has been	falling
we	have been	falling
you	have been	falling
they	have been	falling

Past perfect progressive

I	had been	falling
you	had been	falling
he/she/it	had been	falling
we	had been	falling
you	had been	falling
they	had been	falling

Future

Future simple

I	will	fall
you	will	fall
he/she/it	will	fall
we	will	fall
you	will	fall
they	will	fall

Future progressive

I	will be	falling
you	will be	falling
he/she/it	will be	falling
we	will be	falling
you	will be	falling
they	will be	falling

Future perfect simple

I	will have	fallen
you	will have	fallen
he/she/it	will have	fallen
we	will have	fallen
you	will have	fallen
they	will have	fallen

Future perfect progressive

I	will have been	falling
you	will have been	falling
he/she/it	will have been	falling
we	will have been	falling
you	will have been	falling
they	will have been	falling

Conditional

Conditional I

I	would	fall
you	would	fall
he/she/it	would	fall
we	would	fall
you	would	fall
they	would	fall

Conditional II

I	would have	fallen
you	would have	fallen
he/she/it	would have	fallen
we	would have	fallen
you	would have	fallen
they	would have	fallen

Participle

Present participle

falling

Past participle

fallen

Gerund

falling

Imperative

fall

Perfect infinitive

have fallen

Anwendungsbeispiele

He **fell** badly. *Er **stürzte** schwer.*
A lot of snow **had fallen** that night. *Eine Menge Schnee **war** in dieser Nacht **gefallen**.*
The inflation rate **fell** sharply. *Die Inflationsrate **fiel** deutlich.*
She finally **fell asleep**. *Schließlich **ist** sie **eingeschlafen**.*
His face **fell**. *Er **macht** ein langes Gesicht.*
The bread never **falls** but on the buttered side. *Brot **fällt** immer auf die Butterseite.*

Redewendungen

to fall apart *auseinanderfallen*
to fall behind *zurückfallen/zurückbleiben*
to fall for sb. *sich in jdn. verknallen*
to fall in love (with sb.) *sich (in jdn.) verlieben*
to fall through *ins Wasser fallen*
to fall to pieces *in die Brüche gehen*
to fall under the influence of sb. *unter den Einfluss einer Person geraten*

Ähnliche Verben

to decline *nachlassen/zurückgehen*
to drop *fallen/sinken*
to plunge *dramatisch fallen*
to slip *ausrutschen*
to stumble *straucheln/stolpern*
to trip *stolpern*

Gebrauch

Für eine ganze Reihe von Verbindungen mit fall lässt sich im Deutschen ein einzelnes Vollverb finden: to fall ill/sick *erkranken*, to fall asleep *einschlafen*, to fall in love *sich verlieben*, to fall open *aufklappen*, to fall into debt *sich verschulden* oder to fall into sin *sich versündigen*.

23 feel *fühlen/sich (an)fühlen*

Simple

Present simple

I	feel
you	feel
he/she/it	feels
we	feel
you	feel
they	feel

Past simple

I	felt
you	felt
he/she/it	felt
we	felt
you	felt
they	felt

Present perfect simple

I	have	felt
you	have	felt
he/she/it	has	felt
we	have	felt
you	have	felt
they	have	felt

Past perfect simple

I	had	felt
you	had	felt
he/she/it	had	felt
we	had	felt
you	had	felt
they	had	felt

Progressive

Present progressive

I	am	feeling
you	are	feeling
he/she/it	is	feeling
we	are	feeling
you	are	feeling
they	are	feeling

Past progressive

I	was	feeling
you	were	feeling
he/she/it	was	feeling
we	were	feeling
you	were	feeling
they	were	feeling

Present perfect progressive

I	have been	feeling
you	have been	feeling
he/she/it	has been	feeling
we	have been	feeling
you	have been	feeling
they	have been	feeling

Past perfect progressive

I	had been	feeling
you	had been	feeling
he/she/it	had been	feeling
we	had been	feeling
you	had been	feeling
they	had been	feeling

Future

Future simple

I	will	feel
you	will	feel
he/she/it	will	feel
we	will	feel
you	will	feel
they	will	feel

Future progressive

I	will be	feeling
you	will be	feeling
he/she/it	will be	feeling
we	will be	feeling
you	will be	feeling
they	will be	feeling

Future perfect simple

I	will have	felt
you	will have	felt
he/she/it	will have	felt
we	will have	felt
you	will have	felt
they	will have	felt

Future perfect progressive

I	will have been	feeling
you	will have been	feeling
he/she/it	will have been	feeling
we	will have been	feeling
you	will have been	feeling
they	will have been	feeling

Conditional

Conditional I

I	would	feel
you	would	feel
he/she/it	would	feel
we	would	feel
you	would	feel
they	would	feel

Conditional II

I	would have	felt
you	would have	felt
he/she/it	would have	felt
we	would have	felt
you	would have	felt
they	would have	felt

Participle

Present participle

feeling

Past participle

felt

Gerund

feeling

Imperative

feel

Perfect infinitive

have felt

Anwendungsbeispiele

How do you **feel** today? *Wie **fühlst** du dich heute?*
I **feel** fine, thanks. *Ich **fühle** mich gut, danke.*
My mouth **feels** very dry. *Mein Mund **fühlt sich** sehr trocken **an**.*
It **feels like** silk. *Es **fühlt sich an wie** Seide.*
The doctor **felt** my pulse. *Der Arzt **fühlte** meinen Puls.*
I **felt** as if the world was coming to an end. *Ich **dachte**, die Welt würde untergehen.*
I **feel** that ... *Ich **finde**, dass .../Ich **bin der Meinung**, dass ...*
It **is felt** that ... *Man **ist der Meinung**, dass ...*

Redewendungen

to feel good/bad/sad *sich gut/schlecht/traurig fühlen*
to feel like doing sth. *Lust haben, etw. zu tun*
sb. feels hot/cold *jdm. ist heiß/kalt*

Ähnliche Verben

to believe *glauben*
to guess (AE) *denken/meinen*
to mean *meinen*
to think *denken/meinen*
to touch sth. *etw. berühren*

Gebrauch

Bitte beachten Sie den Unterschied zwischen der einfachen Form und der Verlaufsform. Die Verlaufsform wird dann gebraucht, wenn es sich um eine Aktivität handelt (She**'s feeling** the surface. *Sie **befühlt** die Oberfläche.*) oder wenn man von einem körperlichen oder geistigen Zustand spricht (I**'m feeling** great. *Mir **geht** es ausgezeichnet.*), aber nicht, wenn man eine Meinung zum Ausdruck bringen möchte:
I **feel** that he should go to the police. *Ich **denke**, er sollte zur Polizei gehen.*

Tipps & Tricks

Genauso konjugiert werden u. a. to creep *kriechen*, to feed *füttern*, to flee *fliehen*, to keep *halten*, to leave *verlassen*, to lead *führen*, to lean *sich lehnen*, to mean *meinen*, to read *lesen*, to sleep *schlafen* und to weep *weinen*.

24 find *finden*

Simple

Present simple

I	find
you	find
he/she/it	finds
we	find
you	find
they	find

Past simple

I	found
you	found
he/she/it	found
we	found
you	found
they	found

Present perfect simple

I	have	found
you	have	found
he/she/it	has	found
we	have	found
you	have	found
they	have	found

Past perfect simple

I	had	found
you	had	found
he/she/it	had	found
we	had	found
you	had	found
they	had	found

Progressive

Present progressive

I	am	finding
you	are	finding
he/she/it	is	finding
we	are	finding
you	are	finding
they	are	finding

Past progressive

I	was	finding
you	were	finding
he/she/it	was	finding
we	were	finding
you	were	finding
they	were	finding

Present perfect progressive

I	have been	finding
you	have been	finding
he/she/it	has been	finding
we	have been	finding
you	have been	finding
they	have been	finding

Past perfect progressive

I	had been	finding
you	had been	finding
he/she/it	had been	finding
we	had been	finding
you	had been	finding
they	had been	finding

Future

Future simple

I	will	find
you	will	find
he/she/it	will	find
we	will	find
you	will	find
they	will	find

Future progressive

I	will be	finding
you	will be	finding
he/she/it	will be	finding
we	will be	finding
you	will be	finding
they	will be	finding

Future perfect simple

I	will have	found
you	will have	found
he/she/it	will have	found
we	will have	found
you	will have	found
they	will have	found

Future perfect progressive

I	will have been	finding
you	will have been	finding
he/she/it	will have been	finding
we	will have been	finding
you	will have been	finding
they	will have been	finding

Conditional

Conditional I

I	would	find
you	would	find
he/she/it	would	find
we	would	find
you	would	find
they	would	find

Conditional II

I	would have	found
you	would have	found
he/she/it	would have	found
we	would have	found
you	would have	found
they	would have	found

Participle

Present participle

finding

Past participle

found

Gerund

finding

Imperative

find

Perfect infinitive

have found

Anwendungsbeispiele

I can't **find** my socks. *Ich kann meine Socken nicht* ***finden.***
I'm good at **finding out** the truth. *Ich kann gut die Wahrheit* ***herausfinden.***
They **found** her sleeping on the roof. *Sie* ***fanden*** *sie schlafend auf dem Dach.*
I wish I could **find** more time for her. *Ich wünschte, ich könnte mehr Zeit für sie* ***finden.***
They **were found** murdered. *Sie* ***wurden*** *ermordet* ***aufgefunden.***

Redewendungen

to find sth. easy/interesting/useful *etw. leicht/interessant/nützlich finden*
to find sth. empty *etw. leer vorfinden*
to find sth. hard/difficult *etw. schwierig finden*
to find sb. (not) guilty of sth. *jdn. als (nicht) schuldig befinden*
to find happiness with sb. *mit jdm. glücklich werden*
to find excuses *Ausreden finden*
to find fault with sb./sth. *an jdm./etw. etwas zu kritisieren haben*
to find no reason why ... *keinen Grund finden, warum ...*
to find oneself *zu sich selbst finden*

Ähnliche Verben

to detect sb./sth. *jdn./etw. entdecken*
to discover sb./sth. *jdn./etw. finden*
to think *denken/glauben*
to track down sb./sth. *jdn./etw. aufspüren*

Aufgepasst!

Bitte beachten Sie den Unterschied zwischen den beiden Verben to find (found/found) *finden* und to found (founded/founded) *gründen*:
They **are going to found** a new football club next year. *Nächstes Jahr* ***werden*** *sie einen neuen Fußballverein* ***gründen.***
The company **was founded** in 1935. *Das Unternehmen* ***wurde*** *1935* ***gegründet.***

Tipps & Tricks

Genauso konjugiert wie to find werden to bind *binden*, to grind *zermahlen* und to wind *wickeln/spulen*.

25 fly *fliegen*

-y → -ies vor -s

Simple

Present simple

I	fly
you	fly
he/she/it	flies
we	fly
you	fly
they	fly

Past simple

I	flew
you	flew
he/she/it	flew
we	flew
you	flew
they	flew

Present perfect simple

I	have	flown
you	have	flown
he/she/it	has	flown
we	have	flown
you	have	flown
they	have	flown

Past perfect simple

I	had	flown
you	had	flown
he/she/it	had	flown
we	had	flown
you	had	flown
they	had	flown

Progressive

Present progressive

I	am	flying
you	are	flying
he/she/it	is	flying
we	are	flying
you	are	flying
they	are	flying

Past progressive

I	was	flying
you	were	flying
he/she/it	was	flying
we	were	flying
you	were	flying
they	were	flying

Present perfect progressive

I	have been	flying
you	have been	flying
he/she/it	has been	flying
we	have been	flying
you	have been	flying
they	have been	flying

Past perfect progressive

I	had been	flying
you	had been	flying
he/she/it	had been	flying
we	had been	flying
you	had been	flying
they	had been	flying

Future

Future simple

I	will	fly
you	will	fly
he/she/it	will	fly
we	will	fly
you	will	fly
they	will	fly

Future progressive

I	will be	flying
you	will be	flying
he/she/it	will be	flying
we	will be	flying
you	will be	flying
they	will be	flying

Future perfect simple

I	will have	flown
you	will have	flown
he/she/it	will have	flown
we	will have	flown
you	will have	flown
they	will have	flown

Future perfect progressive

I	will have been	flying
you	will have been	flying
he/she/it	will have been	flying
we	will have been	flying
you	will have been	flying
they	will have been	flying

Conditional

Conditional I

I	would	fly
you	would	fly
he/she/it	would	fly
we	would	fly
you	would	fly
they	would	fly

Conditional II

I	would have	flown
you	would have	flown
he/she/it	would have	flown
we	would have	flown
you	would have	flown
they	would have	flown

Participle

Present participle

flying

Past participle

flown

Gerund

flying

Imperative

fly

Perfect infinitive

have flown

Anwendungsbeispiele

Twenty geese **were flying over** the field. *Zwanzig Gänse **flogen über** das Feld.*
Will you **fly to** Munich or take the train? ***Wirst** du **nach** München **fliegen** oder mit dem Zug fahren?*
Are you **flying out of** JFK? ***Fliegen** Sie **vom** John-F.-Kennedy-Airport **ab**?*
No, we **are flying in from** Newark. *Nein, **wir kommen von** Newark **an**.*
Suddenly the window **flew** open. *Plötzlich **flog** das Fenster auf.*
The flag **was flying on** half-mast. *Die Fahne **wehte auf** Halbmast.*
The days simply **flew by**. *Die Tage **vergingen** wie im Fluge.*
Time **flies.** *Wie die Zeit **vergeht**!*
She **flew at** him. *Sie **ging auf** ihn **los**.*

Redewendungen

to fly into a panic/fury *in Panik/Wut geraten*
to fly to pieces/apart *zerspringen/bersten*
to fly a kite *einen Drachen steigen lassen*
to fly high (AE) *im siebten Himmel sein*
to fly in the face/teeth of sth. *gegen die Norm handeln*

Ähnliche Verben

to be airborne *sich in der Luft befinden (Flugzeug)*
to fail/flunk an exam *durch eine Prüfung fliegen*
to flutter *flattern*
to glide *(dahin)gleiten*
to go by plane *mit dem Flugzeug fliegen*
to pass swiftly *schnell vorüberfahren*
to soar *(hoch) aufsteigen*

Gebrauch

Übrigens: *aus einer Stellung fliegen* (also *gefeuert werden*) heißt to be fired und für *aus der Schule fliegen* sagt man to be/get kicked out of school.

Tipps & Tricks

Genauso wie to fly konjugiert man die Verben to blow *blasen*, to know *kennen/wissen*, to grow *wachsen* und to throw *werfen*.

26 forget *vergessen*

Konsonantenverdoppelung

Simple

Present simple

I	forget
you	forget
he/she/it	forgets
we	forget
you	forget
they	forget

Past simple

I	forgot
you	forgot
he/she/it	forgot
we	forgot
you	forgot
they	forgot

Present perfect simple

I	have	forgotten
you	have	forgotten
he/she/it	has	forgotten
we	have	forgotten
you	have	forgotten
they	have	forgotten

Past perfect simple

I	had	forgotten
you	had	forgotten
he/she/it	had	forgotten
we	had	forgotten
you	had	forgotten
they	had	forgotten

Progressive

Present progressive

I	am	forgetting
you	are	forgetting
he/she/it	is	forgetting
we	are	forgetting
you	are	forgetting
they	are	forgetting

Past progressive

I	was	forgetting
you	were	forgetting
he/she/it	was	forgetting
we	were	forgetting
you	were	forgetting
they	were	forgetting

Present perfect progressive

I	have been	forgetting
you	have been	forgetting
he/she/it	has been	forgetting
we	have been	forgetting
you	have been	forgetting
they	have been	forgetting

Past perfect progressive

I	had been	forgetting
you	had been	forgetting
he/she/it	had been	forgetting
we	had been	forgetting
you	had been	forgetting
they	had been	forgetting

Future

Future simple

I	will	forget
you	will	forget
he/she/it	will	forget
we	will	forget
you	will	forget
they	will	forget

Future progressive

I	will be	forgetting
you	will be	forgetting
he/she/it	will be	forgetting
we	will be	forgetting
you	will be	forgetting
they	will be	forgetting

Future perfect simple

I	will have	forgotten
you	will have	forgotten
he/she/it	will have	forgotten
we	will have	forgotten
you	will have	forgotten
they	will have	forgotten

Future perfect progressive

I	will have been	forgetting
you	will have been	forgetting
he/she/it	will have been	forgetting
we	will have been	forgetting
you	will have been	forgetting
they	will have been	forgetting

Conditional

Conditional I

I	would	forget
you	would	forget
he/she/it	would	forget
we	would	forget
you	would	forget
they	would	forget

Conditional II

I	would have	forgotten
you	would have	forgotten
he/she/it	would have	forgotten
we	would have	forgotten
you	would have	forgotten
they	would have	forgotten

Participle

Present participle

forgetting

Past participle

forgotten

Gerund

forgetting

Imperative

forget

Perfect infinitive

have forgotten

Anwendungsbeispiele

I **forgot** his name. *Ich **habe** seinen Namen **vergessen**.*
She **forgot** to return the books. *Sie **hat vergessen**, die Bücher zurückzugeben.*
Don't forget to lock the door. ***Vergiss nicht**, die Tür abzuschließen.*
I'll never **forget** meeting my husband. *Ich **werde** nie **vergessen**, wie ich meinen Mann kennengelernt habe.*
Don't you **forget** it! ***Merk** dir das!*

Redewendungen

to forget about doing sth. *vergessen, etw. zu tun*
to forget oneself *sich vergessen*
to forget an appointment *einen Termin vergessen/verschwitzen*
to forgive and forget *vergeben und vergessen*

Andere Verben

to bear/keep sth. in mind *etw. nicht vergessen*
to memorize sth. *etw. auswendig lernen*
to recall *sich erinnern*
to recollect *sich besinnen/erinnern*
to remember *sich erinnern*
to remind sb. of sth. *jdn. an etw. erinnern*
to be reminiscent of sth. *sich an etw. erinnern*

Gebrauch

Bitte beachten Sie den Unterschied zwischen to forget und to leave. Forget verwendet man, wenn man vergessen hat, etwas mitzubringen:
I've forgotten to bring your books. *Ich **habe vergessen**, deine Bücher mitzubringen.*
Leave benutzt man, wenn man etwas irgendwo liegen gelassen hat:
I **left** my books in the taxi. *Ich habe meine Bücher im Taxi **liegen lassen**.*
Bei leave muss der Ort genannt werden, an dem man etwas vergessen hat.

Tipps & Tricks

Genauso wie to forget konjugiert man im AE to get.
AE: get/got/gotten; BE: get/got/got.

27 get *bekommen/besorgen/werden*

Konsonantenverdoppelung;
AE Partizip: gotten

Simple

Present simple

I	get
you	get
he/she/it	gets
we	get
you	get
they	get

Past simple

I	got
you	got
he/she/it	got
we	got
you	got
they	got

Present perfect simple

I	have	got
you	have	got
he/she/it	has	got
we	have	got
you	have	got
they	have	got

Past perfect simple

I	had	got
you	had	got
he/she/it	had	got
we	had	got
you	had	got
they	had	got

Progressive

Present progressive

I	am	getting
you	are	getting
he/she/it	is	getting
we	are	getting
you	are	getting
they	are	getting

Past progressive

I	was	getting
you	were	getting
he/she/it	was	getting
we	were	getting
you	were	getting
they	were	getting

Present perfect progressive

I	have been	getting
you	have been	getting
he/she/it	has been	getting
we	have been	getting
you	have been	getting
they	have been	getting

Past perfect progressive

I	had been	getting
you	had been	getting
he/she/it	had been	getting
we	had been	getting
you	had been	getting
they	had been	getting

Future

Future simple

I	will	get
you	will	get
he/she/it	will	get
we	will	get
you	will	get
they	will	get

Future progressive

I	will be	getting
you	will be	getting
he/she/it	will be	getting
we	will be	getting
you	will be	getting
they	will be	getting

Future perfect simple

I	will have	got
you	will have	got
he/she/it	will have	got
we	will have	got
you	will have	got
they	will have	got

Future perfect progressive

I	will have been	getting
you	will have been	getting
he/she/it	will have been	getting
we	will have been	getting
you	will have been	getting
they	will have been	getting

Conditional

Conditional I

I	would	get
you	would	get
he/she/it	would	get
we	would	get
you	would	get
they	would	get

Conditional II

I	would have	got
you	would have	got
he/she/it	would have	got
we	would have	got
you	would have	got
they	would have	got

Participle

Present participle

getting

Past participle

got

Gerund

getting

Imperative

get

Perfect infinitive

have got

Anwendungsbeispiele

Did you **get** what you were looking for? ***Hast** du **bekommen**, wonach du suchtest?*
Could you **get** me a beer? *Kannst du mir ein Bier **holen**?*
Sue **is going to get** the tickets. *Sue **wird** die Tickets **kaufen**.*
I **haven't gotten around** to reading it. (AE) *Ich **bin nicht dazu gekommen**, es zu lesen.*
What time **did** you **get** here? *Wann **bist** du **angekommen**?*
Did you **get** what she said? ***Haben** Sie **verstanden**, was sie gesagt hat?*

Redewendungen

to get well/sick *gesund/krank werden*
to get along with sb. *mit jdm. gut auskommen/zurechtkommen*
to get in/out of the bus *in den Bus einsteigen/aus dem Bus aussteigen*
to get up *aufstehen (z. B. aus dem Bett)*
to get to know sb. better *jdn. besser kennenlernen*
to get sth. done *etw. erledigen lassen*
to get married *heiraten*

Ähnliche Verben

to bring sth. *etw. bringen/holen*
to receive sth. *etw. erhalten/empfangen*
to buy sth. *etw. kaufen*
to obtain sth. *etw. erhalten*
to understand sb./sth. *jdn./etw. verstehen*

Gebrauch

Das Verb to get ist wohl das vielseitigste aller englischen Verben, das in Kombination mit Präpositionen, Substantiven und Adjektiven eine fast unüberschaubare Menge an Bedeutungen annehmen kann. Zudem wird get häufig bei Passivkonstruktionen anstelle von be verwendet:
I **got bitten** by a bee. *Ich **wurde** von einer Biene **gestochen**.*

Tipps & Tricks

Genauso wie die AE-Variante von to get (got/gotten) konjugiert man forget (forgot/forgotten) *vergessen*.

28 give *geben*

Verlaufsform ohne -e

Simple

Present simple

I	give
you	give
he/she/it	gives
we	give
you	give
they	give

Past simple

I	gave
you	gave
he/she/it	gave
we	gave
you	gave
they	gave

Present perfect simple

I	have	given
you	have	given
he/she/it	has	given
we	have	given
you	have	given
they	have	given

Past perfect simple

I	had	given
you	had	given
he/she/it	had	given
we	had	given
you	had	given
they	had	given

Progressive

Present progressive

I	am	giving
you	are	giving
he/she/it	is	giving
we	are	giving
you	are	giving
they	are	giving

Past progressive

I	was	giving
you	were	giving
he/she/it	was	giving
we	were	giving
you	were	giving
they	were	giving

Present perfect progressive

I	have been	giving
you	have been	giving
he/she/it	has been	giving
we	have been	giving
you	have been	giving
they	have been	giving

Past perfect progressive

I	had been	giving
you	had been	giving
he/she/it	had been	giving
we	had been	giving
you	had been	giving
they	had been	giving

Future

Future simple

I	will	give
you	will	give
he/she/it	will	give
we	will	give
you	will	give
they	will	give

Future progressive

I	will be	giving
you	will be	giving
he/she/it	will be	giving
we	will be	giving
you	will be	giving
they	will be	giving

Future perfect simple

I	will have	given
you	will have	given
he/she/it	will have	given
we	will have	given
you	will have	given
they	will have	given

Future perfect progressive

I	will have been	giving
you	will have been	giving
he/she/it	will have been	giving
we	will have been	giving
you	will have been	giving
they	will have been	giving

Conditional

Conditional I

I	would	give
you	would	give
he/she/it	would	give
we	would	give
you	would	give
they	would	give

Conditional II

I	would have	given
you	would have	given
he/she/it	would have	given
we	would have	given
you	would have	given
they	would have	given

Participle

Present participle

giving

Past participle

given

Gerund

giving

Imperative

give

Perfect infinitive

have given

Anwendungsbeispiele

Could you **give** me your e-mail address? *Kannst du mir deine E-Mail-Adresse geben?*
She **gave** it to me. *Sie **hat** sie mir **gegeben**.*
What **did** he **give** you **for** your birthday? *Was **hat** er dir **zum** Geburtstag geschenkt?*
Give me **a break**! (umgs.) ***Hör auf** damit!*

Redewendungen

to give sb. a call *jdn. anrufen*
to give sb. a hand *jdm. helfen*
to give sth. away *etw. verschenken*
to give sth. off *etw. strömt aus (z. B. Gas)*
to give a speech *eine Rede halten*
to give birth (to a child) *(ein Kind) gebären*
sth. gives sb. a headache *etw. verursacht jdm. Kopfschmerzen*
sth. give sb. goose bumps *etw. verursacht jdm. Gänsehaut*

Ähnliche Verben

to hand sb. sth. *jdm etw. (herüber)geben*
to pass sth. to sb. *jdm. etw. (herüber)reichen*
to quit doing sth. *etw. aufgeben (z. B. das Rauchen)*
to surrender *sich ergeben/kapitulieren*

Gebrauch

Steht hinter give sowohl ein Dativ- als auch ein Akkusativobjekt, so steht meist ein direkter Dativ vor dem Akkustiv:
She **gave** Peter the ball. *Sie **gab** Peter den Ball.*
Folgen jedoch zwei Pronomen, so ist die Reihenfolge umgekehrt und vor dem Dativ steht to:
Give it to me! ***Gib** es mir!*

Tipps & Tricks

Genauso wie to give werden die Verben to forbid *verbieten* und to forgive *vergeben* konjugiert.

29 go *gehen/fahren*

3. Person Singular mit **-es**

Simple

Present simple

I	go
you	go
he/she/it	**goes**
we	go
you	go
they	go

Past simple

I	went
you	went
he/she/it	went
we	went
you	went
they	went

Present perfect simple

I	have	gone
you	have	gone
he/she/it	has	gone
we	have	gone
you	have	gone
they	have	gone

Past perfect simple

I	had	gone
you	had	gone
he/she/it	had	gone
we	had	gone
you	had	gone
they	had	gone

Progressive

Present progressive

I	am	going
you	are	going
he/she/it	is	going
we	are	going
you	are	going
they	are	going

Past progressive

I	was	going
you	were	going
he/she/it	was	going
we	were	going
you	were	going
they	were	going

Present perfect progressive

I	have been	going
you	have been	going
he/she/it	has been	going
we	have been	going
you	have been	going
they	have been	going

Past perfect progressive

I	had been	going
you	had been	going
he/she/it	had been	going
we	had been	going
you	had been	going
they	had been	going

Future

Future simple

I	will	go
you	will	go
he/she/it	will	go
we	will	go
you	will	go
they	will	go

Future progressive

I	will be	going
you	will be	going
he/she/it	will be	going
we	will be	going
you	will be	going
they	will be	going

Future perfect simple

I	will have	gone
you	will have	gone
he/she/it	will have	gone
we	will have	gone
you	will have	gone
they	will have	gone

Future perfect progressive

I	will have been	going
you	will have been	going
he/she/it	will have been	going
we	will have been	going
you	will have been	going
they	will have been	going

Conditional

Conditional I

I	would	go
you	would	go
he/she/it	would	go
we	would	go
you	would	go
they	would	go

Conditional II

I	would have	gone
you	would have	gone
he/she/it	would have	gone
we	would have	gone
you	would have	gone
they	would have	gone

Participle

Present participle

going

Past participle

gone

Gerund

going

Imperative

go

Perfect infinitive

have gone

Anwendungsbeispiele

Where **did** you **go** last night. *Wo* ***bist*** *du gestern Abend* ***hingegangen****?*
How often do you **go to** Norway? *Wie häufig* ***fährst*** *du* ***nach*** *Norwegen?*
The shop **has gone out of business.** *Der Laden* ***hat dichtgemacht.***
The milk **has gone** sour. *Die Milch* ***ist*** *sauer.*
I **must be going**. *Ich* ***muss los.***
Just **go** and try. *Versuch's* ***noch mal.***
How**'s** it **going**? *Wie* ***geht's*** *so?*
Go ahead! *Auf* ***geht's****!/Na* ***los!***

Redewendungen

to go by bus/car/train *mit dem Bus/Auto/Zug fahren*
to go for a walk *spazieren gehen*
to go on (a) holiday *Urlaub machen*
to go on a trip/tour/journey *eine Reise machen*
to go to bed *zu Bett gehen*
to go to church/school *in die Kirche/Schule gehen*
to go home *nach Hause gehen*
to go crazy/deaf *verrückt/taub werden*
to go shopping *einkaufen gehen*

Ähnliche Verben

to drive *(selbst) fahren*
to travel *reisen*
to leave *weggehen*
to move *sich bewegen*
to forgo/forego sth. *auf etw. verzichten*
to undergo sth. *etw. durchmachen/ erdulden/sich unterziehen (z. B. Operation)*

Gebrauch

Bitte beachten Sie den Unterschied zwischen to go und to drive. Drive verwendet man nur für die Person, die hinter dem Steuer sitzt und fährt. *Rad fahren* heißt übrigens to go by bike oder to ride a bike.

Tipps & Tricks

Die Form to be going to do sth. in der Vergangenheit besagt, dass man etwas tun wollte, aber nicht getan hat:
I **was going** to clean my car, but it started to rain. *Ich* ***wollte*** *mein Auto* ***putzen****, doch es fing an zu regnen.*

30 grow *wachsen/anbauen*

Simple

Present simple

I	grow
you	grow
he/she/it	grows
we	grow
you	grow
they	grow

Past simple

I	grew
you	grew
he/she/it	grew
we	grew
you	grew
they	grew

Present perfect simple

I	have	grown
you	have	grown
he/she/it	has	grown
we	have	grown
you	have	grown
they	have	grown

Past perfect simple

I	had	grown
you	had	grown
he/she/it	had	grown
we	had	grown
you	had	grown
they	had	grown

Progressive

Present progressive

I	am	growing
you	are	growing
he/she/it	is	growing
we	are	growing
you	are	growing
they	are	growing

Past progressive

I	was	growing
you	were	growing
he/she/it	was	growing
we	were	growing
you	were	growing
they	were	growing

Present perfect progressive

I	have been	growing
you	have been	growing
he/she/it	has been	growing
we	have been	growing
you	have been	growing
they	have been	growing

Past perfect progressive

I	had been	growing
you	had been	growing
he/she/it	had been	growing
we	had been	growing
you	had been	growing
they	had been	growing

Future

Future simple

I	will	grow
you	will	grow
he/she/it	will	grow
we	will	grow
you	will	grow
they	will	grow

Future progressive

I	will be	growing
you	will be	growing
he/she/it	will be	growing
we	will be	growing
you	will be	growing
they	will be	growing

Future perfect simple

I	will have	grown
you	will have	grown
he/she/it	will have	grown
we	will have	grown
you	will have	grown
they	will have	grown

Future perfect progressive

I	will have been	growing
you	will have been	growing
he/she/it	will have been	growing
we	will have been	growing
you	will have been	growing
they	will have been	growing

Conditional

Conditional I

I	would	grow
you	would	grow
he/she/it	would	grow
we	would	grow
you	would	grow
they	would	grow

Conditional II

I	would have	grown
you	would have	grown
he/she/it	would have	grown
we	would have	grown
you	would have	grown
they	would have	grown

Participle

Present participle

growing

Past participle

grown

Gerund

growing

Imperative

grow

Perfect infinitive

have grown

Anwendungsbeispiele

Look, how much she**'s grown**. *Schau, wie* ***groß*** *sie* ***geworden ist!***
We **grow** a lot of vegetables ourselves. *Wir* ***bauen*** *viel Gemüse selbst* ***an.***
The music is strange, but it**'ll grow on** you. *Die Musik ist komisch, aber mit der Zeit* ***wird*** *sie dir schon* ***gefallen.***
When I **grow up** I'm going to be a doctor. *Wenn ich* ***groß bin****, werde ich Arzt.*

Redewendungen

to grow a beard *sich einen Bart wachsen lassen*
to grow old *alt werden*
to grow fat *dick werden*
to grow rapidly/slowly/steadily *schnell/langsam/gleichmäßig ansteigen*
to grow warm *warm werden*
to grow one's hair long *sich die Haare lang wachsen lassen*
to grow apart *sich auseinanderleben*
to grow by ... percent *um ... Prozent zunehmen/wachsen*
to grow up *erwachsen werden*
to grow out of sth. *aus seinen Kleidern herauswachsen/etw. überwinden*
to grow together *zusammenwachsen*

Andere Verben

to decline *sinken*
to decrease *abnehmen*
to diminish sth. *etw. verringern*
to dwindle *schwinden/schrumpfen*
to shrink *schrumpfen*

Gebrauch

To grow ist ein Verb, an das man ein Reihe Adjektive oder Substantive direkt anschließen kann, z. B. to grow taller *größer werden/wachsen* oder to grow coffee/tea *Kaffee/Tee anbauen*.

Tipps & Tricks

Genauso wie to grow werden die Verben to blow *blasen*, to fly *fliegen*, to know *kennen/wissen* und to throw *werfen* konjugiert.

31 hang *hängen/hinhängen*

Simple

Present simple

I	hang
you	hang
he/she/it	hangs
we	hang
you	hang
they	hang

Past simple

I	hung
you	hung
he/she/it	hung
we	hung
you	hung
they	hung

Present perfect simple

I	have	hung
you	have	hung
he/she/it	has	hung
we	have	hung
you	have	hung
they	have	hung

Past perfect simple

I	had	hung
you	had	hung
he/she/it	had	hung
we	had	hung
you	had	hung
they	had	hung

Progressive

Present progressive

I	am	hanging
you	are	hanging
he/she/it	is	hanging
we	are	hanging
you	are	hanging
they	are	hanging

Past progressive

I	was	hanging
you	were	hanging
he/she/it	was	hanging
we	were	hanging
you	were	hanging
they	were	hanging

Present perfect progressive

I	have been	hanging
you	have been	hanging
he/she/it	has been	hanging
we	have been	hanging
you	have been	hanging
they	have been	hanging

Past perfect progressive

I	had been	hanging
you	had been	hanging
he/she/it	had been	hanging
we	had been	hanging
you	had been	hanging
they	had been	hanging

Future

Future simple

I	will	hang
you	will	hang
he/she/it	will	hang
we	will	hang
you	will	hang
they	will	hang

Future progressive

I	will be	hanging
you	will be	hanging
he/she/it	will be	hanging
we	will be	hanging
you	will be	hanging
they	will be	hanging

Future perfect simple

I	will have	hung
you	will have	hung
he/she/it	will have	hung
we	will have	hung
you	will have	hung
they	will have	hung

Future perfect progressive

I	will have been	hanging
you	will have been	hanging
he/she/it	will have been	hanging
we	will have been	hanging
you	will have been	hanging
they	will have been	hanging

Conditional

Conditional I

I	would	hang
you	would	hang
he/she/it	would	hang
we	would	hang
you	would	hang
they	would	hang

Conditional II

I	would have	hung
you	would have	hung
he/she/it	would have	hung
we	would have	hung
you	would have	hung
they	would have	hung

Participle

Present participle

hanging

Past participle

hung

Gerund

hanging

Imperative

hang

Perfect infinitive

have hung

Anwendungsbeispiele

Jamie **hung** the picture **on** the wall. *Jamie **hat** das Bild **an** die Wand **gehängt**.*
The paintings **hung on** the opposite wall. *Die Bilder **hingen an** der gegenüberliegenden Wand.*
He **hung** his shirt **on** the washing line. *Er **hängte** sein Hemd **auf** die Wäscheleine.*
She **hung up** without saying a word. *Sie **legte auf**, ohne ein Wort zu sagen.*
He **was hanged** at the crack of dawn. *Er **wurde** im Morgengrauen **gehängt**.*
Hang on! *Augenblick mal!*

Redewendungen

to hang sth. from a hook/nail *etw. an einem Haken/Nagel aufhängen*
to hang out with sb. *mit jdm. herumhängen*
to hang by a single threat *am seidenen Faden hängen*
to hang out the washing *die Wäsche aufhängen*
to hang up the phone *auflegen*
to hang wallpaper *tapezieren*
to hang one's head *den Kopf hängen lassen*
to hang on sb.'s lips *jdm. an den Lippen hängen*
to hang back from doing sth. *zögern, etw. zu tun*

Ähnliche Verben

to dangle *herabhängen*
to (re)decorate *tapezieren*
to put the phone down *auflegen*

Aufgepasst!

Das Verb to hang kann sowohl mit Objekt als auch ohne verwendet werden und entspricht demnach den deutschen Verben *hängen/hängte/gehängt* (mit Objekt) und *hängen/hing/gehangen* (ohne Objekt). Auch wenn jemand *gehängt* (bzw. *gehenkt*) *wird*, benutzt man to hang. In diesem Fall wird es allerdings regelmäßig konjugiert: hanged/hanged.

32 hear *hören/erfahren*

Simple

Present simple

I	hear
you	hear
he/she/it	hears
we	hear
you	hear
they	hear

Past simple

I	heard
you	heard
he/she/it	heard
we	heard
you	heard
they	heard

Present perfect simple

I	have	heard
you	have	heard
he/she/it	has	heard
we	have	heard
you	have	heard
they	have	heard

Past perfect simple

I	had	heard
you	had	heard
he/she/it	had	heard
we	had	heard
you	had	heard
they	had	heard

Progressive

Present progressive

I	am	hearing
you	are	hearing
he/she/it	is	hearing
we	are	hearing
you	are	hearing
they	are	hearing

Past progressive

I	was	hearing
you	were	hearing
he/she/it	was	hearing
we	were	hearing
you	were	hearing
they	were	hearing

Present perfect progressive

I	have been	hearing
you	have been	hearing
he/she/it	has been	hearing
we	have been	hearing
you	have been	hearing
they	have been	hearing

Past perfect progressive

I	had been	hearing
you	had been	hearing
he/she/it	had been	hearing
we	had been	hearing
you	had been	hearing
they	had been	hearing

Future

Future simple

I	will	hear
you	will	hear
he/she/it	will	hear
we	will	hear
you	will	hear
they	will	hear

Future progressive

I	will be	hearing
you	will be	hearing
he/she/it	will be	hearing
we	will be	hearing
you	will be	hearing
they	will be	hearing

Future perfect simple

I	will have	heard
you	will have	heard
he/she/it	will have	heard
we	will have	heard
you	will have	heard
they	will have	heard

Future perfect progressive

I	will have been	hearing
you	will have been	hearing
he/she/it	will have been	hearing
we	will have been	hearing
you	will have been	hearing
they	will have been	hearing

Conditional

Conditional I

I	would	hear
you	would	hear
he/she/it	would	hear
we	would	hear
you	would	hear
they	would	hear

Conditional II

I	would have	heard
you	would have	heard
he/she/it	would have	heard
we	would have	heard
you	would have	heard
they	would have	heard

Participle

Present participle

hearing

Past participle

heard

Gerund

hearing

Imperative

hear

Perfect infinitive

have heard

Anwendungsbeispiele

Can you **hear** me? *Können Sie mich **hören/verstehen**?*
Have you **heard about** the accident? ***Hast** du **von** dem Unfall **gehört/erfahren**?*
I **haven't heard from** him since then. *Ich **habe** seitdem **nichts** mehr **von** ihm **gehört**.*
The line's terrible. I **can't hear** you. *Die Verbindung ist schrecklich. Ich **kann** dich **nicht verstehen**.*
We **don't hear** much **of** them these days. *Wir **hören** im Moment **nicht** viel **von** ihnen.*
You could **hear** a pin drop. *Man konnte eine Stecknadel fallen **hören**.*
Have you **heard** the one about ...? *Kennst du den (Witz) schon?*

Redewendungen

to hear sb. doing sth. *hören, wie jd. gerade etw. tut*
to make oneself heard *sich Gehör verschaffen*
to hear wedding bells *die Hochzeitsglocken läuten hören*

Ähnliche Verben

to catch sth. *etw. verstehen*
to learn sth. *etw. erfahren*
to listen to sb. *jdm. zuhören*
to overhear sb. *unbeabsichtigt zuhören, wie jd. etw. sagt*
to pick sth. up. *etw. aufschnappen*
to understand sth. *etw. verstehen*

Gebrauch

Es gibt einen Unterschied zwischen to hear und to listen (to). Hear bezeichnet den Vorgang des physischen Hörens oder Verstehens; listen (to) verwendet man für ein gezieltes Zuhören:
I **heard** them talking, but I **didn't listen**. *Ich **habe** sie zwar reden **hören**, **habe** aber **nicht zugehört**.*

33 hit *schlagen/treffen*

Konsonantenverdoppelung

Simple

Present simple

I	hit
you	hit
he/she/it	hits
we	hit
you	hit
they	hit

Past simple

I	hit
you	hit
he/she/it	hit
we	hit
you	hit
they	hit

Present perfect simple

I	have	hit
you	have	hit
he/she/it	has	hit
we	have	hit
you	have	hit
they	have	hit

Past perfect simple

I	had	hit
you	had	hit
he/she/it	had	hit
we	had	hit
you	had	hit
they	had	hit

Progressive

Present progressive

I	am	hitting
you	are	hitting
he/she/it	is	hitting
we	are	hitting
you	are	hitting
they	are	hitting

Past progressive

I	was	hitting
you	were	hitting
he/she/it	was	hitting
we	were	hitting
you	were	hitting
they	were	hitting

Present perfect progressive

I	have been	hitting
you	have been	hitting
he/she/it	has been	hitting
we	have been	hitting
you	have been	hitting
they	have been	hitting

Past perfect progressive

I	had been	hitting
you	had been	hitting
he/she/it	had been	hitting
we	had been	hitting
you	had been	hitting
they	had been	hitting

Future

Future simple

I	will	hit
you	will	hit
he/she/it	will	hit
we	will	hit
you	will	hit
they	will	hit

Future progressive

I	will be	hitting
you	will be	hitting
he/she/it	will be	hitting
we	will be	hitting
you	will be	hitting
they	will be	hitting

Future perfect simple

I	will have	hit
you	will have	hit
he/she/it	will have	hit
we	will have	hit
you	will have	hit
they	will have	hit

Future perfect progressive

I	will have been	hitting
you	will have been	hitting
he/she/it	will have been	hitting
we	will have been	hitting
you	will have been	hitting
they	will have been	hitting

Conditional

Conditional I

I	would	hit
you	would	hit
he/she/it	would	hit
we	would	hit
you	would	hit
they	would	hit

Conditional II

I	would have	hit
you	would have	hit
he/she/it	would have	hit
we	would have	hit
you	would have	hit
they	would have	hit

Participle

Present participle

hitting

Past participle

hit

Gerund

hitting

Imperative

hit

Perfect infinitive

have hit

Anwendungsbeispiele

She **hit** the burglar on the head. *Sie **schlug** dem Einbrecher auf den Kopf.*
Jack **was hit in** the leg. *Jack **wurde am** Bein **getroffen**.*
He **was hit by** a car. *Er **wurde angefahren**.*
The car **hit** a tree. *Der Wagen **fuhr gegen** einen Baum.*
Tokyo **was hit by** an earthquake. *Tokio **wurde von** einem Erdbeben **erschüttert**.*
He **hit** his 455th home run. *Er **erzielte** seinen 455. Homerun. (Baseball)*

Redewendungen

to hit sb. hard *jdn. schwer treffen (auch emotional)*
to hit below the belt *unter die Gürtellinie schlagen*
to hit the right note *den richtigen Ton treffen*
to hit the books (umgs.) *büffeln*
to hit the nail (right) on the head *den Nagel (genau) auf den Kopf treffen*
to hit the jackpot (umgs.) *einen Volltreffer landen*
to hit the road *sich auf den Weg machen/loskommen*
to hit the sack/hay (AE) *sich aufs Ohr hauen/schlafen gehen*

Ähnliche Verben

to beat sb. *jdn. schlagen/verprügeln*
to punch *mit der Faust schlagen*
to slap sb. *jdm. einen Klaps geben*
to smack sb. *jdm. einen Klaps geben*
to strike sb. *schlagen*

Gebrauch

To hit ist eines der Verben, bei denen bei der Verlaufsform der Endkonsonant verdoppelt wird. Dies gilt auch für die Verben to cut *schneiden*, to get *bekommen/holen*, to put *setzen/stellen/legen*, to run *rennen*, to set *setzen*, to sit *sitzen* und to win *gewinnen*.

Tipps & Tricks

Bei einer Reihe von Verben sind die drei Formen gleich, z. B. bei to bet *wetten*, to burst *platzen*, to cast *werfen*, to cost *kosten*, to let *lassen*, to quit *aufhören*, to set *(fest)setzen*, to spread *ausbreiten* und to thrust *stoßen*.

34 hold *halten*

Simple

Present simple

I	hold
you	hold
he/she/it	holds
we	hold
you	hold
they	hold

Past simple

I	**held**
you	**held**
he/she/it	**held**
we	**held**
you	**held**
they	**held**

Present perfect simple

I	have	**held**
you	have	**held**
he/she/it	has	**held**
we	have	**held**
you	have	**held**
they	have	**held**

Past perfect simple

I	had	**held**
you	had	**held**
he/she/it	had	**held**
we	had	**held**
you	had	**held**
they	had	**held**

Progressive

Present progressive

I	am	holding
you	are	holding
he/she/it	is	holding
we	are	holding
you	are	holding
they	are	holding

Past progressive

I	was	holding
you	were	holding
he/she/it	was	holding
we	were	holding
you	were	holding
they	were	holding

Present perfect progressive

I	have been	holding
you	have been	holding
he/she/it	has been	holding
we	have been	holding
you	have been	holding
they	have been	holding

Past perfect progressive

I	had been	holding
you	had been	holding
he/she/it	had been	holding
we	had been	holding
you	had been	holding
they	had been	holding

Future

Future simple

I	will	hold
you	will	hold
he/she/it	will	hold
we	will	hold
you	will	hold
they	will	hold

Future progressive

I	will be	holding
you	will be	holding
he/she/it	will be	holding
we	will be	holding
you	will be	holding
they	will be	holding

Future perfect simple

I	will have	**held**
you	will have	**held**
he/she/it	will have	**held**
we	will have	**held**
you	will have	**held**
they	will have	**held**

Future perfect progressive

I	will have been	holding
you	will have been	holding
he/she/it	will have been	holding
we	will have been	holding
you	will have been	holding
they	will have been	holding

Conditional

Conditional I

I	would	hold
you	would	hold
he/she/it	would	hold
we	would	hold
you	would	hold
they	would	hold

Conditional II

I	would have	**held**
you	would have	**held**
he/she/it	would have	**held**
we	would have	**held**
you	would have	**held**
they	would have	**held**

Participle

Present participle

holding

Past participle

held

Gerund

holding

Imperative

hold

Perfect infinitive

have **held**

Anwendungsbeispiele

She **was holding** a doll in her arms. *Sie **hielt** eine Puppe in den Armen.*
Will the roof **hold** me? ***Wird** das Dach mich **aushalten**?*
The goalkeeper failed to **hold** the ball. *Der Torhüter **hat** den Ball nicht **gehalten**.*
He **held out** his hand to help her. *Er **strecke** seine Hand **aus**, um ihr zu helfen.*
The conference **will be held in** Devon. *Die Konferenz **wird in** Devon **stattfinden**.*
She **held** the office of chairman for 19 years. *19 Jahre lang **bekleidete** sie das Amt der Vorsitzenden.*
Hold the line. ***Bleiben** Sie am Apparat!*
Hold your tongue! ***Halt** deinen Mund!*

Redewendungen

to hold sb. close/tight *jdn. fest (in den Armen) halten*
to hold the door open *die Tür aufhalten*
to hold hands *Händchen halten*
to hold one's breath *den Atem anhalten*
to hold one's nose *sich die Nase zuhalten*

Ähnliche Verben

to carry sth. *etw. tragen*
to clutch sth. *etw. greifen und festhalten*
to grasp sth. *etw. packen*
to grip sth. *etw. ergreifen*

Gebrauch

Das Verb to hold enthält neben seiner Grundbedeutung *halten* alle weiteren Bedeutungsschattierungen des Verbs je nach Sinnzusammenhang, z. B. ***ab**halten*, ***an**halten*, ***auf**halten*, ***aus**halten*, ***bereit**halten*, ***beibe**halten*, ***einbe**halten*, ***fest**halten*, ***zu**halten* und ***zurück**halten*.

35 keep *halten*

Kopulaverb

Simple

Present simple

I	keep
you	keep
he/she/it	keeps
we	keep
you	keep
they	keep

Past simple

I	kept
you	kept
he/she/it	kept
we	kept
you	kept
they	kept

Present perfect simple

I	have	kept
you	have	kept
he/she/it	has	kept
we	have	kept
you	have	kept
they	have	kept

Past perfect simple

I	had	kept
you	had	kept
he/she/it	had	kept
we	had	kept
you	had	kept
they	had	kept

Progressive

Present progressive

I	am	keeping
you	are	keeping
he/she/it	is	keeping
we	are	keeping
you	are	keeping
they	are	keeping

Past progressive

I	was	keeping
you	were	keeping
he/she/it	was	keeping
we	were	keeping
you	were	keeping
they	were	keeping

Present perfect progressive

I	have been	keeping
you	have been	keeping
he/she/it	has been	keeping
we	have been	keeping
you	have been	keeping
they	have been	keeping

Past perfect progressive

I	had been	keeping
you	had been	keeping
he/she/it	had been	keeping
we	had been	keeping
you	had been	keeping
they	had been	keeping

Future

Future simple

I	will	keep
you	will	keep
he/she/it	will	keep
we	will	keep
you	will	keep
they	will	keep

Future progressive

I	will be	keeping
you	will be	keeping
he/she/it	will be	keeping
we	will be	keeping
you	will be	keeping
they	will be	keeping

Future perfect simple

I	will have	kept
you	will have	kept
he/she/it	will have	kept
we	will have	kept
you	will have	kept
they	will have	kept

Future perfect progressive

I	will have been	keeping
you	will have been	keeping
he/she/it	will have been	keeping
we	will have been	keeping
you	will have been	keeping
they	will have been	keeping

Conditional

Conditional I

I	would	keep
you	would	keep
he/she/it	would	keep
we	would	keep
you	would	keep
they	would	keep

Conditional II

I	would have	kept
you	would have	kept
he/she/it	would have	kept
we	would have	kept
you	would have	kept
they	would have	kept

Participle

Present participle

keeping

Past participle

kept

Gerund

keeping

Imperative

keep

Perfect infinitive

have kept

Anwendungsbeispiele

Keep your room tidy. ***Halte*** *dein Zimmer aufgeräumt!*
We decided to **keep** the old car. *Wir haben uns entschieden, das alte Auto zu* ***behalten.***
I listened for a moment but then **kept on** reading. *Einen Moment lang hörte ich zu, doch dann las ich* ***weiter.***
She **kept** him waiting for two hours. *Sie* ***ließ*** *ihn zwei Stunden warten.*
Keep your fingers crossed. ***Drück*** *mir die Daumen!*
Keep cool! ***Bleib*** *cool!*

Redewendungen

to keep (on) doing sth. *mit etw. weitermachen*
to keep sb. from doing sth. *jdn. davon abhalten, etw. zu tun*
to keep sth. in mind *etw. im Gedächtnis behalten*
to keep sth. a secret *etw. geheim halten*
to keep (to the) left/right *sich links/rechts halten*
to keep a promise *ein Versprechen halten*
to keep an appointment *einen Termin einhalten*
to keep a diary *Tagebuch führen*
to keep an eye on sb. *jdn. im Auge behalten*
to keep the ball *im Ballbesitz bleiben*

Ähnliche Verben

to carry on doing sth. *mit etw. weitermachen*
to continue doing sth. *mit etw. weitermachen*
to go on doing sth. *mit etw. weitermachen*
to maintain sth. *(einen Zustand) beibehalten*

Gebrauch

Wie nach fast allen Kombinationen aus Verb und Präposition steht auch nach to keep on das Gerund.

Tipps & Tricks

Genauso konjugiert werden u. a. to feed *füttern*, to flee *fliehen*, to kneel *sich hinknien*, to leave *verlassen*, to lead *führen*, to mean *meinen*, to sleep *schlafen* und to sweep *kehren/fegen*.

36 know *kennen/wissen*

Keine Verlaufsform

Simple

Present simple

I	know
you	know
he/she/it	knows
we	know
you	know
they	know

Past simple

I	knew
you	knew
he/she/it	knew
we	knew
you	knew
they	knew

Present perfect simple

I	have	known
you	have	known
he/she/it	has	known
we	have	known
you	have	known
they	have	known

Past perfect simple

I	had	known
you	had	known
he/she/it	had	known
we	had	known
you	had	known
they	had	known

Progressive

Present progressive

–
–
–
–
–
–

Past progressive

–
–
–
–
–
–

Present perfect progressive

–
–
–
–
–
–

Past perfect progressive

–
–
–
–
–
–

Future

Future simple

I	will	know
you	will	know
he/she/it	will	know
we	will	know
you	will	know
they	will	know

Future progressive

–
–
–
–
–
–

Future perfect simple

I	will have	known
you	will have	known
he/she/it	will have	known
we	will have	known
you	will have	known
they	will have	known

Future perfect progressive

–
–
–
–
–
–

Conditional

Conditional I

I	would	know
you	would	know
he/she/it	would	know
we	would	know
you	would	know
they	would	know

Conditional II

I	would have	known
you	would have	known
he/she/it	would have	known
we	would have	known
you	would have	known
they	would have	known

Participle

Present participle

knowing

Past participle

known

Gerund

knowing

Imperative

know

Perfect infinitive

have known

Anwendungsbeispiele

I've known her for over 20 years. *Ich **kenne** sie seit über 20 Jahren.*
She **knows** some Japanese. *Sie **spricht** etwas Japanisch.*
He just **doesn't know** anything about art. *Er **weiß** einfach **nichts** über Kunst.*
I **know** how to use a computer. *Ich **weiß**, wie man einen Computer benutzt.*
You **should have known** that. *Du **hättest** das **wissen sollen/müssen**.*
Do you **know** the time? ***Wissen** Sie, wie viel Uhr es ist?*
I **know** that **from** experience. *Ich **weiß** das **aus** Erfahrung.*
Do you **know** the poem by heart? ***Kannst** du das Gedicht auswendig?*
I **don't know** much about football. *Ich **verstehe nicht** viel von Fußball.*

Sprichwörter

You never **know** what you can do till you try. *Man **weiß** nie, was man kann, bevor man es versucht.*

Ähnliche Verben

to have knowledge of sth. *von etw. Kenntnis haben*
to be acquainted with sb. *mit jdm. bekannt sein*
to be friends with sb. *mit jdm. befreundet sein*

Aufgepasst!

Um auszudrücken, dass man etwas oder jemanden schon eine Zeit lang kennt, benutzt man im Englischen das Present perfect, während im Deutschen das Präsens verwendet wird:
They'**ve known** each other for a long time. *Sie **kennen** sich schon seit Langem.*
Die Zeitangabe *seit ...* wird mit for (bei einem Zeitraum) oder since (bei einem Zeitpunkt, der immer der Anfangspunkt ist) wiedergegeben.
To know ist ein statisches Verb, das keine Aktivität ausdrückt und somit keine Verlaufsform kennt. Ähnliche Verben ohne ing-Form sind to belong *gehören*, to contain *enthalten*, to need *brauchen*, to own *besitzen*, to prefer *vorziehen*, to seem *scheinen* und to want *wollen*.

Tipps & Tricks

Genauso wie to know werden folgende Verben konjugiert: to blow *blasen*, to fly *fliegen*, to grow *wachsen* und to throw *werfen*.

37 lay *legen*

Simple

Present simple

I	lay
you	lay
he/she/it	lays
we	lay
you	lay
they	lay

Past simple

I	laid
you	laid
he/she/it	laid
we	laid
you	laid
they	laid

Present perfect simple

I	have	laid
you	have	laid
he/she/it	has	laid
we	have	laid
you	have	laid
they	have	laid

Past perfect simple

I	had	laid
you	had	laid
he/she/it	had	laid
we	had	laid
you	had	laid
they	had	laid

Progressive

Present progressive

I	am	laying
you	are	laying
he/she/it	is	laying
we	are	laying
you	are	laying
they	are	laying

Past progressive

I	was	laying
you	were	laying
he/she/it	was	laying
we	were	laying
you	were	laying
they	were	laying

Present perfect progressive

I	have been	laying
you	have been	laying
he/she/it	has been	laying
we	have been	laying
you	have been	laying
they	have been	laying

Past perfect progressive

I	had been	laying
you	had been	laying
he/she/it	had been	laying
we	had been	laying
you	had been	laying
they	had been	laying

Future

Future simple

I	will	lay
you	will	lay
he/she/it	will	lay
we	will	lay
you	will	lay
they	will	lay

Future progressive

I	will be	laying
you	will be	laying
he/she/it	will be	laying
we	will be	laying
you	will be	laying
they	will be	laying

Future perfect simple

I	will have	laid
you	will have	laid
he/she/it	will have	laid
we	will have	laid
you	will have	laid
they	will have	laid

Future perfect progressive

I	will have been	laying
you	will have been	laying
he/she/it	will have been	laying
we	will have been	laying
you	will have been	laying
they	will have been	laying

Conditional

Conditional I

I	would	lay
you	would	lay
he/she/it	would	lay
we	would	lay
you	would	lay
they	would	lay

Conditional II

I	would have	laid
you	would have	laid
he/she/it	would have	laid
we	would have	laid
you	would have	laid
they	would have	laid

Participle

Present participle

laying

Past participle

laid

Gerund

laying

Imperative

lay

Perfect infinitive

have laid

Anwendungsbeispiele

Please **don't lay** your hand **on** my knee. *Bitte **lege** deine Hand **nicht auf** mein Knie.*
She **laid** her coat **on** the floor. *Sie **legte** ihren Mantel **auf** den Boden.*
The terrorists **laid down** their arms. *Die Terroristen **legten** ihre Waffen **nieder**.*
The company **laid off** 50 workers. *Die Firma **entließ** 50 Arbeiter.*
The scene **is laid in** Madrid. *Das Stück **spielt in** Madrid.*
A bricklayer is a man who **lays** bricks. *Ein Maurer ist ein Mann, der Ziegelsteine **mauert**.*

Redewendungen

to lay off smoking *das Rauchen aufgeben*
to lay trouble for oneself *sich in Schwierigkeiten bringen*
to lay sth. somewhere *etw. irgendwo hinlegen*
to lay sth. bare/open *etw. offenlegen*
to lay blame on sb. *jdn. verantwortlich machen*
to lay emphasis/stress on sth. *etw. betonen*
to lay a carpet *einen Teppich verlegen*
to lay an egg *ein Ei legen*
to lay a wreath *einen Kranz niederlegen*
to lay the table *den Tisch decken*
to be laid up *das Bett hüten müssen*

Ähnliche Verben

to place sth. somewhere *etw. irgendwo hinstellen/-setzen/-legen*
to put sth. somewhere *etw. irgendwo hinstellen/-setzen/-legen*
to set sth. somewhere *etw. irgendwo hinstellen/-setzen/-legen*

Gebrauch

Das Verb to lay benötigt immer ein Objekt.

Tipps & Tricks

Bitte beachten Sie den Unterschied zwischen den unregelmäßigen Verben to lay/laid/laid *legen* und to lie/lay/lain *liegen* und dem regelmäßig konjugierten to lie/lied/lied *lügen*.

38 learn *lernen/erfahren*

Im AE regelmäßig

Simple

Present simple

I	learn
you	learn
he/she/it	learns
we	learn
you	learn
they	learn

Past simple

I	learnt
you	learnt
he/she/it	learnt
we	learnt
you	learnt
they	learnt

Present perfect simple

I	have	learnt
you	have	learnt
he/she/it	has	learnt
we	have	learnt
you	have	learnt
they	have	learnt

Past perfect simple

I	had	learnt
you	had	learnt
he/she/it	had	learnt
we	had	learnt
you	had	learnt
they	had	learnt

Progressive

Present progressive

I	am	learning
you	are	learning
he/she/it	is	learning
we	are	learning
you	are	learning
they	are	learning

Past progressive

I	was	learning
you	were	learning
he/she/it	was	learning
we	were	learning
you	were	learning
they	were	learning

Present perfect progressive

I	have been	learning
you	have been	learning
he/she/it	has been	learning
we	have been	learning
you	have been	learning
they	have been	learning

Past perfect progressive

I	had been	learning
you	had been	learning
he/she/it	had been	learning
we	had been	learning
you	had been	learning
they	had been	learning

Future

Future simple

I	will	learn
you	will	learn
he/she/it	will	learn
we	will	learn
you	will	learn
they	will	learn

Future progressive

I	will be	learning
you	will be	learning
he/she/it	will be	learning
we	will be	learning
you	will be	learning
they	will be	learning

Future perfect simple

I	will have	learnt
you	will have	learnt
he/she/it	will have	learnt
we	will have	learnt
you	will have	learnt
they	will have	learnt

Future perfect progressive

I	will have been	learning
you	will have been	learning
he/she/it	will have been	learning
we	will have been	learning
you	will have been	learning
they	will have been	learning

Conditional

Conditional I

I	would	learn
you	would	learn
he/she/it	would	learn
we	would	learn
you	would	learn
they	would	learn

Conditional II

I	would have	learnt
you	would have	learnt
he/she/it	would have	learnt
we	would have	learnt
you	would have	learnt
they	would have	learnt

Participle

Present participle

learning

Past participle

learnt

Gerund

learning

Imperative

learn

Perfect infinitive

have learnt

Anwendungsbeispiele

Did you **learn** anything today at school? ***Hast** du heute etwas in der Schule **gelernt**?*
Yesterday I **learnt** she was pregnant. *Gestern **erfuhr** ich, dass sie schwanger ist.*
She**'ll** never **learn** the truth. *Sie **wird** nie die Wahrheit **erfahren**.*
We **haven't learnt** yet if they arrived safely. *Wir **haben** noch **nicht erfahren**, ob sie sicher angekommen sind.*
Did you **learn** the poem by heart? ***Hast** du das Gedicht auswendig **gelernt**?*

Witz

An English teacher wrote these words on the blackboard because he wanted his students **to learn** something about punctuation: "Woman without her man is nothing". Then he asked them to punctuate the words correctly.
The men wrote: "Woman, without her man, is nothing."
The women wrote: "Woman! Without her, man is nothing."

Ähnliche Verben

to coach sb. *jdn. trainieren/coachen*
to drill sb. *jdn. drillen*
to grasp sth. *etw. begreifen*
to instruct sb. in sth. *jdm. etw. beibringen*
to memorize sth. *sich etw. einprägen*
to pick sth. up *etw. aufschnappen*
to teach sb. *jdn. unterrichten*
to train sb. *jdn. trainieren*

Gebrauch

Bitte beachten Sie den Unterschied zwischen to learn und to study:
Im Sinne von *eine Sprache lernen* verwendet man to learn a language. Möchte man ausdrücken, dass man intensiv *zu Hause lernt,* beispielsweise für eine Prüfung, so sagt man to study (for a test).

Tipps & Tricks

Eine Reihe von Verben wird im BE meist unregelmäßig, doch im AE regelmäßig konjugiert. Zu diesen gehören beispielsweise to dream *träumen*, to kneel *sich hinknien*, to learn *lernen* und to spell *buchstabieren*.

39 lend *(ver)leihen*

Simple

Present simple

I	lend
you	lend
he/she/it	lends
we	lend
you	lend
they	lend

Past simple

I	lent
you	lent
he/she/it	lent
we	lent
you	lent
they	lent

Present perfect simple

I	have	lent
you	have	lent
he/she/it	has	lent
we	have	lent
you	have	lent
they	have	lent

Past perfect simple

I	had	lent
you	had	lent
he/she/it	had	lent
we	had	lent
you	had	lent
they	had	lent

Progressive

Present progressive

I	am	lending
you	are	lending
he/she/it	is	lending
we	are	lending
you	are	lending
they	are	lending

Past progressive

I	was	lending
you	were	lending
he/she/it	was	lending
we	were	lending
you	were	lending
they	were	lending

Present perfect progressive

I	have been	lending
you	have been	lending
he/she/it	has been	lending
we	have been	lending
you	have been	lending
they	have been	lending

Past perfect progressive

I	had been	lending
you	had been	lending
he/she/it	had been	lending
we	had been	lending
you	had been	lending
they	had been	lending

Future

Future simple

I	will	lend
you	will	lend
he/she/it	will	lend
we	will	lend
you	will	lend
they	will	lend

Future progressive

I	will be	lending
you	will be	lending
he/she/it	will be	lending
we	will be	lending
you	will be	lending
they	will be	lending

Future perfect simple

I	will have	lent
you	will have	lent
he/she/it	will have	lent
we	will have	lent
you	will have	lent
they	will have	lent

Future perfect progressive

I	will have been	lending
you	will have been	lending
he/she/it	will have been	lending
we	will have been	lending
you	will have been	lending
they	will have been	lending

Conditional

Conditional I

I	would	lend
you	would	lend
he/she/it	would	lend
we	would	lend
you	would	lend
they	would	lend

Conditional II

I	would have	lent
you	would have	lent
he/she/it	would have	lent
we	would have	lent
you	would have	lent
they	would have	lent

Participle

Present participle

lending

Past participle

lent

Gerund

lending

Imperative

lend

Perfect infinitive

have lent

Anwendungsbeispiele

I **lent** my camera **to** Jane. *Ich **habe** Jane meine Kamera **geliehen**.*
The new furniture **lent** the room a nice atmosphere. *Die neuen Möbel **verliehen** dem Raum eine schöne Atmosphäre.*
Could you **lend** me **a hand**? *Könntest du mir **behilflich sein**?*
Please **lend** him **an ear**. *Bitte **schenken** Sie ihm **Gehör**.*
The documents **lent** more credibility to her story. *Die Dokumente **verliehen** ihrer Geschichte mehr Glaubwürdigkeit.*
The garden **lends** itself **to** meditation. *Der Garten **eignet sich gut zur** Meditation.*
A bank **lends** out money **at** interest. *Eine Bank **verleiht** Geld **gegen** Zinsen.*

Sprichwörter

Lend your money and lose a friend. ***Verleih** dein Geld und verliere einen Freund.*

Ähnliche Verben

to beg *(er)bitten/betteln*
to contribute sth. to sth. *etw. zu etw. beisteuern*
to give *geben*
to loan (AE) *Geld ausleihen*
to provide sth. *etw. bereitstellen/zur Verfügung stellen*

Gebrauch

Bitte verwechseln Sie nicht die beiden Verben to lend und to borrow. Borrow sagt man, wenn man etwas von jemandem leihen möchte:
Can I **borrow** your bicycle for an hour? *Kann ich mir dein Rad für eine Stunde **leihen**?*
Lend bezeichnet die entgegengesetzte Richtung, wenn man etwas jemandem ausleiht:
Could you **lend** me your bicycle for an hour? *Kannst du mir dein Rad für eine Stunde **leihen**?*

Tipps & Tricks

Genauso wie to lend konjugiert man to bend *biegen/krümmen*, to send *senden* und to spend *ausgeben*.

40 lie *liegen*

ing-Form mit -y

Simple

Present simple

I	lie
you	lie
he/she/it	lies
we	lie
you	lie
they	lie

Past simple

I	lay
you	lay
he/she/it	lay
we	lay
you	lay
they	lay

Present perfect simple

I	have	lain
you	have	lain
he/she/it	has	lain
we	have	lain
you	have	lain
they	have	lain

Past perfect simple

I	had	lain
you	had	lain
he/she/it	had	lain
we	had	lain
you	had	lain
they	had	lain

Progressive

Present progressive

I	am	lying
you	are	lying
he/she/it	is	lying
we	are	lying
you	are	lying
they	are	lying

Past progressive

I	was	lying
you	were	lying
he/she/it	was	lying
we	were	lying
you	were	lying
they	were	lying

Present perfect progressive

I	have been	lying
you	have been	lying
he/she/it	has been	lying
we	have been	lying
you	have been	lying
they	have been	lying

Past perfect progressive

I	had been	lying
you	had been	lying
he/she/it	had been	lying
we	had been	lying
you	had been	lying
they	had been	lying

Future

Future simple

I	will	lie
you	will	lie
he/she/it	will	lie
we	will	lie
you	will	lie
they	will	lie

Future progressive

I	will be	lying
you	will be	lying
he/she/it	will be	lying
we	will be	lying
you	will be	lying
they	will be	lying

Future perfect simple

I	will have	lain
you	will have	lain
he/she/it	will have	lain
we	will have	lain
you	will have	lain
they	will have	lain

Future perfect progressive

I	will have been	lying
you	will have been	lying
he/she/it	will have been	lying
we	will have been	lying
you	will have been	lying
they	will have been	lying

Conditional

Conditional I

I	would	lie
you	would	lie
he/she/it	would	lie
we	would	lie
you	would	lie
they	would	lie

Conditional II

I	would have	lain
you	would have	lain
he/she/it	would have	lain
we	would have	lain
you	would have	lain
they	would have	lain

Participle

Present participle

lying

Past participle

lain

Gerund

lying

Imperative

lie

Perfect infinitive

have lain

Anwendungsbeispiele

Don't lie in the sun for too long. ***Lieg*** *nicht zu lange* ***in*** *der Sonne.*
She **was lying on** the bed reading a book. *Sie* ***lag auf*** *dem Bett und las ein Buch.*
The beauty of the book **lies in** its language. *Die Schönheit des Buches* ***liegt in*** *seiner Sprache.*
He **lay back against** the pillow. *Er* ***legte sich zurück ins*** *Kissen.*
The town **lies** east of the harbour. *Die Stadt* ***liegt*** *östlich des Hafens.*

Redewendungen

to lie around *herumliegen*
to lie down *sich hinlegen*
to lie on one's back *auf seinem Rücken liegen*
to lie off the coast *vor der Küste liegen*
to lie still/awake *still/wach liegen*
to lie low *untergetaucht sein*
to lie heavily on one's stomach *jdm. schwer im Magen liegen*
to lie through one's teeth *wie gedruckt lügen*

Ähnliche Verben

to chill out (AE) *sich beruhigen*
to relax *sich entspannen*
to repose *sich ausruhen*
to rest *(aus)ruhen*
to sleep/be asleep *schlafen*
to stretch out *sich ausstrecken*

Aufgepasst!

Bitte beachten Sie den Unterschied zwischen den unregelmäßigen Verben to lie/lay/lain *liegen* und to lay/laid/laid *legen* und dem regelmäßig konjugierten to lie/lied/lied *lügen*.

41 look *aussehen/schauen*

Kopulaverb

Simple

Present simple

I	look
you	look
he/she/it	looks
we	look
you	look
they	look

Past simple

I	looked
you	looked
he/she/it	looked
we	looked
you	looked
they	looked

Present perfect simple

I	have	looked
you	have	looked
he/she/it	has	looked
we	have	looked
you	have	looked
they	have	looked

Past perfect simple

I	had	looked
you	had	looked
he/she/it	had	looked
we	had	looked
you	had	looked
they	had	looked

Progressive

Present progressive

I	am	looking
you	are	looking
he/she/it	is	looking
we	are	looking
you	are	looking
they	are	looking

Past progressive

I	was	looking
you	were	looking
he/she/it	was	looking
we	were	looking
you	were	looking
they	were	looking

Present perfect progressive

I	have been	looking
you	have been	looking
he/she/it	has been	looking
we	have been	looking
you	have been	looking
they	have been	looking

Past perfect progressive

I	had been	looking
you	had been	looking
he/she/it	had been	looking
we	had been	looking
you	had been	looking
they	had been	looking

Future

Future simple

I	will	look
you	will	look
he/she/it	will	look
we	will	look
you	will	look
they	will	look

Future progressive

I	will be	looking
you	will be	looking
he/she/it	will be	looking
we	will be	looking
you	will be	looking
they	will be	looking

Future perfect simple

I	will have	looked
you	will have	looked
he/she/it	will have	looked
we	will have	looked
you	will have	looked
they	will have	looked

Future perfect progressive

I	will have been	looking
you	will have been	looking
he/she/it	will have been	looking
we	will have been	looking
you	will have been	looking
they	will have been	looking

Conditional

Conditional I

I	would	look
you	would	look
he/she/it	would	look
we	would	look
you	would	look
they	would	look

Conditional II

I	would have	looked
you	would have	looked
he/she/it	would have	looked
we	would have	looked
you	would have	looked
they	would have	looked

Participle

Present participle

looking

Past participle

looked

Gerund

looking

Imperative

look

Perfect infinitive

have looked

Anwendungsbeispiele

It's five o'clock, he said, **looking at** his watch. *Es ist fünf Uhr, sagte er, indem er* ***auf*** *seine Uhr* ***schaute.***
We all just **looked at** her. *Wir* ***schauten*** *sie alle einfach nur* ***an.***
It **looks as if/as though/like** it's going to rain any moment. *Es* ***sieht so aus, als*** *würde es in jedem Moment regnen.*
I **look forward to** meeting you. *Ich* ***freue mich (darauf)****, dich zu treffen.*
I'm just **looking.** *Ich* ***schaue mich*** *nur mal* ***um.***

Redewendungen

to look tired/happy/stupid *müde/glücklich/dumm aussehen*
to look sb. in the eye *jdm. in die Augen schauen*
to look after a child *sich um ein Kind kümmern*
to look for the key *nach dem Schlüssel suchen*
to look over an essay *einen Aufsatz durchsehen/beurteilen*
to look through the pockets *die Taschen durchsuchen*
to look sth. up in a dictionary *etw. im Wörterbuch nachschlagen*
to look up to sb. *zu jdm. aufsehen/jdn. bewundern*
to look down on sb. *auf jdn. herabsehen*

Ähnliche Verben

to observe sb./sth. *jdn./etw. beobachten*
to seek sth. *etw. suchen*
to see sth. *etw. sehen*
to watch *schauen (TV)*

Gebrauch

Als Kopulaverb verwendet man to look mit einem Adjektiv (und nicht mit einem Adverb) oder mit einem direkten Objekt:
He **looks** wonderful. *Sie* ***sieht*** *wunderbar* ***aus.***
He really **looks** his age. *Man* ***sieht*** *ihm sein Alter wirklich* ***an.***

Tipps & Tricks

Did und Grundform, das ist Norm – nach did steht nie die Past tense-Form!

42 lose *verlieren*

Verlaufsform ohne **-e**

Simple

Present simple

I	lose
you	lose
he/she/it	loses
we	lose
you	lose
they	lose

Past simple

I	lost
you	lost
he/she/it	lost
we	lost
you	lost
they	lost

Present perfect simple

I	have	lost
you	have	lost
he/she/it	has	lost
we	have	lost
you	have	lost
they	have	lost

Past perfect simple

I	had	lost
you	had	lost
he/she/it	had	lost
we	had	lost
you	had	lost
they	had	lost

Progressive

Present progressive

I	am	losing
you	are	losing
he/she/it	is	losing
we	are	losing
you	are	losing
they	are	losing

Past progressive

I	was	losing
you	were	losing
he/she/it	was	losing
we	were	losing
you	were	losing
they	were	losing

Present perfect progressive

I	have been	losing
you	have been	losing
he/she/it	has been	losing
we	have been	losing
you	have been	losing
they	have been	losing

Past perfect progressive

I	had been	losing
you	had been	losing
he/she/it	had been	losing
we	had been	losing
you	had been	losing
they	had been	losing

Future

Future simple

I	will	lose
you	will	lose
he/she/it	will	lose
we	will	lose
you	will	lose
they	will	lose

Future progressive

I	will be	losing
you	will be	losing
he/she/it	will be	losing
we	will be	losing
you	will be	losing
they	will be	losing

Future perfect simple

I	will have	lost
you	will have	lost
he/she/it	will have	lost
we	will have	lost
you	will have	lost
they	will have	lost

Future perfect progressive

I	will have been	losing
you	will have been	losing
he/she/it	will have been	losing
we	will have been	losing
you	will have been	losing
they	will have been	losing

Conditional

Conditional I

I	would	lose
you	would	lose
he/she/it	would	lose
we	would	lose
you	would	lose
they	would	lose

Conditional II

I	would have	lost
you	would have	lost
he/she/it	would have	lost
we	would have	lost
you	would have	lost
they	would have	lost

Participle

Present participle

losing

Past participle

lost

Gerund

losing

Imperative

lose

Perfect infinitive

have lost

Anwendungsbeispiele

I've lost your telephone number. *Ich **habe** deine Telefonnummer **verloren**.*
Lucy **has lost** her appetite. *Lucy **hat** ihren Appetit **verloren**.*
Have you **lost** your marbles? ***Hast** du **nicht mehr** alle Tassen im Schrank?*
I've lost my voice. *Ich **bin** heiser.*
She**'s lost** a son in the war. *Sie **hat** einen Sohn im Krieg **verloren**.*
You've got nothing to **lose**. *Du hast nichts zu **verlieren**.*
He**'s lost** ten pounds. *Er **hat** zehn Pfund **abgenommen**.*

Redewendungen

to lose a game/an election *ein Spiel/eine Wahl verlieren*
to lose blood *Blut verlieren*
to lose confidence/hope *das Vertrauen/die Hoffnung verlieren*
to lose consciousness *das Bewusstsein verlieren*
to lose face *das Gesicht verlieren*
to lose weight *Gewicht verlieren/abnehmen*
to lose touch with sb. *den Kontakt zu jdm. verlieren*
to lose one's train of thought *den Gedankengang verlieren*
to lose out to sb. *jdm. unterlegen sein*
to be lost in thoughts *sich in Gedanken verlieren/gedankenverloren sein*

Andere Verben

to discover sth. *etw. entdecken*
to find sth. *etw. finden*
to regain sth. *etw. zurückgewinnen*
to uncover sth. *etw. aufdecken/freilegen*

Aufgepasst!

Bitte verwechseln Sie to lose nicht mit dem Adjektiv loose, das *locker* oder *lose* bedeutet, wie in to hang **loose** *lose herunterhängen* oder **loose** morals *lockere Moral*.

Tipps & Tricks

Das Verb to lose konjugiert man genauso wie to shoot *schießen*.

43 love *lieben/mögen*

Verlaufsform eher selten

Simple

Present simple

I	love
you	love
he/she/it	loves
we	love
you	love
they	love

Past simple

I	loved
you	loved
he/she/it	loved
we	loved
you	loved
they	loved

Present perfect simple

I	have	loved
you	have	loved
he/she/it	has	loved
we	have	loved
you	have	loved
they	have	loved

Past perfect simple

I	had	loved
you	had	loved
he/she/it	had	loved
we	had	loved
you	had	loved
they	had	loved

Progressive

Present progressive

I	am	loving
you	are	loving
he/she/it	is	loving
we	are	loving
you	are	loving
they	are	loving

Past progressive

I	was	loving
you	were	loving
he/she/it	was	loving
we	were	loving
you	were	loving
they	were	loving

Present perfect progressive

I	have been	loving
you	have been	loving
he/she/it	has been	loving
we	have been	loving
you	have been	loving
they	have been	loving

Past perfect progressive

I	had been	loving
you	had been	loving
he/she/it	had been	loving
we	had been	loving
you	had been	loving
they	had been	loving

Future

Future simple

I	will	love
you	will	love
he/she/it	will	love
we	will	love
you	will	love
they	will	love

Future progressive

I	will be	loving
you	will be	loving
he/she/it	will be	loving
we	will be	loving
you	will be	loving
they	will be	loving

Future perfect simple

I	will have	loved
you	will have	loved
he/she/it	will have	loved
we	will have	loved
you	will have	loved
they	will have	loved

Future perfect progressive

I	will have been	loving
you	will have been	loving
he/she/it	will have been	loving
we	will have been	loving
you	will have been	loving
they	will have been	loving

Conditional

Conditional I

I	would	love
you	would	love
he/she/it	would	love
we	would	love
you	would	love
they	would	love

Conditional II

I	would have	loved
you	would have	loved
he/she/it	would have	loved
we	would have	loved
you	would have	loved
they	would have	loved

Participle

Present participle

loving

Past participle

loved

Gerund

loving

Imperative

love

Perfect infinitive

have loved

Anwendungsbeispiele

I **love** you. *Ich **liebe** dich.*
She**'s loved** him for over ten years. *Sie **liebt** ihn seit über zehn Jahren.*
He **loves** going out. *Er geht **gern** aus.*
I'd love to have a hot bath now. *Ich **würde** jetzt **gern** ein heißes Bad nehmen.*
Please, **send my love to** her. *Bitte **grüße** sie recht **herzlich**.*
We **loved** having you with us. *Wir **haben uns** sehr über ihren Besuch **gefreut**.*
Love it or hate it. *Ob's dir **passt** oder nicht.*
I **would have loved** to see it. *Ich **hätte** es **gern** gesehen.*

Redewendungen

to love sb. dearly/passionately *jdn. von ganzem Herzen/leidenschaftlich lieben*
to be in love with sb. *in jdn. verliebt sein*
to feel loved *sich geliebt fühlen*
to be a loved one *eine nahestehende Person sein*

Andere Verben

to despise sb./sth. *jdn./etw. verachten*
to detest sb./sth. *jdn./etw. verabscheuen*
to dislike sb./sth. *jdn./etw. nicht mögen*
to hate sb./sth. *jdn./etw. hassen*
to loathe sb./sth. *jdn./etw. verabscheuen*
to be sick of sb./sth. *jdn./etw. satthaben*

Gebrauch

To love gehört wie to hate *hassen*, to enjoy *genießen*, to like *mögen* und to dislike *nicht mögen* zu den Verben des Mögens und Hassens und sollte daher nicht in der Verlaufsform verwendet werden. Jede Sprache ist jedoch ständigen Veränderungen unterworfen und so kann man vor allem im AE einen Satz wie I'm really loving it. *Ich liebe das wirklich sehr* durchaus gelegentlich sehen oder hören.

44 make *machen/tun/herstellen*

Verlaufsform ohne -e

Simple

Present simple

I	make
you	make
he/she/it	makes
we	make
you	make
they	make

Past simple

I	made
you	made
he/she/it	made
we	made
you	made
they	made

Present perfect simple

I	have	made
you	have	made
he/she/it	has	made
we	have	made
you	have	made
they	have	made

Past perfect simple

I	had	made
you	had	made
he/she/it	had	made
we	had	made
you	had	made
they	had	made

Progressive

Present progressive

I	am	making
you	are	making
he/she/it	is	making
we	are	making
you	are	making
they	are	making

Past progressive

I	was	making
you	were	making
he/she/it	was	making
we	were	making
you	were	making
they	were	making

Present perfect progressive

I	have been	making
you	have been	making
he/she/it	has been	making
we	have been	making
you	have been	making
they	have been	making

Past perfect progressive

I	had been	making
you	had been	making
he/she/it	had been	making
we	had been	making
you	had been	making
they	had been	making

Future

Future simple

I	will	make
you	will	make
he/she/it	will	make
we	will	make
you	will	make
they	will	make

Future progressive

I	will be	making
you	will be	making
he/she/it	will be	making
we	will be	making
you	will be	making
they	will be	making

Future perfect simple

I	will have	made
you	will have	made
he/she/it	will have	made
we	will have	made
you	will have	made
they	will have	made

Future perfect progressive

I	will have been	making
you	will have been	making
he/she/it	will have been	making
we	will have been	making
you	will have been	making
they	will have been	making

Conditional

Conditional I

I	would	make
you	would	make
he/she/it	would	make
we	would	make
you	would	make
they	would	make

Conditional II

I	would have	made
you	would have	made
he/she/it	would have	made
we	would have	made
you	would have	made
they	would have	made

Participle

Present participle

making

Past participle

made

Gerund

making

Imperative

make

Perfect infinitive

have made

Anwendungsbeispiele

Who **made** this? *Wer **hat** das **gemacht**?*
He **was making** breakfast when I called. *Er **machte gerade** das Frühstück, als ich anrief.*
She **made** her own wedding dress. *Sie **nähte** ihr eigenes Hochzeitskleid.*
This dress **is made of** silk. *Dieses Kleid **ist aus** Seide.*
They **have been making** toys for over 100 years. *Seit über 100 Jahren **stellen** sie Spielzeug **her**.*

Redewendungen

to make sb. laugh *jdn. zum Lachen bringen*
to make sb. do sth. *jdn. zwingen, etw. zu tun*
to make up one's mind *sich entscheiden*
to make an appointment *einen Termin vereinbaren*
to make money *Geld verdienen*
to make a phone call *einen Anruf tätigen*
to make sense *Sinn ergeben*

Ähnliche Verben

to do sth. *etw. tun/machen*
to generate sth. *etw. erzeugen*
to manufacture sth. *etw. herstellen*
to produce sth. *etw. produzieren*

Gebrauch

Die Verben to make und to do werden häufig für feststehende Redewendungen verwendet. Leider stimmen sie nicht immer mit den deutschen Entsprechungen überein. Hier eine kleine Liste mit Phrasen, die im Englischen mit do, im Deutschen aber mit *machen* gebildet werden: to **do** one's homework *die Hausaufgaben **machen***, to **do** nothing *nichts **machen***, to **do** the washing up *den Abwasch **machen***, to **do** business with sb. *mit jdm. Geschäfte **machen***.

Tipps & Tricks

Die Aussprache von make/made/made ist genauso wie die von pay/paid/paid *zahlen* und lay/laid/laid *legen*.

45 meet *(sich) treffen/(sich) kennenlernen*

Simple

Present simple

I	meet
you	meet
he/she/it	meets
we	meet
you	meet
they	meet

Past simple

I	met
you	met
he/she/it	met
we	met
you	met
they	met

Present perfect simple

I	have	met
you	have	met
he/she/it	has	met
we	have	met
you	have	met
they	have	met

Past perfect simple

I	had	met
you	had	met
he/she/it	had	met
we	had	met
you	had	met
they	had	met

Progressive

Present progressive

I	am	meeting
you	are	meeting
he/she/it	is	meeting
we	are	meeting
you	are	meeting
they	are	meeting

Past progressive

I	was	meeting
you	were	meeting
he/she/it	was	meeting
we	were	meeting
you	were	meeting
they	were	meeting

Present perfect progressive

I	have been	meeting
you	have been	meeting
he/she/it	has been	meeting
we	have been	meeting
you	have been	meeting
they	have been	meeting

Past perfect progressive

I	had been	meeting
you	had been	meeting
he/she/it	had been	meeting
we	had been	meeting
you	had been	meeting
they	had been	meeting

Future

Future simple

I	will	meet
you	will	meet
he/she/it	will	meet
we	will	meet
you	will	meet
they	will	meet

Future progressive

I	will be	meeting
you	will be	meeting
he/she/it	will be	meeting
we	will be	meeting
you	will be	meeting
they	will be	meeting

Future perfect simple

I	will have	met
you	will have	met
he/she/it	will have	met
we	will have	met
you	will have	met
they	will have	met

Future perfect progressive

I	will have been	meeting
you	will have been	meeting
he/she/it	will have been	meeting
we	will have been	meeting
you	will have been	meeting
they	will have been	meeting

Conditional

Conditional I

I	would	meet
you	would	meet
he/she/it	would	meet
we	would	meet
you	would	meet
they	would	meet

Conditional II

I	would have	met
you	would have	met
he/she/it	would have	met
we	would have	met
you	would have	met
they	would have	met

Participle

Present participle

meeting

Past participle

met

Gerund

meeting

Imperative

meet

Perfect infinitive

have met

Anwendungsbeispiele

Let's **meet in front of** the theatre. *Lasst uns uns* ***vor*** *dem Theater* ***treffen****.*
I **met** her **in** a pub. *Ich* ***habe*** *sie* ***in*** *einem Pub* ***kennengelernt****.*
I'd like you **to meet** Jane. *Ich* ***möchte*** *Ihnen Jane* ***vorstellen****.*
She **met** me **at** the station. *Sie* ***holte*** *mich* ***vom*** *Bahnhof* ***ab****.*
There's more to it than **meets** the eye. *Da* ***steckt*** *mehr* ***dahinter****.*

Redewendungen

to meet sb. for lunch/a drink *jdn. zum Mittagessen/auf einen Drink treffen*
to meet a challenge *sich einer Herausforderung stellen*
to meet a deadline *einen Termin einhalten*
to meet an expectation *einer Erwartung gerecht werden*
to meet a problem *auf ein Problem stoßen*
to meet with approval *auf Zustimmung stoßen*

Ähnliche Verben

to bump into sb. (umgs.) *jdn. zufällig treffen*
to encounter sb./sth. *jdm./etw. begegnen*
to hit sth. *etw. treffen*
to run into sb. *jdn. zufällig treffen*
to strike sb./sth. *etw./jdn. schlagen*

Gebrauch

Möchte man einen Fremden begrüßen, sagt man Nice to **meet** you! *Nett, Sie* ***kennenzulernen****!* Auf die Frage eines Dritten, ob man sich bereits kenne, entgegnet man mit No, we **haven't met**. *Nein, wir* ***kennen*** *uns* ***noch nicht*** oder mit Yes, we've **met**. *Ja, wir* ***kennen*** *uns.*
Wenn man sich dann wieder verabschiedet, sagt man noch mal (It was) nice to **meet** you oder Nice **meeting** you. *Es war nett, Sie* ***kennenzulernen****.*
Das Gerund (meeting) steht nur hier, weil ein Gerund häufig in die Vergangenheit gerichtet ist, ein Infinitiv mit to dagegen in die Zukunft.

Tipps & Tricks

Genauso konjugiert werden u. a. to breed *brüten/züchten*, to kneel *sich hinknien*, to leave *verlassen*, to lead *führen*, to lean *sich lehnen*, to leap *springen*, to mean *meinen*, to sweep *kehren/fegen* und to weep *weinen*.

46 **must** *müssen* – **must not** *nicht dürfen*

Unvollständiges Hilfsverb; Ersatzform: **to have to (do sth.)**

Simple

Present simple

I	must/have to
you	must/have to
he/she/it	must/has to
we	must/have to
you	must/have to
they	must/have to

Past simple

I	had to
you	had to
he/she/it	had to
we	had to
you	had to
they	had to

Present perfect simple

I	have	had to
you	have	had to
he/she/it	has	had to
we	have	had to
you	have	had to
they	have	had to

Past perfect simple

I	had	had to
you	had	had to
he/she/it	had	had to
we	had	had to
you	had	had to
they	had	had to

Progressive

Present progressive

–
–
–
–
–
–

Past progressive

–
–
–
–
–
–

Present perfect progressive

–
–
–
–
–
–

Past perfect progressive

–
–
–
–
–
–

Future

Future simple

I	will	have to
you	will	have to
he/she/it	will	have to
we	will	have to
you	will	have to
they	will	have to

Future progressive

–
–
–
–
–
–

Future perfect simple

I	will have	had to
you	will have	had to
he/she/it	will have	had to
we	will have	had to
you	will have	had to
they	will have	had to

Future perfect progressive

–
–
–
–
–
–

Conditional

Conditional I

I	would	have to
you	would	have to
he/she/it	would	have to
we	would	have to
you	would	have to
they	would	have to

Conditional II

I	would have	had to
you	would have	had to
he/she/it	would have	had to
we	would have	had to
you	would have	had to
they	would have	had to

Participle

Present participle

having to

Past participle

had to

Gerund

having to

Imperative

–

Perfect infinitive

have had to

Anwendungsbeispiele

You really **must** see this film. *Du **musst** dir unbedingt diesen Film ansehen.*
I **must** go now. *Ich **muss** jetzt gehen.*
She **must** still be under 18. *Sie **muss** noch unter 18 sein.*
She **must** have seen the accident. *Sie **muss** den Unfall gesehen haben.*
You **mustn't** smoke in here. *Man **darf** hier drin **nicht** rauchen.*
Smoke, if you **must**. *Dann rauche eben, wenn du **unbedingt musst**.*
We **must never** forget how terrible our situation was. *Wir **dürfen nie** vergessen, wie schrecklich unsere Lage war.*
You **must** be out of your mind. *Du **hast wohl** den Verstand verloren.*
You**'ve got to** study harder if you want to pass the exam. *Du **musst** einfach mehr lernen, wenn du das Examen schaffen willst.*
You **don't have to** do that. *Du **musst/brauchst** das **nicht** tun.*

Witz

Postman: "I'm exhaused. I**'ve had to** walk five miles to deliver this letter."
Farmer: "Why didn't you send it by post?"

Ähnliche Verben

to need *brauchen/müssen*
to be essential *unbedingt erforderlich sein*
to be necessary *notwendig sein*

Gebrauch

Bitte beachten Sie den kleinen Unterschied zwischen must und have to:
Must ist meist eine Verpflichtung oder ein Wunsch, der von innen kommt (You **must** read this book. *Du **musst** dieses Buch unbedingt lesen.*), während have to eine oft lästige Pflicht ist, die von außen an einen herangetragen wird (I **have to** do my homework. *Ich **muss** meine Hausaufgaben machen.*).
Die Verneinung *nicht müssen* heißt don't have to do sth., needn't do sth. oder don't need to do sth.

Tipps & Tricks

Wie alle Hilfsverben, hat auch must kein -s in der dritten Person Singular. Fragen werden wie im Deutschen gebildet, indem man Subjekt und Hilfsverb vertauscht:
Must I clean all windows? ***Muss** ich alle Fenster putzen?*

47 need *brauchen/müssen*

Vollverb, im BE auch Hilfsverb; keine Verlaufsform

Simple

Present simple

I	need
you	need
he/she/it	needs
we	need
you	need
they	need

Past simple

I	needed
you	needed
he/she/it	needed
we	needed
you	needed
they	needed

Present perfect simple

I	have	needed
you	have	needed
he/she/it	has	needed
we	have	needed
you	have	needed
they	have	needed

Past perfect simple

I	had	needed
you	had	needed
he/she/it	had	needed
we	had	needed
you	had	needed
they	had	needed

Progressive

Present progressive

–
–
–
–
–
–

Past progressive

–
–
–
–
–
–

Present perfect progressive

–
–
–
–
–
–

Past perfect progressive

–
–
–
–
–
–

Future

Future simple

I	will	need
you	will	need
he/she/it	will	need
we	will	need
you	will	need
they	will	need

Future progressive

–
–
–
–
–
–

Future perfect simple

I	will have	needed
you	will have	needed
he/she/it	will have	needed
we	will have	needed
you	will have	needed
they	will have	needed

Future perfect progressive

–
–
–
–
–
–

Conditional

Conditional I

I	would	need
you	would	need
he/she/it	would	need
we	would	need
you	would	need
they	would	need

Conditional II

I	would have	needed
you	would have	needed
he/she/it	would have	needed
we	would have	needed
you	would have	needed
they	would have	needed

Participle

Present participle

needing

Past participle

needed

Gerund

needing

Imperative

–

Perfect infinitive

have needed

Anwendungsbeispiele

I **need** someting to drink. *Ich **brauche** etwas zu trinken.*
I **need** to talk to you. *Ich **muss** mal mit dir reden.*
I **need** my bike fixed. *Ich **muss** mein Rad reparieren lassen.*
Need I fill in a form? (BE)/Do I have to ... (AE) ***Muss** ich ein Formular ausfüllen?*
You **needn't** do that. (BE)/You **didn't need** to do that. (AE) *Du **brauchtest** das **nicht** zu tun.*
She **needn't** have come. (BE)/She **didn't need** to come. (AE) *Sie **hätte nicht** zu kommen **brauchen**.*
Your windows **need** cleaning. (BE) *Deine Fenster **müssen** mal geputzt werden.*
Need I say more? ***Muss** ich noch mehr sagen?*

Redewendungen

to need sth. desperately/urgently *etw. unbedingt/dringend benötigen*
to need to do sth. *etw. tun müssen*
sth. needs to be done *etw. muss getan werden*

Ähnliche Verben

to demand sth. *etw. verlangen*
to have to do sth. *etw. tun müssen*
must do sth. *etw. tun müssen*
to require sth. *etw. brauchen/verlangen*
to want sth. *etw. wollen*
to be essential *unbedingt erforderlich sein*
to be necessary *notwendig sein*

Gebrauch

Bitte beachten Sie folgenden Unterschied: You **needn't** have done it. *Du hättest es nicht zu tun brauchen* heißt, dass man etwas getan hat, was nicht notwendig gewesen ist. You **didn't need** to do it. *Du brauchtest/man brauchte das nicht zu tun* heißt, dass es allgemein nicht notwendig war, etwas zu tun.

Tipps & Tricks

Im AE wird to need nur als Vollverb gebraucht (Frage und Verneinung mit do/does/did). Im BE kann man es auch als Hilfsverb verwenden. Hier gelten dann die Regeln für Hilfsverben (▶ Grammatik rund ums Verb, 3.1).

48 pay *(be)zahlen*

Simple

Present simple

I	pay
you	pay
he/she/it	pays
we	pay
you	pay
they	pay

Past simple

I	paid
you	paid
he/she/it	paid
we	paid
you	paid
they	paid

Present perfect simple

I	have	paid
you	have	paid
he/she/it	has	paid
we	have	paid
you	have	paid
they	have	paid

Past perfect simple

I	had	paid
you	had	paid
he/she/it	had	paid
we	had	paid
you	had	paid
they	had	paid

Progressive

Present progressive

I	am	paying
you	are	paying
he/she/it	is	paying
we	are	paying
you	are	paying
they	are	paying

Past progressive

I	was	paying
you	were	paying
he/she/it	was	paying
we	were	paying
you	were	paying
they	were	paying

Present perfect progressive

I	have been	paying
you	have been	paying
he/she/it	has been	paying
we	have been	paying
you	have been	paying
they	have been	paying

Past perfect progressive

I	had been	paying
you	had been	paying
he/she/it	had been	paying
we	had been	paying
you	had been	paying
they	had been	paying

Future

Future simple

I	will	pay
you	will	pay
he/she/it	will	pay
we	will	pay
you	will	pay
they	will	pay

Future progressive

I	will be	paying
you	will be	paying
he/she/it	will be	paying
we	will be	paying
you	will be	paying
they	will be	paying

Future perfect simple

I	will have	paid
you	will have	paid
he/she/it	will have	paid
we	will have	paid
you	will have	paid
they	will have	paid

Future perfect progressive

I	will have been	paying
you	will have been	paying
he/she/it	will have been	paying
we	will have been	paying
you	will have been	paying
they	will have been	paying

Conditional

Conditional I

I	would	pay
you	would	pay
he/she/it	would	pay
we	would	pay
you	would	pay
they	would	pay

Conditional II

I	would have	paid
you	would have	paid
he/she/it	would have	paid
we	would have	paid
you	would have	paid
they	would have	paid

Participle

Present participle

paying

Past participle

paid

Gerund

paying

Imperative

pay

Perfect infinitive

have paid

Anwendungsbeispiele

How much **did** you **pay for** that? *Wie viel **hast** du **dafür bezahlt**?*

It **pays** to know a computer expert. *Es **macht sich bezahlt**, einen Computerfachmann zu kennen.*

I **paid** € 1000 **into** your account. *Ich **habe** € 1000 **auf** dein Konto **eingezahlt**.*

Pay the driver. *Beim Fahrer **zahlen**.*

Redewendungen

to pay (in) cash *bar bezahlen*
to pay in dollars/euros *in Dollar/Euro zahlen*
to pay by cheque/credit card *mit Scheck/Kreditkarte bezahlen*
to pay sb. for sth. *jdn. für etw. bezahlen/jdm. für etw. Geld geben*
to be/get paid weekly/monthly *wöchentlich/monatlich ausgezahlt werden*
to pay back sth. *etw. zurückzahlen*
to pay sb. back for sth. *es jdm. für etw. heimzahlen*
to pay off sth. *etw. komplett abzahlen*
to pay attention (to sth.) *(auf etw.) achtgeben/aufpassen*
to pay dearly for sth. *teuer für etw. bezahlen*

Ähnliche Verben

to compensate sb. for sth. *jdn. für etw. entschädigen*
to reimburse sb. for sth. *jdn. für etw. finanziell entschädigen*
to settle (an account) *(ein Konto) ausgleichen*
to spend *ausgeben*

Gebrauch

Dem Verb to pay folgt ein direktes Substantiv oder Personalpronomen, wenn man eine Person bezahlt:

I **paid** him € 20. *Ich **habe** ihm € 20 **bezahlt**.*

Spricht man von der Sache, für die man etwas bezahlt hat, heißt es to pay ... for:

I **paid** € 20 **for** the book. *Ich **habe** € 20 **für** das Buch **bezahlt**.*

Tipps & Tricks

Die Aussprache von pay/paid/paid ist genauso wie die von lay/laid/laid *legen* und make/made/made *machen*.

49 put *setzen/stellen/legen*

Konsonantenverdoppelung

Simple

Present simple

I	put
you	put
he/she/it	puts
we	put
you	put
they	put

Past simple

I	put
you	put
he/she/it	put
we	put
you	put
they	put

Present perfect simple

I	have	put
you	have	put
he/she/it	has	put
we	have	put
you	have	put
they	have	put

Past perfect simple

I	had	put
you	had	put
he/she/it	had	put
we	had	put
you	had	put
they	had	put

Progressive

Present progressive

I	am	putting
you	are	putting
he/she/it	is	putting
we	are	putting
you	are	putting
they	are	putting

Past progressive

I	was	putting
you	were	putting
he/she/it	was	putting
we	were	putting
you	were	putting
they	were	putting

Present perfect progressive

I	have been	putting
you	have been	putting
he/she/it	has been	putting
we	have been	putting
you	have been	putting
they	have been	putting

Past perfect progressive

I	had been	putting
you	had been	putting
he/she/it	had been	putting
we	had been	putting
you	had been	putting
they	had been	putting

Future

Future simple

I	will	put
you	will	put
he/she/it	will	put
we	will	put
you	will	put
they	will	put

Future progressive

I	will be	putting
you	will be	putting
he/she/it	will be	putting
we	will be	putting
you	will be	putting
they	will be	putting

Future perfect simple

I	will have	put
you	will have	put
he/she/it	will have	put
we	will have	put
you	will have	put
they	will have	put

Future perfect progressive

I	will have been	putting
you	will have been	putting
he/she/it	will have been	putting
we	will have been	putting
you	will have been	putting
they	will have been	putting

Conditional

Conditional I

I	would	put
you	would	put
he/she/it	would	put
we	would	put
you	would	put
they	would	put

Conditional II

I	would have	put
you	would have	put
he/she/it	would have	put
we	would have	put
you	would have	put
they	would have	put

Participle

Present participle

putting

Past participle

put

Gerund

putting

Imperative

put

Perfect infinitive

have put

Anwendungsbeispiele

He **put** the books **on** the table. *Er **legte** die Bücher **auf** den Tisch.*
She **put** too much milk **in** my coffee. *Sie **hat** zu viel Milch **in** meinen Kaffee **getan**.*
You'd better **put on** a coat. *Du solltest dir lieber einen Mantel **anziehen**.*
How shall I **put** it? *Wie soll ich es **ausdrücken**?*
I cannot **put** it **into** words. *Ich kann es nicht **in** Worte **fassen**.*
I **put** everything **on** paper. *Ich **habe** alles **zu** Papier **gebracht**.*

Redewendungen

to put on a dress *ein Kleid anziehen*
to put off a date *eine Verabredung verschieben*
to put down a note *eine Nachricht aufschreiben/eine Notiz machen*
to put out the fire *das Feuer löschen*
to put up a house *ein Haus errichten*
to put sth. simply *etw. einfach ausdrücken*
to put sb. to bed *jdn. ins Bett bringen*
to put away sth. *etw. wegräumen*
to put the phone down *(den Hörer) auflegen*
to put on weight *(an Gewicht) zunehmen*

Ähnliche Verben

to express sth. *etw. ausdrücken*
to lay sth. on/over sth. *etw. auf etw. legen*
to place sth. somewhere *etw. irgendwo hinstellen/hinlegen*
to position sth. *etw. in die richtige Stellung bringen/positionieren*
to set *(fest)setzen/stellen*

Gebrauch

To put ist ein sehr vielseitiges Verb; es lässt sich mit fast allen Präpositionen verbinden und nimmt dabei eine Vielzahl von Bedeutungen an, z. B. to put **aside** ***weg**legen*, to put **on** ***an**ziehen*, to put **together** ***zusammen**setzen* usw.

Tipps & Tricks

Bei einer Reihe von Verben sind die drei Verbformen gleich, z. B. bei to bet *wetten*, to bid *bieten*, to cast *werfen*, to cost *kosten*, to cut *schneiden*, to hit *schlagen*, to let *lassen*, to set *festsetzen* und to thrust *stoßen*.

50 read *lesen*

Simple

Present simple

I	read
you	read
he/she/it	reads
we	read
you	read
they	read

Past simple

I	**read**
you	**read**
he/she/it	**read**
we	**read**
you	**read**
they	**read**

Present perfect simple

I	have	**read**
you	have	**read**
he/she/it	has	**read**
we	have	**read**
you	have	**read**
they	have	**read**

Past perfect simple

I	had	**read**
you	had	**read**
he/she/it	had	**read**
we	had	**read**
you	had	**read**
they	had	**read**

Progressive

Present progressive

I	am	reading
you	are	reading
he/she/it	is	reading
we	are	reading
you	are	reading
they	are	reading

Past progressive

I	was	reading
you	were	reading
he/she/it	was	reading
we	were	reading
you	were	reading
they	were	reading

Present perfect progressive

I	have been	reading
you	have been	reading
he/she/it	has been	reading
we	have been	reading
you	have been	reading
they	have been	reading

Past perfect progressive

I	had been	reading
you	had been	reading
he/she/it	had been	reading
we	had been	reading
you	had been	reading
they	had been	reading

Future

Future simple

I	will	read
you	will	read
he/she/it	will	read
we	will	read
you	will	read
they	will	read

Future progressive

I	will be	reading
you	will be	reading
he/she/it	will be	reading
we	will be	reading
you	will be	reading
they	will be	reading

Future perfect simple

I	will have	**read**
you	will have	**read**
he/she/it	will have	**read**
we	will have	**read**
you	will have	**read**
they	will have	**read**

Future perfect progressive

I	will have been	reading
you	will have been	reading
he/she/it	will have been	reading
we	will have been	reading
you	will have been	reading
they	will have been	reading

Conditional

Conditional I

I	would	read
you	would	read
he/she/it	would	read
we	would	read
you	would	read
they	would	read

Conditional II

I	would have	**read**
you	would have	**read**
he/she/it	would have	**read**
we	would have	**read**
you	would have	**read**
they	would have	**read**

Participle

Present participle

reading

Past participle

read

Gerund

reading

Imperative

read

Perfect infinitive

have **read**

Anwendungsbeispiele

I **read** a 150 pages last night. *Gestern Abend* ***habe*** *ich 150 Seiten* ***gelesen****.*
I was shocked when I **read about** the accident. *Ich war geschockt, als ich (in der Zeitung)* ***von*** *dem Unfall* ***las****.*
Mum, will you **read** me a fairy tail? *Mama,* ***liest*** *du mir ein Märchen* ***vor****?*
The sign on the fence **read**: "No trespassing". *Auf dem Schild am Zaun* ***stand****: „Betreten verboten".*

Redewendungen

to read a book/the newspaper *ein Buch/die Zeitung lesen*
to read sth. aloud *etw. laut vorlesen*
to read sb.'s mind/thoughts *jds. Gedanken lesen*
to read between the lines *zwischen den Zeilen lesen*
to read over/through sth. *sich etw. durchlesen*
to read music *Noten lesen*
to read sth. into sth. *etw. in etw. hineinlesen/-interpretieren*

Ähnliche Verben

to browse through sth. *etw. durchblättern*
to flick/leaf through sth. *etw. durchblättern*
to peruse sth. *etw. sorgfältig durchlesen*
to recite sth. *etw. vortragen/aufsagen (z. B. ein Gedicht)*
to scan sth. *etw. kritisch prüfen*
to study sth. *etw. studieren/lernen*

Aufgepasst!

Die Besonderheit des Verbs to read liegt in seiner Aussprache. Um welche Form es sich handelt, muss man anhand des Kontextes (z. B. wenn eine Zeitangabe wie yesterday oder last night in der Nähe steht) herausfinden. Übrigens: Die englische Stadt Reading spricht sich aus wie das Partizip von read. Die Stadt in Nordkalifornien schreibt man hingegen Redding.

Tipps & Tricks

Genauso konjugiert werden u. a. to deal *handeln/dealen*, to feed *füttern*, to feel *fühlen*, to flee *fliehen*, to keep *halten*, to leave *verlassen*, to lead *führen*, to meet *treffen/kennenlernen*, to mean *meinen* und to weep *weinen*.

51 remember *sich erinnern*

Verlaufsform selten;
she/it aus Platzgründen nicht aufgeführt

Simple

Present simple

I	remember
you	remember
he	remembers
we	remember
you	remember
they	remember

Past simple

I	remembered
you	remembered
he	remembered
we	remembered
you	remembered
they	remembered

Present perfect simple

I	have	remembered
you	have	remembered
he	has	remembered
we	have	remembered
you	have	remembered
they	have	remembered

Past perfect simple

I	had	remembered
you	had	remembered
he	had	remembered
we	had	remembered
you	had	remembered
they	had	remembered

Progressive

Present progressive

I	am	remembering
you	are	remembering
he	is	remembering
we	are	remembering
you	are	remembering
they	are	remembering

Past progressive

I	was	remembering
you	were	remembering
he	was	remembering
we	were	remembering
you	were	remembering
they	were	remembering

Present perfect progressive

I	have been	remembering
you	have been	remembering
he	has been	remembering
we	have been	remembering
you	have been	remembering
they	have been	remembering

Past perfect progressive

I	had been	remembering
you	had been	remembering
he	had been	remembering
we	had been	remembering
you	had been	remembering
they	had been	remembering

Future

Future simple

I	will	remember
you	will	remember
he	will	remember
we	will	remember
you	will	remember
they	will	remember

Future progressive

I	will be	remembering
you	will be	remembering
he	will be	remembering
we	will be	remembering
you	will be	remembering
they	will be	remembering

Future perfect simple

I	will have	remembered
you	will have	remembered
he	will have	remembered
we	will have	remembered
you	will have	remembered
they	will have	remembered

Future perfect progressive

I	will have been	remembering
you	will have been	remembering
he	will have been	remembering
we	will have been	remembering
you	will have been	remembering
they	will have been	remembering

Conditional

Conditional I

I	would	remember
you	would	remember
he	would	remember
we	would	remember
you	would	remember
they	would	remember

Conditional II

I	would have	remembered
you	would have	remembered
he	would have	remembered
we	would have	remembered
you	would have	remembered
they	would have	remembered

Participle

Present participle

remembering

Past participle

remembered

Gerund

remembering

Imperative

remember

Perfect infinitive

have remembered

Anwendungsbeispiele

Do you **remember** aunt Jane? *Kannst du dich* ***an*** *Tante Jane* ***erinnern****?*
I **remember** calling her. *Ich* ***erinnere*** *mich* ***daran****, sie angerufen zu haben.*
Please **remember** to call her. *Bitte* ***denk daran****, sie anzurufen.*
I **remember** her **as** a young girl. *Ich* ***habe*** *sie* ***als*** *kleines Mädchen* ***in Erinnerung****.*
I must **remember** this. *Das muss ich mir* ***merken****.*
As far as I can **remember**. *Soweit ich mich* ***erinnern*** *kann.*
Remember me? (umgs.) ***Kennst*** *du* ***mich noch****?*

Redewendungen

to be a sight to remember *ein unvergesslicher Anblick sein*
to remember sth. rightly/correctly *sich an etw. richtig erinnern*
to remember doing sth. *sich daran erinnern, etw. getan zu haben*
to remember to do sth. *daran denken, etw. zu tun*
to remember sb. in one's will *jdn. in seinem Testament bedenken*
to get oneself remembered *sich in Erinnerung bringen*

Andere Verben

to forget *vergessen*
to fail to remember sth. *sich an etw. nicht erinnern können*
to leave sth. *etw. liegen lassen/vergessen*
to neglect to do sth. *versäumen, etw. zu tun*
to overlook sth. *etw. übersehen*

Gebrauch

To remember ist ein kognitives Verb, das einen Denkprozess ausdrückt und in der Regel nicht in der Verlaufsform verwendet wird. Ähnliche Verben, die nur selten in der ing-Form stehen, sind to conclude *schlussfolgern*, to notice *bemerken*, to realize *sich bewusst werden*, to recognize *wiedererkennen*, to regret *bedauern* und to understand *verstehen*.

Tipps & Tricks

Zum Unterschied zwischen to remember und to remind: Mit dem reflexiven remember erinnert man sich an etwas oder jemanden. To remind drückt hingegen aus, dass ein anderer jemanden erinnert.

52 run *rennen/laufen*

Konsonantenverdoppelung

Simple

Present simple

I	run
you	run
he/she/it	runs
we	run
you	run
they	run

Past simple

I	ran
you	ran
he/she/it	ran
we	ran
you	ran
they	ran

Present perfect simple

I	have	run
you	have	run
he/she/it	has	run
we	have	run
you	have	run
they	have	run

Past perfect simple

I	had	run
you	had	run
he/she/it	had	run
we	had	run
you	had	run
they	had	run

Progressive

Present progressive

I	am	running
you	are	running
he/she/it	is	running
we	are	running
you	are	running
they	are	running

Past progressive

I	was	running
you	were	running
he/she/it	was	running
we	were	running
you	were	running
they	were	running

Present perfect progressive

I	have been	running
you	have been	running
he/she/it	has been	running
we	have been	running
you	have been	running
they	have been	running

Past perfect progressive

I	had been	running
you	had been	running
he/she/it	had been	running
we	had been	running
you	had been	running
they	had been	running

Future

Future simple

I	will	run
you	will	run
he/she/it	will	run
we	will	run
you	will	run
they	will	run

Future progressive

I	will be	running
you	will be	running
he/she/it	will be	running
we	will be	running
you	will be	running
they	will be	running

Future perfect simple

I	will have	run
you	will have	run
he/she/it	will have	run
we	will have	run
you	will have	run
they	will have	run

Future perfect progressive

I	will have been	running
you	will have been	running
he/she/it	will have been	running
we	will have been	running
you	will have been	running
they	will have been	running

Conditional

Conditional I

I	would	run
you	would	run
he/she/it	would	run
we	would	run
you	would	run
they	would	run

Conditional II

I	would have	run
you	would have	run
he/she/it	would have	run
we	would have	run
you	would have	run
they	would have	run

Participle

Present participle

running

Past participle

run

Gerund

running

Imperative

run

Perfect infinitive

have run

Anwendungsbeispiele

They **ran up** the hill. *Sie **liefen** den Hügel **hinauf**.*
Your nose **is running**. *Deine Nase **läuft**.*
This program **will run on** any PC. *Dieses Programm **wird auf** allen PCs **laufen**.*
The bus to Bath **doesn't run on** Sundays. *Der Bus nach Bath **fährt** sonntags **nicht**.*
She's **running for** president. *Sie **kandidiert für** das Amt des Präsidenten.*
He waited for one hour with the engine **running**. *Er wartete eine Stunde bei **laufendem** Motor.*
He **ran after** her. *Er **lief hinter** ihr **her**.*

Redewendungen

to run away (from home) *(von zu Hause) weglaufen*
to run out of control *außer Kontrolle geraten*
to run out of gas (AE) *kein Benzin mehr haben*
to run a bath *sich Badewasser einlassen*
to run a check/test *einen Check/Test durchführen*
to run a fever/temperature *Fieber/Temperatur haben*
to run a red light *bei Rot über die Ampel fahren*

Ähnliche Verben

to amble *bummeln*
to hike *wandern*
to race *rennen*
to rush *eilen/hetzen*
to sprint *sprinten*

Gebrauch

Bitte beachten Sie, dass to run neben *rennen*, *laufen* und *fließen* auch ganz andere Bedeutungen, wie *kandidieren* (*für ein Amt*), *leiten* (*ein Unternehmen*) oder *durchführen* (*ein Experiment*), annehmen kann.

Tipps & Tricks

Ähnlich wie to run werden folgende Verben konjugiert: to begin *beginnen*, to drink *trinken*, to ring *klingeln*, to sing *singen*, to sink *sinken*, to spring *springen*, to shrink *schrumpfen*, to stink *stinken* und to swim *schwimmen*.

53 say *sagen*

Simple

Present simple

I	say
you	say
he/she/it	says
we	say
you	say
they	say

Past simple

I	said
you	said
he/she/it	said
we	said
you	said
they	said

Present perfect simple

I	have	said
you	have	said
he/she/it	has	said
we	have	said
you	have	said
they	have	said

Past perfect simple

I	had	said
you	had	said
he/she/it	had	said
we	had	said
you	had	said
they	had	said

Progressive

Present progressive

I	am	saying
you	are	saying
he/she/it	is	saying
we	are	saying
you	are	saying
they	are	saying

Past progressive

I	was	saying
you	were	saying
he/she/it	was	saying
we	were	saying
you	were	saying
they	were	saying

Present perfect progressive

I	have been	saying
you	have been	saying
he/she/it	has been	saying
we	have been	saying
you	have been	saying
they	have been	saying

Past perfect progressive

I	had been	saying
you	had been	saying
he/she/it	had been	saying
we	had been	saying
you	had been	saying
they	had been	saying

Future

Future simple

I	will	say
you	will	say
he/she/it	will	say
we	will	say
you	will	say
they	will	say

Future progressive

I	will be	saying
you	will be	saying
he/she/it	will be	saying
we	will be	saying
you	will be	saying
they	will be	saying

Future perfect simple

I	will have	said
you	will have	said
he/she/it	will have	said
we	will have	said
you	will have	said
they	will have	said

Future perfect progressive

I	will have been	saying
you	will have been	saying
he/she/it	will have been	saying
we	will have been	saying
you	will have been	saying
they	will have been	saying

Conditional

Conditional I

I	would	say
you	would	say
he/she/it	would	say
we	would	say
you	would	say
they	would	say

Conditional II

I	would have	said
you	would have	said
he/she/it	would have	said
we	would have	said
you	would have	said
they	would have	said

Participle

Present participle

saying

Past participle

said

Gerund

saying

Imperative

say

Perfect infinitive

have said

Anwendungsbeispiele

What **did** you **say** to him? *Was **hast** du ihm **gesagt**?*
He **said** he didn't meet him. *Er **sagte**, er habe ihn nicht getroffen.*
I've got something to **say to** you. *Ich muss Ihnen etwas **sagen**.*
She didn't know how to **say** it. *Sie wusste nicht, wie sie es **ausdrücken** sollte.*
They have little to **say to** each other. *Sie haben sich nicht viel zu **sagen**.*
It **says** here that they got married in June. *Hier **steht**, dass sie im Juni heirateten.*
My watch **says** 8:50. *Meine Uhr **sagt** 8 Uhr 50.*
What do you **say**? *Was **meinst** du?*
Hard to **say**. *Schwer zu **sagen**.*
That goes without **saying**. *Das versteht sich **von selbst**.*

Redewendungen

to say hello/goodbye/thank you *Hallo/Auf Wiedersehen/Danke sagen*
to have sth./nothing to say *etw./nichts zu sagen haben*
to say grace *das Tischgebet sprechen*

Ähnliche Verben

to add *hinzufügen*
to express sth. *etw. ausdrücken*
to mention sth. *etw. erwähnen*
to remark *bemerken/äußern*
to tell sb. sth. *jdm. etw. sagen*

Gebrauch

Zum Unterschied zwischen to say und to tell: Nach tell steht für gewöhnlich ein Objekt, meist ein Name oder ein Personalpronomen (he **told** Jack *er **sagte** Jack*, they **told** him *sie **sagten** ihm* etc.) oder eine Wendung wie a story *eine Geschichte*, the truth *die Wahrheit* usw., während nach say zwischen Verb und Personalpronomen ein to eingeschoben werden muss (he **said to** him *er **sagte** (**zu**) ihm*).

Tipps & Tricks

Genauso wie to say konjugiert man die Verben to lay *legen* und to pay *zahlen*. Sie werden allerdings anders ausgesprochen.

54 seem *scheinen*

Keine Verlaufsform;
Kopulaverb

Simple

Present simple

I	seem	
you	seem	
he/she/it	seems	
we	seem	
you	seem	
they	seem	

Past simple

I	seemed
you	seemed
he/she/it	seemed
we	seemed
you	seemed
they	seemed

Present perfect simple

I	have	seemed
you	have	seemed
he/she/it	has	seemed
we	have	seemed
you	have	seemed
they	have	seemed

Past perfect simple

I	had	seemed
you	had	seemed
he/she/it	had	seemed
we	had	seemed
you	had	seemed
they	had	seemed

Progressive

Present progressive

–
–
–
–
–
–

Past progressive

–
–
–
–
–
–

Present perfect progressive

–
–
–
–
–
–

Past perfect progressive

–
–
–
–
–
–

Future

Future simple

I	will	seem
you	will	seem
he/she/it	will	seem
we	will	seem
you	will	seem
they	will	seem

Future progressive

–
–
–
–
–
–

Future perfect simple

I	will have	seemed
you	will have	seemed
he/she/it	will have	seemed
we	will have	seemed
you	will have	seemed
they	will have	seemed

Future perfect progressive

–
–
–
–
–
–

Conditional

Conditional I

I	would	seem
you	would	seem
he/she/it	would	seem
we	would	seem
you	would	seem
they	would	seem

Conditional II

I	would have	seemed
you	would have	seemed
he/she/it	would have	seemed
we	would have	seemed
you	would have	seemed
they	would have	seemed

Participle

Present participle

seeming

Past participle

seemed

Gerund

seeming

Imperative

seem

Perfect infinitive

have seemed

Anwendungsbeispiele

She **seems** very nice. *Sie **scheint** sehr nett zu sein.*
He **seems (to be)** a good lawyer. *Er **scheint** ein guter Anwalt **zu sein**.*
She is 18, but **seems** much younger. *Sie ist 18, **wirkt** aber viel jünger.*
I **seem** to hear voices. *Mir **scheint**, als hörte ich Stimmen.*
I **seem** to have lost my purse. *Ich **scheine** mein Portemonnaie verloren zu haben.*
I can't **seem** to get this right. *Wie es **aussieht**, kriege ich das nie hin.*
Strawberries do not **seem** to grow here. *Erdbeeren wachsen hier **anscheinend** nicht.*
There **seems** to have been a mistake. *Da liegt **anscheinend** ein Irrtum vor.*
It **seems like** a good idea. *Das **scheint** eine gute Idee zu sein.*
It **seems** to me that this is far too expensive. *Ich **finde**, das ist viel zu teuer.*
It should/would **seem** that she actually stole the money. *Es **scheint** so, dass sie tatsächlich das Geld gestohlen hat.*

Redewendungen

to seem right *richtig zu sein scheinen*
to seem unlikely *unwahrscheinlich zu sein scheinen*
to seem as if/as though ... *so scheinen, als ob ...*
to seem impossible *unmöglich scheinen*

Ähnliche Verben

to appear (to be) sb./sth. *scheinen, jd./etw. zu sein*
to look sth. *wie etw. aussehen*
to sound sth. *wie etw. klingen*

Gebrauch

Das Verb to seem ist ein Kopulaverb, an das man ein Adjektiv (kein Adverb!) oder ein Substantiv direkt oder mit like anschließen kann:
It **seems** difficult. *Es **scheint** schwierig zu sein.*
Seems (like) a good idea. ***Scheint** eine gute Idee zu sein.*

Tipps & Tricks

Weitere häufig verwendete Kopulaverben sind: to appear *scheinen*, to be *sein*, to become *werden*, to feel *fühlen*, to get *hier: werden*, to look *aussehen*, to smell *riechen*, to sound *klingen* und to taste *fühlen*.

55 set *(fest)setzen/stellen*

Konsonantenverdoppelung

Simple

Present simple

I	set
you	set
he/she/it	sets
we	set
you	set
they	set

Past simple

I	set
you	set
he/she/it	set
we	set
you	set
they	set

Present perfect simple

I	have	set
you	have	set
he/she/it	has	set
we	have	set
you	have	set
they	have	set

Past perfect simple

I	had	set
you	had	set
he/she/it	had	set
we	had	set
you	had	set
they	had	set

Progressive

Present progressive

I	am	setting
you	are	setting
he/she/it	is	setting
we	are	setting
you	are	setting
they	are	setting

Past progressive

I	was	setting
you	were	setting
he/she/it	was	setting
we	were	setting
you	were	setting
they	were	setting

Present perfect progressive

I	have been	setting
you	have been	setting
he/she/it	has been	setting
we	have been	setting
you	have been	setting
they	have been	setting

Past perfect progressive

I	had been	setting
you	had been	setting
he/she/it	had been	setting
we	had been	setting
you	had been	setting
they	had been	setting

Future

Future simple

I	will	set
you	will	set
he/she/it	will	set
we	will	set
you	will	set
they	will	set

Future progressive

I	will be	setting
you	will be	setting
he/she/it	will be	setting
we	will be	setting
you	will be	setting
they	will be	setting

Future perfect simple

I	will have	set
you	will have	set
he/she/it	will have	set
we	will have	set
you	will have	set
they	will have	set

Future perfect progressive

I	will have been	setting
you	will have been	setting
he/she/it	will have been	setting
we	will have been	setting
you	will have been	setting
they	will have been	setting

Conditional

Conditional I

I	would	set
you	would	set
he/she/it	would	set
we	would	set
you	would	set
they	would	set

Conditional II

I	would have	set
you	would have	set
he/she/it	would have	set
we	would have	set
you	would have	set
they	would have	set

Participle

Present participle

setting

Past participle

set

Gerund

setting

Imperative

set

Perfect infinitive

have set

Anwendungsbeispiele

Remember to **set** the alarm for 5 am. *Vergiss nicht, den Wecker auf fünf Uhr zu stellen.*
He **hasn't set** a date for the test. *Er **hat** noch keinen Termin für den Test **festgesetzt**.*
I want to **set up** my own business. *Ich möchte mein eigenes Unternehmen gründen.*
Jurassic Park **is set on** an island. *Jurassic Park **spielt auf** einer Insel.*
And then she **sat** the glass **to** her lips. *Und dann **setzte** sie das Glas **an** ihre Lippen.*

Redewendungen

to set off trouble *Streit verursachen*
to set an example *ein Beispiel geben*
to set a record *einen Rekord aufstellen*
to set the table *den Tisch decken*
to set a broken bone *einen gebrochenen Knochen richten*
to set a poem to music *ein Gedicht vertonen*
to set in motion *in Bewegung setzen*
to set on fire *in Brand setzen*
to set oneself a goal *sich ein Ziel setzen*
to set out on a journey/voyage *zu einer (längeren) Reise aufbrechen*

Ähnliche Verben

to lay sth. on/over sth. *etw. über etw. legen*
to put sth. somewhere *hinsetzen/hinstellen/hinlegen*
to place sth. somewhere *hinstellen/hinlegen*
to position sth. *etw. in die richtige Stellung bringen/positionieren*

Gebrauch

To set ist ein schwieriges Verb, da es in Kombination mit einer Präposition oft eine wörtliche und eine übertragene Bedeutung annimmt. So bedeutet beispielsweise to set **off** *auslösen*, *hervorheben* oder *sich auf dem Weg machen*.

Tipps & Tricks

Bei einer Reihe von Verben sind die drei Verbformen gleich, z. B. bei to bet *wetten*, to burst *platzen*, to cast *werfen*, to cost *kosten*, to cut *schneiden*, to hit *schlagen*, to quit *aufhören* und to shut *schließen*.

56 shall *sollen/werden*

Unvollständiges Hilfsverb;
Ersatzform: **to be supposed to (do sth.)**

Simple

Present simple

I	shall
you	shall
he/she/it	shall
we	shall
you	shall
they	shall

Past simple

I	should
you	should
he/she/it	should
we	should
you	should
they	should

Present perfect simple

I	have	been supposed to
you	have	been supposed to
he/she/it	has	been supposed to
we	have	been supposed to
you	have	been supposed to
they	have	been supposed to

Past perfect simple

I	had	been supposed to
you	had	been supposed to
he/she/it	had	been supposed to
we	had	been supposed to
you	had	been supposed to
they	had	been supposed to

Progressive

Present progressive

–
–
–
–
–
–

Past progressive

–
–
–
–
–
–

Present perfect progressive

–
–
–
–
–
–

Past perfect progressive

–
–
–
–
–
–

Future

Future simple

I	will be supposed to
you	will be supposed to
he/she/it	will be supposed to
we	will be supposed to
you	will be supposed to
they	will be supposed to

Future progressive

–
–
–
–
–
–

Future perfect simple

I	will have been supposed to
you	will have been supposed to
he/she/it	will have been supposed to
we	will have been supposed to
you	will have been supposed to
they	will have been supposed to

Future perfect progressive

–
–
–
–
–
–

Conditional

Conditional I

I	should
you	should
he/she/it	should
we	should
you	should
they	should

Conditional II

I	should have
you	should have
he/she/it	should have
we	should have
you	should have
they	should have

Participle

Present participle

being supposed to

Past participle

been supposed to

Gerund

being supposed to

Imperative

–

Perfect infinitive

have been supposed to

Anwendungsbeispiele

Shall I leave the light on? ***Soll** ich das Licht anlassen?*
We **shall** need an umbrella. (BE) *Wir **werden** einen Schirm brauchen.*
There **shouldn't be** any problems. *Es **dürfte** eigentlich keine Probleme geben.*
She **should have done** it later. *Sie **hätte** es später **tun sollen**.*
My teacher suggested that I (**should**) see a doctor. *Mein Lehrer meinte, **es wäre besser**, wenn ich zum Arzt ginge.*
It is necessary that his mother **should** be informed. (BE) *Es ist notwendig, dass man seine Mutter informiert.*
How **am I supposed** to find her? *Wie **soll** ich sie finden?*
Your father said you **are supposed to** come home immediately. *Dein Vater sagt, du **sollst** sofort nach Hause kommen.*
You'**d** better see a doctor. *Du **solltest** besser zum Arzt gehen.*

Witz

What **should** one do if a child falls down the stairs?
Run and get a book on bringing up children.

Ähnliche Verben

to be to do sth. *etw. tun dürfen/sollen*
ought to do sth. *etw. tun sollen (stärker als* should*)*
had better do sth. *etw. (unbedingt) tun sollen*

Aufgepasst!

Die Past tense-Form should kommt fast nur in der indirekten Rede vor:
He said I **should** see a dentist. *Er sagte, ich **solle/sollte** zum Arzt gehen.*
Bitte beachten Sie auch, dass im BE shall in der ersten Person Singular und Plural *werden* heißt. Das Verb *sollen* zu übersetzen, ist schwierig. Da shall nur bei Fragen und in Verneinungen *sollen* heißt und should meist mit *sollte* übertragen wird, muss man für einen Satz wie *Was **sollen** wir tun?* die Ersatzform What are we **supposed to do**? wählen.

Tipps & Tricks

Wie alle Hilfsverben hat auch shall kein -s in der dritten Person Singular und keine Verlaufsform. Fragen werden wie im Deutschen gebildet, indem man Subjekt und Hilfsverb vertauscht:
What shall I say? *Was soll ich sagen?*

57 shine *scheinen/leuchten*

Simple

Present simple

I	shine
you	shine
he/she/it	shines
we	shine
you	shine
they	shine

Past simple

I	shone
you	shone
he/she/it	shone
we	shone
you	shone
they	shone

Present perfect simple

I	have	shone
you	have	shone
he/she/it	has	shone
we	have	shone
you	have	shone
they	have	shone

Past perfect simple

I	had	shone
you	had	shone
he/she/it	had	shone
we	had	shone
you	had	shone
they	had	shone

Progressive

Present progressive

I	am	shining
you	are	shining
he/she/it	is	shining
we	are	shining
you	are	shining
they	are	shining

Past progressive

I	was	shining
you	were	shining
he/she/it	was	shining
we	were	shining
you	were	shining
they	were	shining

Present perfect progressive

I	have been	shining
you	have been	shining
he/she/it	has been	shining
we	have been	shining
you	have been	shining
they	have been	shining

Past perfect progressive

I	had been	shining
you	had been	shining
he/she/it	had been	shining
we	had been	shining
you	had been	shining
they	had been	shining

Future

Future simple

I	will	shine
you	will	shine
he/she/it	will	shine
we	will	shine
you	will	shine
they	will	shine

Future progressive

I	will be	shining
you	will be	shining
he/she/it	will be	shining
we	will be	shining
you	will be	shining
they	will be	shining

Future perfect simple

I	will have	shone
you	will have	shone
he/she/it	will have	shone
we	will have	shone
you	will have	shone
they	will have	shone

Future perfect progressive

I	will have been	shining
you	will have been	shining
he/she/it	will have been	shining
we	will have been	shining
you	will have been	shining
they	will have been	shining

Conditional

Conditional I

I	would	shine
you	would	shine
he/she/it	would	shine
we	would	shine
you	would	shine
they	would	shine

Conditional II

I	would have	shone
you	would have	shone
he/she/it	would have	shone
we	would have	shone
you	would have	shone
they	would have	shone

Participle

Present participle

shining

Past participle

shone

Gerund

shining

Imperative

shine

Perfect infinitive

have shone

Anwendungsbeispiele
The moon **was shining** when I entered the hallway. *Der Mond **schien gerade**, als ich in die Eingangshalle trat.*
The light of the lamp **shone in** my eyes. *Das Licht der Lampe **schien** mir **in** die Augen.*
Her body **was shining with** sweat. *Ihr Körper **glänzte vor** Schweiß.*
He had **shining** black hair. *Er hatte **glänzendes** schwarzes Haar.*
She **shines at** chemistry. *Sie **ist hervorragend in** Chemie.*

Redewendungen
to shine through the window *durch das Fenster hineinscheinen*
to shine with wits *geistreich sein*
to shine a beam of light at sb. *jdn. anstrahlen*
to shine a torch (BE)/flashlight (AE) into sth. *mit einer Taschenlampe in etw. hineinleuchten*

Ähnliche Verben
to beam (at sb.) *strahlen/jdn. anstrahlen*
to glow *glühen*
to gleam *glänzen/leuchten*
to radiate *strahlen*
to glitter *glitzern*
to sparkle *funkeln*
to glare *grell scheinen*
to twinkle *blitzen*
to shimmer *schimmern*

Gebrauch
Das Verb to shine/shone/shone ist unregelmäßig. Dennoch gibt es auch die regelmäßige Form to shine/shined/shined. Sie hat die Bedeutung *polieren*:
The shoes **were** perfectly **shined.** *Die Schuhe **waren** perfekt **poliert.***

58 show *zeigen*

Simple

Present simple

I	show
you	show
he/she/it	shows
we	show
you	show
they	show

Past simple

I	showed
you	showed
he/she/it	showed
we	showed
you	showed
they	showed

Present perfect simple

I	have	shown
you	have	shown
he/she/it	has	shown
we	have	shown
you	have	shown
they	have	shown

Past perfect simple

I	had	shown
you	had	shown
he/she/it	had	shown
we	had	shown
you	had	shown
they	had	shown

Progressive

Present progressive

I	am	showing
you	are	showing
he/she/it	is	showing
we	are	showing
you	are	showing
they	are	showing

Past progressive

I	was	showing
you	were	showing
he/she/it	was	showing
we	were	showing
you	were	showing
they	were	showing

Present perfect progressive

I	have been	showing
you	have been	showing
he/she/it	has been	showing
we	have been	showing
you	have been	showing
they	have been	showing

Past perfect progressive

I	had been	showing
you	had been	showing
he/she/it	had been	showing
we	had been	showing
you	had been	showing
they	had been	showing

Future

Future simple

I	will	show
you	will	show
he/she/it	will	show
we	will	show
you	will	show
they	will	show

Future progressive

I	will be	showing
you	will be	showing
he/she/it	will be	showing
we	will be	showing
you	will be	showing
they	will be	showing

Future perfect simple

I	will have	shown
you	will have	shown
he/she/it	will have	shown
we	will have	shown
you	will have	shown
they	will have	shown

Future perfect progressive

I	will have been	showing
you	will have been	showing
he/she/it	will have been	showing
we	will have been	showing
you	will have been	showing
they	will have been	showing

Conditional

Conditional I

I	would	show
you	would	show
he/she/it	would	show
we	would	show
you	would	show
they	would	show

Conditional II

I	would have	shown
you	would have	shown
he/she/it	would have	shown
we	would have	shown
you	would have	shown
they	would have	shown

Participle

Present participle

showing

Past participle

shown

Gerund

showing

Imperative

show

Perfect infinitive

have shown

Anwendungsbeispiele

She **showed** me her new jacket. *Sie **zeigte** mir ihre neue Jacke.*
I **showed** my passport **to** the officer. *Ich **zeigte** dem Beamten meinen Reisepass.*
It **showed** no signs of improvement. *Es **wies** keine Anzeichen einer Verbesserung **auf**.*
His sadness **showed** in his face. *Man **sah** ihm seine Traurigkeit **an**.*
He **has shown** himself to be a good listener. *Er **hat** sich als guter Zuhörer **erwiesen**.*
The fight **will be shown on** TV. *Der Kampf **wird im** Fernsehen **übertragen werden**.*
She **showed up at** the party quite late. *Sie **tauchte** sehr spät **auf** der Party **auf**.*

Redewendungen

to show compassion for sb. *mit jdm. Mitleid haben*
to show sb. respect *jdm. Respekt zollen*
to show sb. the way *jdm. den Weg zeigen*
to show sb. around *jdn. herumführen (und alles zeigen)*
to show off *angeben*

Ähnliche Verben

to demonstrate sth. *etw. zeigen/beweisen*
to display sth. *etw. auslegen/ausstellen*
to exhibit sth. *etw. ausstellen*
to indicate *andeuten/aufweisen*
to manifest sth. *manifestieren/deutlich zeigen*
to present sth. *etw. präsentieren*
to prove sth. *etw. beweisen*
to reveal *zeigen/sehen lassen*

Gebrauch

Gelegentlich, vor allem im AE, kann man auch das Partizip showed hören oder lesen.

Tipps & Tricks

Genauso wie to show konjugiert man die Verben to mow *mähen*, to sew *nähen* und to sow *sähen*. Auch bei diesen Verben gibt es bereits das regelmäßige Partizip mit derselben Bedeutung.

59 sit *sitzen/sich setzen*

Konsonantenverdoppelung

Simple

Present simple

I	sit
you	sit
he/she/it	sits
we	sit
you	sit
they	sit

Past simple

I	sat
you	sat
he/she/it	sat
we	sat
you	sat
they	sat

Present perfect simple

I	have	sat
you	have	sat
he/she/it	has	sat
we	have	sat
you	have	sat
they	have	sat

Past perfect simple

I	had	sat
you	had	sat
he/she/it	had	sat
we	had	sat
you	had	sat
they	had	sat

Progressive

Present progressive

I	am	sitting
you	are	sitting
he/she/it	is	sitting
we	are	sitting
you	are	sitting
they	are	sitting

Past progressive

I	was	sitting
you	were	sitting
he/she/it	was	sitting
we	were	sitting
you	were	sitting
they	were	sitting

Present perfect progressive

I	have been	sitting
you	have been	sitting
he/she/it	has been	sitting
we	have been	sitting
you	have been	sitting
they	have been	sitting

Past perfect progressive

I	had been	sitting
you	had been	sitting
he/she/it	had been	sitting
we	had been	sitting
you	had been	sitting
they	had been	sitting

Future

Future simple

I	will	sit
you	will	sit
he/she/it	will	sit
we	will	sit
you	will	sit
they	will	sit

Future progressive

I	will be	sitting
you	will be	sitting
he/she/it	will be	sitting
we	will be	sitting
you	will be	sitting
they	will be	sitting

Future perfect simple

I	will have	sat
you	will have	sat
he/she/it	will have	sat
we	will have	sat
you	will have	sat
they	will have	sat

Future perfect progressive

I	will have been	sitting
you	will have been	sitting
he/she/it	will have been	sitting
we	will have been	sitting
you	will have been	sitting
they	will have been	sitting

Conditional

Conditional I

I	would	sit
you	would	sit
he/she/it	would	sit
we	would	sit
you	would	sit
they	would	sit

Conditional II

I	would have	sat
you	would have	sat
he/she/it	would have	sat
we	would have	sat
you	would have	sat
they	would have	sat

Participle

Present participle
sitting

Past participle
sat

Gerund

sitting

Imperative

sit

Perfect infinitive

have sat

Anwendungsbeispiele

He **was sitting at** the table when I came in. *Er **saß am** Tisch, als ich hereinkam.*
She **sat in** a café reading a book. *Sie **saß in** einem Café und las ein Buch.*
I **sat next to** her. *Ich **setzte** mich **neben** sie.*
The house **is sitting on** an old cemetary. *Das Haus **steht auf** einem alten Friedhof.*
She was the first women to **sit on** the committee. *Sie war die erste Frau, die **im** Komitee **saß**.*
Don't just **sit** here. ***Sitz** nicht tatenlos herum!*

Redewendungen

to sit around *herumsitzen*
to sit back *sich zurücklehnen/die Hände in den Schoß legen*
to sit by *tatenlos danebenstehen*
to sit in an armchair/on the sofa *im Sessel/auf dem Sofa sitzen*
to sit at the desk/table *am Schreibtisch/Tisch sitzen*
to sit on one's hands *nichts tun/keinen Finger krumm machen*
to sit on the fence *sich nicht entscheiden können*
to sit well on sb. *jdm. gut passen (Kleidung)*

Ähnliche Verben

to perch *sich setzen/niederlassen*
to squat *in der Hocke sitzen*
to take a seat *sich (hin)setzen*

Gebrauch

To sit bedeutet *sitzen* oder *sich (hin)setzen* gleichermaßen. In einigen Fällen wird es im Deutschen auch mit *stehen* wiedergegeben:
The house **has sat** empty for many years. *Das Haus **steht** seit vielen Jahren leer.*
Your coffee mug **is sitting** right on your desk. *Dein Kaffeebecher **steht** genau auf deinem Schreibtisch.*

Tipps & Tricks

Das Verb to spit *spucken* konjugiert man genauso wie to sit.

60 smell *riechen*

Im AE regelmäßig

Simple

Present simple

I	smell
you	smell
he/she/it	smells
we	smell
you	smell
they	smell

Past simple

I	smelt
you	smelt
he/she/it	smelt
we	smelt
you	smelt
they	smelt

Present perfect simple

I	have	smelt
you	have	smelt
he/she/it	has	smelt
we	have	smelt
you	have	smelt
they	have	smelt

Past perfect simple

I	had	smelt
you	had	smelt
he/she/it	had	smelt
we	had	smelt
you	had	smelt
they	had	smelt

Progressive

Present progressive

I	am	smelling
you	are	smelling
he/she/it	is	smelling
we	are	smelling
you	are	smelling
they	are	smelling

Past progressive

I	was	smelling
you	were	smelling
he/she/it	was	smelling
we	were	smelling
you	were	smelling
they	were	smelling

Present perfect progressive

I	have been	smelling
you	have been	smelling
he/she/it	has been	smelling
we	have been	smelling
you	have been	smelling
they	have been	smelling

Past perfect progressive

I	had been	smelling
you	had been	smelling
he/she/it	had been	smelling
we	had been	smelling
you	had been	smelling
they	had been	smelling

Future

Future simple

I	will	smell
you	will	smell
he/she/it	will	smell
we	will	smell
you	will	smell
they	will	smell

Future progressive

I	will be	smelling
you	will be	smelling
he/she/it	will be	smelling
we	will be	smelling
you	will be	smelling
they	will be	smelling

Future perfect simple

I	will have	smelt
you	will have	smelt
he/she/it	will have	smelt
we	will have	smelt
you	will have	smelt
they	will have	smelt

Future perfect progressive

I	will have been	smelling
you	will have been	smelling
he/she/it	will have been	smelling
we	will have been	smelling
you	will have been	smelling
they	will have been	smelling

Conditional

Conditional I

I	would	smell
you	would	smell
he/she/it	would	smell
we	would	smell
you	would	smell
they	would	smell

Conditional II

I	would have	smelt
you	would have	smelt
he/she/it	would have	smelt
we	would have	smelt
you	would have	smelt
they	would have	smelt

Participle

Present participle

smelling

Past participle

smelt

Gerund

smelling

Imperative

smell

Perfect infinitive

have smelt

Anwendungsbeispiele

I can **smell** gas. *Hier **riecht** es **nach** Gas.*
You **smell** good. *Du **riechst** gut.*
It **smelt of/like** fish. *Es **roch nach** Fisch.*
His breath **smells**. *Er hat Mund**geruch**.*

Redewendungen

to smell bad/strange *schlecht/komisch riechen*
to smell a rat *Lunte/den Braten riechen*
to smell fishy/odd/wrong *verdächtig sein*
to smell to high heaven *zum Himmel stinken*
to smell trouble/danger *Ärger/Gefahr riechen*
to smell sth. a mile off *etw. schon von Weitem riechen*

Ähnliche Verben

to pong of sth. (BE) *nach etw. miefen*
to reek *übel riechen*
to scent sth. *etw. wittern*
to stink *stinken*

Gebrauch

Verben, die eine Sinneswahrnehmung ausdrücken, wie to smell *riechen*, to taste *schmecken* und to touch *berühren*, können nur dann in der Verlaufsform stehen, wenn es sich tatsächlich um eine Aktivität handelt. Bei dem folgenden Satz ist eine ing-Form nicht möglich, da die Suppe nichts tut.
The soup **smells** bad. *Die Suppe **riecht** schlecht.*
Es geht hier vielmehr um eine Eigenheit der Suppe, also steht keine ing-Form. Es folgt ein Adjektiv (kein Adverb!), da sich bad auf die Suppe bezieht und nicht auf das Riechen. Vergleichen Sie hingegen:
The cat **is smelling** the flowers carefully. *Die Katze **riecht** vorsichtig an den Blumen.*
Die Katze verrichtet eine Aktivität; es folgt ein Adverb, das sich auf smell bezieht.

Tipps & Tricks

Eine Reihe von Verben wird im BE meist unregelmäßig, doch im AE regelmäßig konjugiert. Zu diesen gehören z. B. to dwell *wohnen*, to dream *träumen*, to kneel *sich hinknien*, to learn *lernen* und to spell *buchstabieren*.

61 speak *sprechen/reden*

Simple

Present simple

I	speak
you	speak
he/she/it	speaks
we	speak
you	speak
they	speak

Past simple

I	spoke
you	spoke
he/she/it	spoke
we	spoke
you	spoke
they	spoke

Present perfect simple

I	have	spoken
you	have	spoken
he/she/it	has	spoken
we	have	spoken
you	have	spoken
they	have	spoken

Past perfect simple

I	had	spoken
you	had	spoken
he/she/it	had	spoken
we	had	spoken
you	had	spoken
they	had	spoken

Progressive

Present progressive

I	am	speaking
you	are	speaking
he/she/it	is	speaking
we	are	speaking
you	are	speaking
they	are	speaking

Past progressive

I	was	speaking
you	were	speaking
he/she/it	was	speaking
we	were	speaking
you	were	speaking
they	were	speaking

Present perfect progressive

I	have been	speaking
you	have been	speaking
he/she/it	has been	speaking
we	have been	speaking
you	have been	speaking
they	have been	speaking

Past perfect progressive

I	had been	speaking
you	had been	speaking
he/she/it	had been	speaking
we	had been	speaking
you	had been	speaking
they	had been	speaking

Future

Future simple

I	will	speak
you	will	speak
he/she/it	will	speak
we	will	speak
you	will	speak
they	will	speak

Future progressive

I	will be	speaking
you	will be	speaking
he/she/it	will be	speaking
we	will be	speaking
you	will be	speaking
they	will be	speaking

Future perfect simple

I	will have	spoken
you	will have	spoken
he/she/it	will have	spoken
we	will have	spoken
you	will have	spoken
they	will have	spoken

Future perfect progressive

I	will have been	speaking
you	will have been	speaking
he/she/it	will have been	speaking
we	will have been	speaking
you	will have been	speaking
they	will have been	speaking

Conditional

Conditional I

I	would	speak
you	would	speak
he/she/it	would	speak
we	would	speak
you	would	speak
they	would	speak

Conditional II

I	would have	spoken
you	would have	spoken
he/she/it	would have	spoken
we	would have	spoken
you	would have	spoken
they	would have	spoken

Participle

Present participle

speaking

Past participle

spoken

Gerund

speaking

Imperative

speak

Perfect infinitive

have spoken

Anwendungsbeispiele

She **speaks** English fluently. *Sie **spricht** fließend Englisch.*

But he **speaks with** a German accent. *Aber er **spricht mit** einem deutschen Akzent.*

Can I **speak to** Ms Carlton, please? *Kann ich bitte **mit** Frau Carlton **sprechen**?*

They **are** not **speaking to** each other. *Zurzeit **reden** sie nicht **miteinander**.*

I **couldn't speak a word** of Chinese when I arrived. *Als ich ankam, **konnte** ich **kein Wort** Chinesisch.*

Actions **speak** louder than words. *Taten **sagen** mehr als Worte.*

Redewendungen

to speak on the phone *telefonieren*

to speak up *lauter sprechen*

to speak ill/well of sb. *schlecht/gut von jdm. reden*

to speak the truth *die Wahrheit sagen*

to speak in tongues *in Zungen reden (biblisch)*

Ähnliche Verben

to chat *plaudern*

to converse *sich unterhalten*

to gossip *schwätzen*

to talk *reden/sich unterhalten*

to blab *plappern*

to babble *plappern/schwatzen*

Gebrauch

Die Verben to speak und to talk sind in ihrer Verwendung häufig austauschbar, wobei speak das formellere Wort ist. Talk lässt eher an eine lockere Konversation zwischen mehreren Menschen denken. Möchte man sagen, dass man eine oder mehrere Sprachen spricht, kann nur speak verwendet werden:

He **speaks** Russian and Chinese. *Er **spricht** Russisch und Chinesisch.*

Tipps & Tricks

Ähnlich wie to speak werden folgende Verben konjugiert: to break *zerbrechen*, to choose *wählen*, to freeze *frieren*, to steal *stehlen*, to wake *aufwachen* und im BE to weave *weben*.

62 strike *schlagen/treffen/streiken*

Verlaufsform ohne -e

Simple

Present simple

I	strike
you	strike
he/she/it	strikes
we	strike
you	strike
they	strike

Past simple

I	struck
you	struck
he/she/it	struck
we	struck
you	struck
they	struck

Present perfect simple

I	have	struck
you	have	struck
he/she/it	has	struck
we	have	struck
you	have	struck
they	have	struck

Past perfect simple

I	had	struck
you	had	struck
he/she/it	had	struck
we	had	struck
you	had	struck
they	had	struck

Progressive

Present progressive

I	am	striking
you	are	striking
he/she/it	is	striking
we	are	striking
you	are	striking
they	are	striking

Past progressive

I	was	striking
you	were	striking
he/she/it	was	striking
we	were	striking
you	were	striking
they	were	striking

Present perfect progressive

I	have been	striking
you	have been	striking
he/she/it	has been	striking
we	have been	striking
you	have been	striking
they	have been	striking

Past perfect progressive

I	had been	striking
you	had been	striking
he/she/it	had been	striking
we	had been	striking
you	had been	striking
they	had been	striking

Future

Future simple

I	will	strike
you	will	strike
he/she/it	will	strike
we	will	strike
you	will	strike
they	will	strike

Future progressive

I	will be	striking
you	will be	striking
he/she/it	will be	striking
we	will be	striking
you	will be	striking
they	will be	striking

Future perfect simple

I	will have	struck
you	will have	struck
he/she/it	will have	struck
we	will have	struck
you	will have	struck
they	will have	struck

Future perfect progressive

I	will have been	striking
you	will have been	striking
he/she/it	will have been	striking
we	will have been	striking
you	will have been	striking
they	will have been	striking

Conditional

Conditional I

I	would	strike
you	would	strike
he/she/it	would	strike
we	would	strike
you	would	strike
they	would	strike

Conditional II

I	would have	struck
you	would have	struck
he/she/it	would have	struck
we	would have	struck
you	would have	struck
they	would have	struck

Participle

Present participle

striking

Past participle

struck

Gerund

striking

Imperative

strike

Perfect infinitive

have struck

Anwendungsbeispiele

She **struck** her head **against** a branch. *Sie **hat** sich den Kopf **an** einem Ast **gestoßen**.*
He **was struck by** a stone. *Er **wurde von** einem Stein **getroffen**.*
A funny idea **has** just **struck** me. *Ein witziger Gedanke **ist** mir da gerade **gekommen**.*
The old clock began to **strike** midnight. *Die alte Uhr fing an, Mitternacht zu **schlagen**.*
The tree **was struck by** lightning. *Der Baum **wurde vom** Blitz **getroffen**.*
A large earthquake could **strike** Tokyo. *Ein großes Erdbeben könnte Tokio **heimsuchen**.*
How does it **strike** you? *Was **hältst** du **davon**?*
They**'re striking for** more rights. *Sie **streiken für** mehr Rechte.*

Redewendungen

to strike sb. in the face *jdn. ins Gesicht schlagen*
to be struck with horror/terror *plötzlich sehr ängstlich sein*
to strike a deal/bargain with sb. *mit jdm. eine Vereinbarung treffen*
to strike oil *auf Öl stoßen*
to strike a match *ein Streichholz anzünden*
to strike home *ins Schwarze treffen*

Ähnliche Verben

to beat sb. *jdn. schlagen/verprügeln*
to hit sb. *jdn. schlagen*
to punch sb. *jdn. mit der Faust schlagen*
to slap sb. *jdm. einen Klaps geben*

Gebrauch

Im Sinne von *schlagen/treffen* ist im gesprochenen Englisch das Verb to hit weitaus häufiger als to strike anzutreffen.

63 take *nehmen/bringen*

Verlaufsform ohne **-e**

Simple

Present simple

I	take
you	take
he/she/it	takes
we	take
you	take
they	take

Past simple

I	took
you	took
he/she/it	took
we	took
you	took
they	took

Present perfect simple

I	have	taken
you	have	taken
he/she/it	has	taken
we	have	taken
you	have	taken
they	have	taken

Past perfect simple

I	had	taken
you	had	taken
he/she/it	had	taken
we	had	taken
you	had	taken
they	had	taken

Progressive

Present progressive

I	am	taking
you	are	taking
he/she/it	is	taking
we	are	taking
you	are	taking
they	are	taking

Past progressive

I	was	taking
you	were	taking
he/she/it	was	taking
we	were	taking
you	were	taking
they	were	taking

Present perfect progressive

I	have been	taking
you	have been	taking
he/she/it	has been	taking
we	have been	taking
you	have been	taking
they	have been	taking

Past perfect progressive

I	had been	taking
you	had been	taking
he/she/it	had been	taking
we	had been	taking
you	had been	taking
they	had been	taking

Future

Future simple

I	will	take
you	will	take
he/she/it	will	take
we	will	take
you	will	take
they	will	take

Future progressive

I	will be	taking
you	will be	taking
he/she/it	will be	taking
we	will be	taking
you	will be	taking
they	will be	taking

Future perfect simple

I	will have	taken
you	will have	taken
he/she/it	will have	taken
we	will have	taken
you	will have	taken
they	will have	taken

Future perfect progressive

I	will have been	taking
you	will have been	taking
he/she/it	will have been	taking
we	will have been	taking
you	will have been	taking
they	will have been	taking

Conditional

Conditional I

I	would	take
you	would	take
he/she/it	would	take
we	would	take
you	would	take
they	would	take

Conditional II

I	would have	taken
you	would have	taken
he/she/it	would have	taken
we	would have	taken
you	would have	taken
they	would have	taken

Participle

Present participle

taking

Past participle

taken

Gerund

taking

Imperative

take

Perfect infinitive

have taken

Anwendungsbeispiele

Please, **take** an apple. *Bitte,* ***nimm*** *doch einen Apfel.*
Take the next on the right. ***Nehmen*** *Sie die Nächste rechts!*
Could you **take** me **home**? *Kannst du mich* ***nach Hause bringen****?*
It **took** him three hours to do his homework. *Er* ***brauchte*** *drei Stunden für seine Hausaufgaben.*
I can't **take** it anymore. *Ich kann es nicht mehr* ***ertragen****.*
I'**m taking** Translation I next year. *Nächstes Jahr* ***belege*** *ich Übersetzen I.*

Redewendungen

to take sb./sth. personally/seriously *jdn./etw. persönlich/ernst nehmen*
to take off the shoes *die Schuhe ausziehen*
to take sb. out (for dinner) *jdn. (zum Abendessen) ausführen/einladen*
to take a bath/shower *baden/duschen*
to take the bus/train *mit dem Bus/Zug fahren*
to take a photo/picture *ein Foto/Bild machen/fotografieren*
to take a test/an exam *einen Test/ein Examen schreiben*
to take sb. by the hand *jdn. an/bei der Hand nehmen*

Ähnliche Verben

to bring *(mit)bringen*
to last *dauern*
to mistake sb. for. sb. *jdn. verwechseln*
to overtake sb. *jdn. überholen*

Gebrauch

Bitte beachten Sie den Unterschied zwischen to take und to bring: Vereinfacht gesagt, bezeichnet bring eine Bewegung zum Sprecher, während take eine Bewegung in die andere Richtung ausdrückt.
Ferner gibt es einen Unterschied zwischen to take und to last: Take wird verwendet, wenn eine Person eine bestimmte Zeit für eine Handlung braucht; last steht bei unpersönlichen Dingen:
The film **lasts** an hour and a half. *Der Film* ***dauert*** *anderthalb Stunden.*

Tipps & Tricks

Die Verben to mistake *verwechseln*, overtake *überholen* und to shake *schütteln* werden genauso wie to take konjugiert.

64 tell *erzählen/sagen*

Simple

Present simple

I	tell
you	tell
he/she/it	tells
we	tell
you	tell
they	tell

Past simple

I	told
you	told
he/she/it	told
we	told
you	told
they	told

Present perfect simple

I	have	told
you	have	told
he/she/it	has	told
we	have	told
you	have	told
they	have	told

Past perfect simple

I	had	told
you	had	told
he/she/it	had	told
we	had	told
you	had	told
they	had	told

Progressive

Present progressive

I	am	telling
you	are	telling
he/she/it	is	telling
we	are	telling
you	are	telling
they	are	telling

Past progressive

I	was	telling
you	were	telling
he/she/it	was	telling
we	were	telling
you	were	telling
they	were	telling

Present perfect progressive

I	have been	telling
you	have been	telling
he/she/it	has been	telling
we	have been	telling
you	have been	telling
they	have been	telling

Past perfect progressive

I	had been	telling
you	had been	telling
he/she/it	had been	telling
we	had been	telling
you	had been	telling
they	had been	telling

Future

Future simple

I	will	tell
you	will	tell
he/she/it	will	tell
we	will	tell
you	will	tell
they	will	tell

Future progressive

I	will be	telling
you	will be	telling
he/she/it	will be	telling
we	will be	telling
you	will be	telling
they	will be	telling

Future perfect simple

I	will have	told
you	will have	told
he/she/it	will have	told
we	will have	told
you	will have	told
they	will have	told

Future perfect progressive

I	will have been	telling
you	will have been	telling
he/she/it	will have been	telling
we	will have been	telling
you	will have been	telling
they	will have been	telling

Conditional

Conditional I

I	would	tell
you	would	tell
he/she/it	would	tell
we	would	tell
you	would	tell
they	would	tell

Conditional II

I	would have	told
you	would have	told
he/she/it	would have	told
we	would have	told
you	would have	told
they	would have	told

Participle

Present participle

telling

Past participle

told

Gerund

telling

Imperative

tell

Perfect infinitive

have told

Anwendungsbeispiele

Tell me exactly what she said. ***Sag*** *mir genau, was sie gesagt hat.*
What **did** she **tell** you? *Was* ***hat*** *sie dir* ***gesagt****?*
I **told** you so. *Ich* ***habe*** *es dir doch gleich* ***gesagt****.*
Has she **told** you **about** his accident. ***Hat*** *sie dir* ***von*** *seinem Unfall* ***erzählt****?*
I've been told he has left the country. *Mir* ***ist gesagt worden****, er habe das Land verlassen.*
She **told** them not to open the door. *Sie* ***sagte*** *ihnen, sie sollten die Tür nicht öffnen.*
How can you **tell** a Rolls **from** a Bentley? *Wie kann man einen Rolls* ***von*** *einem Bentley* ***unterscheiden****?*
I can't **tell** them **apart**. *Ich kann sie nicht* ***auseinanderhalten****.*
You can never **tell**. *Man kann nie* ***wissen****.*

Redewendungen

to tell a lie/the truth *lügen/die Wahrheit sagen*
to tell a tale *ein Märchen erzählen*
to tell a joke *einen Witz machen*
to tell the difference *einen Unterschied feststellen*

Ähnliche Verben

to distinguish between *unterscheiden zwischen*
to express sth. *etw. ausdrücken*
to mention sth. *etw. erwähnen*
to remark *bemerken/äußern*
to say sth. *etw. sagen*

Gebrauch

Das Verb to tell benötigt immer ein Objekt (meist ein Personalpronomen oder in wenigen Ausnahmen ein Substantiv). Man verwendet tell nicht vor a word *Wort*, a name *Name*, a sentence *Satz* oder a phrase *Ausdruck*.

Tipps & Tricks

Genauso wie to tell konjugiert man das Verb to sell *verkaufen*.

65 think *denken/glauben*

Simple

Present simple

I	think
you	think
he/she/it	thinks
we	think
you	think
they	think

Past simple

I	thought
you	thought
he/she/it	thought
we	thought
you	thought
they	thought

Present perfect simple

I	have	thought
you	have	thought
he/she/it	has	thought
we	have	thought
you	have	thought
they	have	thought

Past perfect simple

I	had	thought
you	had	thought
he/she/it	had	thought
we	had	thought
you	had	thought
they	had	thought

Progressive

Present progressive

I	am	thinking
you	are	thinking
he/she/it	is	thinking
we	are	thinking
you	are	thinking
they	are	thinking

Past progressive

I	was	thinking
you	were	thinking
he/she/it	was	thinking
we	were	thinking
you	were	thinking
they	were	thinking

Present perfect progressive

I	have been	thinking
you	have been	thinking
he/she/it	has been	thinking
we	have been	thinking
you	have been	thinking
they	have been	thinking

Past perfect progressive

I	had been	thinking
you	had been	thinking
he/she/it	had been	thinking
we	had been	thinking
you	had been	thinking
they	had been	thinking

Future

Future simple

I	will	think
you	will	think
he/she/it	will	think
we	will	think
you	will	think
they	will	think

Future progressive

I	will be	thinking
you	will be	thinking
he/she/it	will be	thinking
we	will be	thinking
you	will be	thinking
they	will be	thinking

Future perfect simple

I	will have	thought
you	will have	thought
he/she/it	will have	thought
we	will have	thought
you	will have	thought
they	will have	thought

Future perfect progressive

I	will have been	thinking
you	will have been	thinking
he/she/it	will have been	thinking
we	will have been	thinking
you	will have been	thinking
they	will have been	thinking

Conditional

Conditional I

I	would	think
you	would	think
he/she/it	would	think
we	would	think
you	would	think
they	would	think

Conditional II

I	would have	thought
you	would have	thought
he/she/it	would have	thought
we	would have	thought
you	would have	thought
they	would have	thought

Participle

Present participle

thinking

Past participle

thought

Gerund

thinking

Imperative

think

Perfect infinitive

have thought

Anwendungsbeispiele

I **think** you're right. *Ich **denke**, du hast recht.*
What do you **think**? *Was **meinst** du?*
I'll be thinking of you. *Ich **werde an** dich **denken**.*
They **are thinking of** selling their house. *Sie **überlegen**, ihr Haus zu verkaufen.*
I **think** so. *Ich **denke/glaube** schon.*
I **thought** he was from Spain. *Ich **dachte**, er sei aus Spanien.*
I **think** it best to go now. *Ich **halte** es **für** das Beste, jetzt zu gehen.*
The boy **thought** no harm. *Der Junge **hatte** nichts Böses **im Sinn**.*
I can't **think straight** anymore. *Ich kann nicht mehr **klar denken**.*

Redewendungen

to think sb. to be sth. *jdn. für etw. halten*
to think highly of sb. *viel von jdm. halten*
to think oneself lucky *sich glücklich schätzen*
to think for oneself *selbstständig denken*
to be unable to hear oneself think *sein eigenes Wort nicht verstehen*

Ähnliche Verben

to assume *annehmen*
to believe *glauben*
to contemplate *nachdenken*
to guess (AE) *denken/meinen*
to ponder *nachdenken*
to reflect *reflektieren*

Aufgepasst!

Bitte beachten Sie, dass to think in der einfachen Zeitform *denken/glauben/meinen* bedeutet, während es in der Verlaufsform *nachdenken/überlegen/reflektieren* meint. Die ing-Form wird also nur verwendet, wenn man ausdrücken möchte, dass es sich um die intensive Aktivität des Nachdenkens handelt.

Tipps & Tricks

Ähnlich konjugiert wie to think werden die Verben to bring *bringen*, to catch *fangen*, to buy *kaufen*, to fight *kämpfen*, to seek *suchen* und to teach *lehren*.

66 throw *werfen*

Simple

Present simple

I	throw
you	throw
he/she/it	throws
we	throw
you	throw
they	throw

Past simple

I	threw
you	threw
he/she/it	threw
we	threw
you	threw
they	threw

Present perfect simple

I	have	thrown
you	have	thrown
he/she/it	has	thrown
we	have	thrown
you	have	thrown
they	have	thrown

Past perfect simple

I	had	thrown
you	had	thrown
he/she/it	had	thrown
we	had	thrown
you	had	thrown
they	had	thrown

Progressive

Present progressive

I	am	throwing
you	are	throwing
he/she/it	is	throwing
we	are	throwing
you	are	throwing
they	are	throwing

Past progressive

I	was	throwing
you	were	throwing
he/she/it	was	throwing
we	were	throwing
you	were	throwing
they	were	throwing

Present perfect progressive

I	have been	throwing
you	have been	throwing
he/she/it	has been	throwing
we	have been	throwing
you	have been	throwing
they	have been	throwing

Past perfect progressive

I	had been	throwing
you	had been	throwing
he/she/it	had been	throwing
we	had been	throwing
you	had been	throwing
they	had been	throwing

Future

Future simple

I	will	throw
you	will	throw
he/she/it	will	throw
we	will	throw
you	will	throw
they	will	throw

Future progressive

I	will be	throwing
you	will be	throwing
he/she/it	will be	throwing
we	will be	throwing
you	will be	throwing
they	will be	throwing

Future perfect simple

I	will have	thrown
you	will have	thrown
he/she/it	will have	thrown
we	will have	thrown
you	will have	thrown
they	will have	thrown

Future perfect progressive

I	will have been	throwing
you	will have been	throwing
he/she/it	will have been	throwing
we	will have been	throwing
you	will have been	throwing
they	will have been	throwing

Conditional

Conditional I

I	would	throw
you	would	throw
he/she/it	would	throw
we	would	throw
you	would	throw
they	would	throw

Conditional II

I	would have	thrown
you	would have	thrown
he/she/it	would have	thrown
we	would have	thrown
you	would have	thrown
they	would have	thrown

Participle

Present participle

throwing

Past participle

thrown

Gerund

throwing

Imperative

throw

Perfect infinitive

have thrown

Anwendungsbeispiele

Someone **threw** a snowball at the bus. *Jemand **warf** einen Schneeball an den Bus.*
She **threw herself onto** the couch. *Sie **warf sich auf** die Couch.*
The bus stopped suddenly and I was **thrown forward.** *Der Bus stoppte plötzlich und ich **wurde nach vorn geworfen.***
He finally **threw** his old coat **away.** *Schließlich **warf** er seinen alten Mantel **fort.***

Redewendungen

to throw a tantrum *einen Wutanfall bekommen*
to throw sb. into prison/jail *jdn. ins Gefängnis werfen*
to throw oneself at sb. *sich jdm. an den Hals werfen*
to throw doubt on sth. *etw. in Zweifel ziehen*
to throw a look/smile at sb. *jdm. einen Blick/ein Lächeln zuwerfen*
to throw a party *eine Party schmeißen*
to throw (the) dice/a six *würfeln/eine Sechs werfen*
to throw money away on sth. *Geld für etw. zum Fenster hinauswerfen*
to throw up *sich übergeben*

Andere Verben

to catch sth. *etw. fangen*
to drop sth. *etw. werfen/fallen lassen*
to grab sth. *etw. (hastig) ergreifen*
to grasp sth. *etw. packen*
to seize sb./sth. *jdn./etw. ergreifen*

Gebrauch

Das Verb throw wird im Großen und Ganzen wie das deutsche *werfen* verwendet, auch im Zusammenhang mit einer Reihe von Präpositionen, z. B. to throw **away** ***weg**werfen*, to throw **down** ***herunter**werfen*, to throw **out** ***heraus**werfen*, to throw **overboard** ***über Bord** werfen*.

Tipps & Tricks

Genauso wie to throw konjugiert man die Verben to blow *blasen*, to fly *fliegen*, to grow *wachsen* und to know *wissen/kennen*.

67 wear *tragen*

Simple

Present simple

I	wear
you	wear
he/she/it	wears
we	wear
you	wear
they	wear

Past simple

I	wore
you	wore
he/she/it	wore
we	wore
you	wore
they	wore

Present perfect simple

I	have	worn
you	have	worn
he/she/it	has	worn
we	have	worn
you	have	worn
they	have	worn

Past perfect simple

I	had	worn
you	had	worn
he/she/it	had	worn
we	had	worn
you	had	worn
they	had	worn

Progressive

Present progressive

I	am	wearing
you	are	wearing
he/she/it	is	wearing
we	are	wearing
you	are	wearing
they	are	wearing

Past progressive

I	was	wearing
you	were	wearing
he/she/it	was	wearing
we	were	wearing
you	were	wearing
they	were	wearing

Present perfect progressive

I	have been	wearing
you	have been	wearing
he/she/it	has been	wearing
we	have been	wearing
you	have been	wearing
they	have been	wearing

Past perfect progressive

I	had been	wearing
you	had been	wearing
he/she/it	had been	wearing
we	had been	wearing
you	had been	wearing
they	had been	wearing

Future

Future simple

I	will	wear
you	will	wear
he/she/it	will	wear
we	will	wear
you	will	wear
they	will	wear

Future progressive

I	will be	wearing
you	will be	wearing
he/she/it	will be	wearing
we	will be	wearing
you	will be	wearing
they	will be	wearing

Future perfect simple

I	will have	worn
you	will have	worn
he/she/it	will have	worn
we	will have	worn
you	will have	worn
they	will have	worn

Future perfect progressive

I	will have been	wearing
you	will have been	wearing
he/she/it	will have been	wearing
we	will have been	wearing
you	will have been	wearing
they	will have been	wearing

Conditional

Conditional I

I	would	wear
you	would	wear
he/she/it	would	wear
we	would	wear
you	would	wear
they	would	wear

Conditional II

I	would have	worn
you	would have	worn
he/she/it	would have	worn
we	would have	worn
you	would have	worn
they	would have	worn

Participle

Present participle

wearing

Past participle

worn

Gerund

wearing

Imperative

wear

Perfect infinitive

have worn

Anwendungsbeispiele

I **was wearing** a blue shirt to the party. *Bei der Party* ***trug*** *ich ein blaues Hemd.*
Does your teacher **wear** glasses? ***Trägt*** *deine Lehrerin eine Brille?*
She **wore** her hair loose. *Sie* ***trug*** *ihr Haar offen.*
My boots **are worn out**. *Meine Stiefel* ***sind verschlissen****.*
I'm totally **worn out**. *Ich* ***bin*** *total* ***erschöpft****.*
These trousers are starting to **wear at** the knees. *Diese Hose* ***wird an*** *den Knien schon ganz* ***dünn****.*
After an hour the pain **wore off**. *Nach einer Stunde* ***ließ*** *der Schmerz* ***nach****.*
In his family she**'s wearing** the trousers (BE)/pants (AE). *In seiner Familie* ***hat*** *sie die Hosen* ***an****.*
She didn't want to join us at first, but we finally **wore** her **down**. *Zunächst wollte sie sich uns nicht anschließen, doch schließlich* ***haben*** *wir sie* ***kleingekriegt****.*

Witz

"Mum, now that I'm fifteen, can I **wear** eye-shadow and lipstick and mascara and perfume and high-heeled shoes?"
"No, Robert, better not."

Ähnliche Verben

to have sth. on *etw. anhaben*
to put sth. on *etw. anziehen*
to be clothed in *gekleidet sein in/tragen*
to be dressed in *gekleidet sein in/tragen*

Gebrauch

Im Sinne von *tragen* verwendet man to wear nur für Kleidung, die man anhat. Für Dinge oder Lasten, die man mit den Händen trägt, verwendet man to carry oder to bear, wobei Letzteres auch für emotionale Dinge gilt:
His bad manners were more than I could **bear**. *Seine schlechten Manieren waren mehr, als ich* ***ertragen*** *konnte.*

Tipps & Tricks

Das Verb to wear wird genauso konjugiert wie to bear *tragen/ertragen*, to swear *schwören* und to tear *zerreißen*.

68 win *gewinnen*

Konsonantenverdoppelung

Simple

Present simple

I	win
you	win
he/she/it	wins
we	win
you	win
they	win

Past simple

I	won
you	won
he/she/it	won
we	won
you	won
they	won

Present perfect simple

I	have	won
you	have	won
he/she/it	has	won
we	have	won
you	have	won
they	have	won

Past perfect simple

I	had	won
you	had	won
he/she/it	had	won
we	had	won
you	had	won
they	had	won

Progressive

Present progressive

I	am	winning
you	are	winning
he/she/it	is	winning
we	are	winning
you	are	winning
they	are	winning

Past progressive

I	was	winning
you	were	winning
he/she/it	was	winning
we	were	winning
you	were	winning
they	were	winning

Present perfect progressive

I	have been	winning
you	have been	winning
he/she/it	has been	winning
we	have been	winning
you	have been	winning
they	have been	winning

Past perfect progressive

I	had been	winning
you	had been	winning
he/she/it	had been	winning
we	had been	winning
you	had been	winning
they	had been	winning

Future

Future simple

I	will	win
you	will	win
he/she/it	will	win
we	will	win
you	will	win
they	will	win

Future progressive

I	will be	winning
you	will be	winning
he/she/it	will be	winning
we	will be	winning
you	will be	winning
they	will be	winning

Future perfect simple

I	will have	won
you	will have	won
he/she/it	will have	won
we	will have	won
you	will have	won
they	will have	won

Future perfect progressive

I	will have been	winning
you	will have been	winning
he/she/it	will have been	winning
we	will have been	winning
you	will have been	winning
they	will have been	winning

Conditional

Conditional I

I	would	win
you	would	win
he/she/it	would	win
we	would	win
you	would	win
they	would	win

Conditional II

I	would have	won
you	would have	won
he/she/it	would have	won
we	would have	won
you	would have	won
they	would have	won

Participle

Present participle

winning

Past participle

won

Gerund

winning

Imperative

win

Perfect infinitive

have won

Anwendungsbeispiele

Who **won** the match? *Wer* ***hat*** *das Spiel* ***gewonnen****?*

I **won at** poker last night. *Gestern Abend* ***habe*** *ich* ***beim*** *Pokern* ***gewonnen****.*

She**'s won in** the lottery. *Sie* ***hat in*** *der Lotterie* ***gewonnen****.*

Who**'s winning**? *Wer* ***gewinnt/ist am Gewinnen****?*

They are **winning** by 2–1. *Sie* ***führen*** *2 zu 1.*

Redewendungen

to win by 20 points *mit 20 Punkten (Unterschied) gewinnen*

to win a battle *eine Schlacht gewinnen*

to win a case *einen Fall gewinnen*

to win an election *eine Wahl gewinnen*

to win sb.'s approval/support *jds. Anerkennung/Unterstützung gewinnen*

to win popularity *sich beliebt machen*

to win sb.'s heart *jds. Herz gewinnen*

to win sth. back *etw. zurückgewinnen*

to win out over sb. *sich gegen jdn. durchsetzen/über jdn. siegen*

to win a war *einen Krieg gewinnen*

Ähnliche Verben

to come/be first *Erste(r) sein*

to finish first *als Erste(r) ankommen*

to be victorious in sth. *bei etw. siegreich sein*

to gain victory *den Sieg erringen*

to succeed in sth. *bei etw. erfolgreich sein*

to triumph *triumphieren*

Gebrauch

Das Verb to win kann in manchen Redewendungen auch mit *bekommen* oder *erhalten* übersetzt werden, z. B. to win sb.'s approval *jds. Anerkennung erhalten* oder to win a scholarship *ein Stipendium erhalten*.

Tipps & Tricks

Genauso wie to win konjugiert man to cling *festhalten*, to dig *graben*, to fling *werfen/schleudern*, to spin *drehen/spinnen*, to stick *kleben*, to sting *stechen*, to swing *schwingen* und to wring *auswringen*.

69 work *arbeiten*

Simple

Present simple

I	work
you	work
he/she/it	works
we	work
you	work
they	work

Past simple

I	worked
you	worked
he/she/it	worked
we	worked
you	worked
they	worked

Present perfect simple

I	have	worked
you	have	worked
he/she/it	has	worked
we	have	worked
you	have	worked
they	have	worked

Past perfect simple

I	had	worked
you	had	worked
he/she/it	had	worked
we	had	worked
you	had	worked
they	had	worked

Progressive

Present progressive

I	am	working
you	are	working
he/she/it	is	working
we	are	working
you	arc	working
they	are	working

Past progressive

I	was	working
you	were	working
he/she/it	was	working
we	were	working
you	were	working
they	were	working

Present perfect progressive

I	have been	working
you	have been	working
he/she/it	has been	working
we	have been	working
you	have been	working
they	have been	working

Past perfect progressive

I	had been	working
you	had been	working
he/she/it	had been	working
we	had been	working
you	had been	working
they	had been	working

Future

Future simple

I	will	work
you	will	work
he/she/it	will	work
we	will	work
you	will	work
they	will	work

Future progressive

I	will be	working
you	will be	working
he/she/it	will be	working
we	will be	working
you	will be	working
they	will be	working

Future perfect simple

I	will have	worked
you	will have	worked
he/she/it	will have	worked
we	will have	worked
you	will have	worked
they	will have	worked

Future perfect progressive

I	will have been	working
you	will have been	working
he/she/it	will have been	working
we	will have been	working
you	will have been	working
they	will have been	working

Conditional

Conditional I

I	would	work
you	would	work
he/she/it	would	work
we	would	work
you	would	work
they	would	work

Conditional II

I	would have	worked
you	would have	worked
he/she/it	would have	worked
we	would have	worked
you	would have	worked
they	would have	worked

Participle

Present participle

working

Past participle

worked

Gerund

working

Imperative

work

Perfect infinitive

have worked

Anwendungsbeispiele

I **work for** a computer company. *Ich **arbeite bei** einer Computerfirma.*
I **work as** a computer programmer. *Ich **arbeite als** Programmierer.*
I'**ve been working** here for five years. *Ich **arbeite** hier schon seit fünf Jahren.*
It took me three days **to work** it **out**. *Ich habe drei Tage gebraucht, um das **auszuarbeiten**.*
The printer **doesn't work**. *Der Drucker **geht/funktioniert nicht**.*

Redewendungen

to work in publishing/education *im Verlagswesen/Erziehungswesen arbeiten*
to work at a problem *an einem Problem arbeiten*
to work part-time/full-time *Teilzeit/Vollzeit arbeiten*
to work from home *zu Hause arbeiten*
to work one's way up *sich hocharbeiten*
to work one's fingers to the bone *sich den Rücken krumm arbeiten*
to work out a solution *eine Lösung erarbeiten*
to work up a plan *einen Plan erarbeiten*
to work like a horse *schuften wie ein Pferd*
to work wonders with sb./sth. *bei jdm./etw. Wunder wirken*

Andere Verben

to be unemployed *arbeitslos sein*
to idle *faulenzen*
to laze around *faulenzen*
to relax *sich entspannen*

Aufgepasst!

Um auszudrücken, dass man schon seit einer bestimmten Zeit bei einer Firma arbeitet, verwendet man am besten das Present perfect progressive:
I've been working for XP-Consult for 15 years/since 2005. *Ich **arbeite** für XP-Consult **schon** seit 15 Jahren/seit 2005.*

70 write *schreiben*

Simple

Present simple

I	write
you	write
he/she/it	writes
we	write
you	write
they	write

Past simple

I	wrote
you	wrote
he/she/it	wrote
we	wrote
you	wrote
they	wrote

Present perfect simple

I	have	written
you	have	written
he/she/it	has	written
we	have	written
you	have	written
they	have	written

Past perfect simple

I	had	written
you	had	written
he/she/it	had	written
we	had	written
you	had	written
they	had	written

Progressive

Present progressive

I	am	writing
you	are	writing
he/she/it	is	writing
we	are	writing
you	are	writing
they	are	writing

Past progressive

I	was	writing
you	were	writing
he/she/it	was	writing
we	were	writing
you	were	writing
they	were	writing

Present perfect progressive

I	have been	writing
you	have been	writing
he/she/it	has been	writing
we	have been	writing
you	have been	writing
they	have been	writing

Past perfect progressive

I	had been	writing
you	had been	writing
he/she/it	had been	writing
we	had been	writing
you	had been	writing
they	had been	writing

Future

Future simple

I	will	write
you	will	write
he/she/it	will	write
we	will	write
you	will	write
they	will	write

Future progressive

I	will be	writing
you	will be	writing
he/she/it	will be	writing
we	will be	writing
you	will be	writing
they	will be	writing

Future perfect simple

I	will have	written
you	will have	written
he/she/it	will have	written
we	will have	written
you	will have	written
they	will have	written

Future perfect progressive

I	will have been	writing
you	will have been	writing
he/she/it	will have been	writing
we	will have been	writing
you	will have been	writing
they	will have been	writing

Conditional

Conditional I

I	would	write
you	would	write
he/she/it	would	write
we	would	write
you	would	write
they	would	write

Conditional II

I	would have	written
you	would have	written
he/she/it	would have	written
we	would have	written
you	would have	written
they	would have	written

Participle

Present participle

writing

Past participle

wrote

Gerund

writing

Imperative

write

Perfect infinitive

have written

Anwendungsbeispiele

Who **wrote** Hamlet? *Wer* ***schrieb*** *Hamlet?*
Did you **write** this letter? ***Hast*** *du diesen Brief* ***geschrieben****?*
Pete sat in a café **writing** e-mails. *Pete saß in einem Café und* ***schrieb*** *E-Mails.*
She **wrote** him a postcard. *Sie* ***schrieb*** *ihm eine Postkarte.*
He **wrote** an essay about Hemingway. *Er* ***hat*** *einen Aufsatz über Hemingway* ***geschrieben****.*
He **wrote** everything **down**. *Er* ***hat*** *alles* ***aufgeschrieben/notiert****.*
The book **is** very poorly **written**. *Das Buch* ***ist*** *sehr schlecht* ***geschrieben****.*
It **is written** that you shall not steal. *Es* ***steht geschrieben****, dass man nicht stehlen soll.*
He **wrote off** his new car. *Er* ***hat*** *seinen neuen Wagen* ***zu Schrott gefahren****.*

Redewendungen

to write clearly/legibly *deutlich/lesbar schreiben*
to write a cheque (BE)/check (AE) *einen Scheck ausstellen*
to write a book/a poem *ein Buch/Gedicht schreiben*
to write a prescription/receipt *ein Rezept/eine Quittung ausstellen*
to write a test/thesis *einen Test/eine Doktorarbeit schreiben*
to write sth. in German *etw. auf Deutsch verfassen*
to write for a living *von der Schriftstellerei leben/Schriftsteller(in) sein*

Ähnliche Verben

to draft sth. *etw. entwerfen*
to copy sth. *etw. kopieren*
to note sth. down *etw. notieren*
to scribble *kritzeln*
to take sth. down *etw. aufschreiben*
to rewrite sth. *etw. umschreiben*
to underwrite sth. *seine Zustimmung zu etw. geben*

Aufgepasst!

To write wird genauso ausgesprochen wie right *rechts*. Das -w ist nicht hörbar.

Tipps & Tricks

Genauso wie to write konjugiert man to arise *aufstehen/auftauchen*, to drive *fahren*, to ride *reiten/fahren*, to rise *sich erheben/aufstehen*, to stride *schreiten* und to strive *streben*.

Unregelmäßige Verben

Hier finden Sie die wichtigsten englischen unregelmäßigen Verben mit ihrer deutschen Übersetzung alphabetisch aufgelistet. Manchmal gibt es zwei Formen im britischen Englisch (BE). In Klammern stehen jene Formen, die eher im amerikanischen Englisch (AE) verwendet werden.

Infinitiv	Past simple	Past participle	Deutsch
arise	arose	arisen	*aufstehen/entstehen*
awake	awoke	awoken	*aufwachen*
be	was/were	been	*sein*
bear	bore	borne/born	*tragen/gebären*
beat	beat	beaten	*schlagen*
become	became	become	*werden*
begin	began	begun	*beginnen/anfangen*
bend	bent	bent	*(sich) bücken/biegen*
bet	bet	bet	*wetten*
bid	bade/bid	bid/bidden	*bieten*
bind	bound	bound	*binden*
bite	bit	bitten	*beißen*
bleed	bled	bled	*bluten*
blow	blew	blown	*blasen/wehen*
break	broke	broken	*(zer)brechen/kaputtgehen*
breed	bred	bred	*züchten*
bring	brought	brought	*bringen*
broadcast	broadcast	broadcast	*senden (TV)*
build	built	built	*bauen*
burn	burnt/burned	burnt/burned	*(ver)brennen*
burst	burst	burst	*platzen*
buy	bought	bought	*kaufen*
cast	cast	cast	*werfen*
catch	caught	caught	*fangen*
choose	chose	chosen	*(aus)wählen*
cling	clung	clung	*festhalten*
come	came	come	*kommen*
cost	cost	cost	*kosten*
creep	crept	crept	*kriechen*
cut	cut	cut	*schneiden*

Infinitiv	Past simple	Past participle	Deutsch
deal	dealt	dealt	*handeln/dealen*
dig	dug	dug	*graben*
dive	dived (AE: dove)	dived	*tauchen*
do	did	done	*tun/machen*
draw	drew	drawn	*zeichnen/ziehen*
dream	dreamt/dreamed	dreamt/dreamed	*träumen*
drink	drank	drunk	*trinken*
drive	drove	driven	*(selbst) fahren*
dwell	dwelt/dwelled	dwelt/dwelled	*wohnen*
eat	ate	eaten	*essen*
fall	fell	fallen	*fallen*
feed	fed	fed	*füttern*
feel	felt	felt	*(sich) (an)fühlen*
fight	fought	fought	*kämpfen*
find	found	found	*finden*
flee	fled	fled	*fliehen*
fling	flung	flung	*schleudern*
fly	flew	flown	*fliegen*
forbid	forbade/forbad	forbidden	*verbieten*
forecast	forecast	forecast	*vorhersagen*
for(e)go	for(e)went	for(e)gone	*verzichten*
foresee	foresaw	foreseen	*vorhersehen*
forget	forgot	forgotten	*vergessen*
forgive	forgave	forgiven	*vergeben*
freeze	froze	frozen	*frieren*
get	got	got (AE: gotten)	*holen/bekommen*
give	gave	given	*geben*
go	went	gone	*gehen/fahren*
grind	ground	ground	*(zer)mahlen*
grow	grew	grown	*wachsen/(an)bauen*
hang	hung/hanged	hung/hanged	*aufhängen/hängen*
have	had	had	*haben*
hear	heard	heard	*hören*
hide	hid	hidden/hid	*(sich) verstecken*
hit	hit	hit	*schlagen/treffen*
hold	held	held	*halten*
hurt	hurt	hurt	*verletzen/wehtun*

Infinitiv	Past simple	Past participle	Deutsch
keep	kept	kept	*(be)halten/weitermachen*
kneel	knelt (AE: kneeled)	knelt (AE: kneeled)	*sich hinknien*
know	knew	known	*kennen/wissen*
lay	laid	laid	*legen/Tisch decken*
lead	led	led	*führen/leiten*
lean	leaned/leant	leaned/leant	*lehnen/sich neigen*
leap	leapt (AE: leaped)	leapt (AE: leaped)	*springen*
learn	learnt (AE: learned)	learnt (AE: learned)	*lernen*
leave	left	left	*(ver-, zurück)lassen/ weggehen*
lend	lent	lent	*(ver)leihen*
let	let	let	*lassen*
lie	lay	lain	*liegen*
light	lit/lighted	lit/lighted	*anzünden*
lose	lost	lost	*verlieren*
make	made	made	*machen*
mean	meant	meant	*bedeuten/meinen*
meet	met	met	*treffen/kennenlernen*
mislay	mislaid	mislaid	*verlegen*
mistake	mistook	mistaken	*falsch verstehen*
misunderstand	misunderstood	misunderstood	*missverstehen*
mow	mowed	mown/mowed	*mähen*
overcome	overcame	overcome	*überwinden/überwältigen*
oversleep	overslept	overslept	*verschlafen*
overtake	overtook	overtaken	*überholen*
pay	paid	paid	*(be)zahlen*
prove	proved	proved (AE: proven)	*beweisen*
put	put	put	*setzen/stellen/legen*
quit	quit	quit	*aufgeben/aufhören*
read	read	read	*lesen*
redo	redid	redone	*nochmals tun*
repay	repaid	repaid	*zurückzahlen*
ride	rode	ridden	*fahren/reiten*
ring	rang	rung	*klingeln/anrufen*
rise	rose	risen	*(auf)steigen*
run	ran	run	*laufen/rennen*

Infinitiv	Past simple	Past participle	Deutsch
saw	sawed	sawn/sawed	*sägen*
say	said	said	*sagen*
see	saw	seen	*sehen*
seek	sought	sought	*suchen*
sell	sold	sold	*verkaufen*
send	sent	sent	*schicken/senden*
set	set	set	*(fest)setzen/stellen*
sew	sewed	sewn/sewed	*nähen*
shake	shook	shaken	*schütteln*
shine	shone/shined	shone/shined	*scheinen/polieren*
shoot	shot	shot	*schießen*
show	showed	shown/showed	*zeigen*
shrink	shrank/shrunk	shrunk	*schrumpfen/einlaufen*
shut	shut	shut	*schließen*
sing	sang	sung	*singen*
sink	sank/sunk	sunk	*sinken*
sit	sat	sat	*sitzen*
sleep	slept	slept	*schlafen*
slide	slid	slid	*rutschen*
sling	slung	slung	*schleudern*
slit	slit	slit	*aufschlitzen*
smell	smelt (AE: smelled)	smelt (AE: smelled)	*riechen*
sow	sowed	sown/sowed	*säen*
speak	spoke	spoken	*sprechen*
spell	spelt (AE: spelled)	spelt (AE: spelled)	*buchstabieren*
spend	spent	spent	*ausgeben/verbringen*
spill	spilt (AE: spilled)	spilt (AE: spilled)	*verschütten*
spin	span/spun	spun	*spinnen/drehen*
spit	spat (AE: spit)	spat (AE: spit)	*spucken*
split	split	split	*spalten*
spoil	spoiled/spoilt	spoiled/spoilt	*verderben*
spread	spread	spread	*aus-/verbreiten*
spring	sprang (AE: sprung)	sprung	*springen*
stand	stood	stood	*stehen*
steal	stole	stolen	*stehlen*
stick	stuck	stuck	*kleben/hängen bleiben*
sting	stung	stung	*stechen*
stink	stank/stunk	stunk	*stinken*
stride	strode	stridden	*schreiten*

Infinitiv	Past simple	Past participle	Deutsch
strike	struck	struck (AE: stricken)	*schlagen*
strive	strove/strived	striven/strived	*sich bemühen*
swear	swore	sworn	*schwören*
sweep	swept	swept	*kehren/fegen*
swim	swam	swum	*schwimmen*
swing	swung	swung	*schwingen*
take	took	taken	*nehmen/bringen*
teach	taught	taught	*lehren*
tear	tore	torn	*(zer)reißen*
tell	told	told	*erzählen/sagen*
think	thought	thought	*denken/glauben*
throw	threw	thrown	*werfen*
thrust	thrust	thrust	*stoßen*
undergo	underwent	undergone	*durchmachen/erdulden*
understand	understood	understood	*verstehen*
underwrite	underwrote	underwritten	*Zustimmung geben*
undo	undid	undone	*rückgängig machen*
wake	woke	woken	*aufwachen*
wear	wore	worn	*tragen (Kleidung)*
weave	wove	woven	*weben*
weep	wept	wept	*weinen*
win	won	won	*gewinnen*
wind	wound	wound	*wickeln/spulen*
withdraw	withdrew	withdrawn	*abheben (Geld)*
wring	wrung	wrung	*auswringen*
write	wrote	written	*schreiben*

Verben mit Präposition

Im Englischen kommen manche Verben bisweilen in Verbindung mit Präpositionen vor. Die Präpositionen führen oftmals zu einer Bedeutungsänderung des Verbs. Einige Verben ziehen immer dieselbe Präposition nach sich, andere werden hingegen in Verbindung mit verschiedenen Präpositionen verwendet. Gehen Verb und Präposition eine untrennbare Verbindung ein, spricht man auch von einem Phrasal verb. In diesem Fall nimmt das Verb häufig eine übertragene Bedeutung an. Im Folgenden haben wir für Sie die wichtigsten Phrasal verbs aufgelistet. Die Angabe (+ -ing) signalisiert, dass nach der Präposition ein Verb als Gerund stehen kann bzw. muss.

▸ account **for** sth. *sich etw. erklären*	How do you account for the missing cash? *Wie erklärst du dir das fehlende Geld?*
accuse sb. **of** (+ -ing) sth. *jdn. wegen etw. beschuldigen/jdn. beschuldigen, etw. getan zu haben*	The police accused Mike of robbing a bank. *Die Polizei beschuldigte Mike, eine Bank ausgeraubt zu haben.*
adapt **to** sb./sth. *sich an etw./jdn. anpassen*	I found it difficult to adapt to the local customs. *Ich fand es schwierig, mich den Gebräuchen anzupassen.*
agree **with** sb. *mit jdm. einer Meinung sein*	She never agrees with him. *Sie ist nie seiner Meinung.*
apologize **for** (+ -ing) sth. *sich für etw. entschuldigen*	You will have to apologize for that. *Du wirst dich dafür entschuldigen müssen.*
ask **after** sb. *sich nach jdm. erkundigen*	Jack asked after you when you were gone. *Jack hat sich nach dir erkundigt, als du weg warst.*
▸ believe **in** (+ -ing) sth. *an etw. glauben*	Do you believe in God? *Glaubst du an Gott?*
belong **to** sb. *zu jdm. gehören*	This bag belongs to Lilian. *Diese Tasche gehört Lilian.*
break **down** *kaputtgehen*	My car has broken down three times this year. *Mein Auto ist dieses Jahr schon drei Mal kaputtgegangen.*

bring sth. **up** .... I hate it when he brings up that subject.
etw. zur Sprache bringen/ erwähnen — *Ich hasse es, wenn er dieses Thema zur Sprache bringt.*

▸ carry **out** sth. .... They carried out lots of repairs.
etw. durchführen — *Sie haben viele Reparaturen durchgeführt.*

close sth. **down** .... They've closed down the factory.
etw. schließen/stilllegen/ den Betrieb einstellen — *Sie haben die Fabrik stillgelegt.*

come **across** sth. .... I came across some old photos when I tidied my room.
zufällig auf etw. stoßen — *Ich bin zufällig auf ein paar Fotos gestoßen, als ich mein Zimmer aufräumte.*

come **down with** sth. .... After her trip to Peru she came down with a bad cold.
sich etw. einfangen/krank werden — *Nach ihrer Reise nach Peru bekam sie eine schlimme Erkältung.*

concentrate **on** (+ -ing) sth. ... Why don't you concentrate on your work?
sich auf etw. konzentrieren — *Warum konzentrierst du dich nicht auf deine Arbeit?*

consist **of** sth. .... This cake consists of eggs, flour and sugar.
aus etw. bestehen — *Dieser Kuchen besteht aus Eiern, Mehl und Zucker.*

cope **with** sth. .... How do you cope with all this work?
etw. bewältigen — *Wie bewältigst du nur all die Arbeit?*

▸ deal **with** sth. .... I'll deal with that later.
sich mit etw. befassen/um etw. kümmern — *Ich kümmere mich später darum.*

drop **in (on)** sb. .... Do you mind if I drop in on you for a coffee sometime?
bei jdm. (unerwartet) vorbeischauen — *Hast du was dagegen, wenn ich mal auf einen Kaffee bei dir vorbeischaue?*

drop **out of** sth. .... I dropped out of school when I was 14.
etw. abbrechen (Schule, Universität) — *Mit 14 habe ich die Schule abgebrochen.*

▸ flick/flip **through** sth. *etw. durchblättern*	The only thing she did was flicking/flipping through some magazines. *Das Einzige, was sie tat, war, ein paar Magazine durchzublättern.*
▸ get **along with** sb. *mit jdm. (gut) auskommen*	I never got along with her. *Ich bin nie gut mit ihr ausgekommen.*
get **over** sth. *über etw. hinwegkommen (Krankheit, Angst)*	Will he ever get over his fears? *Wird er je über seine Ängste hinwegkommen?*
give **in to** sb./sth. *jdm./etw. nachgeben*	Never give in to your brother's demands. *Gib nie den Forderungen deines Bruders nach.*
grow **out of** sth. *sich aus etw. entwickeln*	My interest in astronomy grew out of playing with space ships a lot. *Mein Interesse an Astronomie entwickelte sich daraus, dass ich viel mit Raumschiffen spielte.*
▸ hand **down** sth. **to** sb. *jdm. etw. weitergeben/überliefern/vererben*	This ring was handed down to me from my grandmother. *Diesen Ring habe ich von meiner Großmutter geerbt.*
▸ insist **on** (+ -ing) sth. *auf etw. bestehen*	She insisted on going to the zoo. *Sie bestand darauf, in den Zoo zu gehen.*
▸ keep **on** (+ -ing) sth. *fortfahren, etw. zu tun/weitermachen*	If he keeps on being so lazy he'll be kicked out of the team. *Wenn er weiterhin so faul ist, wird er aus dem Team geworfen werden.*
▸ leave sth. **out** *etw. auslassen/weglassen*	She didn't leave anything out. *Sie hat nichts ausgelassen.*
look **after** sb. *sich um jdn. kümmern*	I usually look after her dog when she's away on holiday. *Ich kümmere mich für gewöhnlich um ihren Hund, wenn sie im Urlaub ist.*
look **up to** sb. *jdn. bewundern*	I've always looked up to my older sister. *Ich habe meine ältere Schwester immer bewundert.*

▸ make **up for** sth. ... *etw. wiedergutmachen/entschädigen*	After he had broken the vase, he bought her a present to make up for it. *Nachdem er die Vase kaputt gemacht hatte, kaufte er ihr ein Geschenk als Wiedergutmachung.*
make **up** sth. ... *etw. erfinden (Geschichte)*	The whole story was made up. *Die ganze Geschichte war erfunden.*
▸ name sb./sth. **after** sb./sth. ... *jdn./etw. nach jdm./etw. benennen*	He named his car after his first girlfriend. *Er nannte sein Auto nach seiner ersten Freundin.*
▸ pass **away** ... *sterben*	He passed away last Friday. *Er ist am vergangenen Freitag gestorben.*
pass **out** ... *das Bewusstsein verlieren/in Ohnmacht fallen*	When she heard the news she passed out. *Als sie die Nachricht erfuhr, fiel sie in Ohnmacht.*
put **down** sb. ... *jdn. kritisieren/schlechtmachen*	Stop putting me down in front of my boss. *Hör auf, mich in Gegenwart meines Chefs schlechtzumachen.*
put **off** sth. ... *etw. verschieben*	The concert was put off until next Sunday. *Das Konzert wurde auf den nächsten Sonntag verschoben.*
put sb. **through** (to sb.) ... *jdn. durchstellen/verbinden (Telefon)*	Hold the line, I'll put you through. *Bleiben Sie dran, ich verbinde Sie.*
put **up with** sb./sth. ... *jdn./etw. ertragen*	She's really difficult to put up with. *Sie ist wirklich schwer zu ertragen.*
▸ see sb. **off** ... *jdn. verabschieden/zum Bahnhof etc. bringen*	The whole family went to the station to see aunt Jane off. *Die ganze Familie fuhr zum Bahnhof, um Tante Jane zu verabschieden.*
settle **down** ... *sich (häuslich) niederlassen*	He finally settled down in a small town in Nebraska and got married. *Schließlich ließ er sich in einem kleinen Ort in Nebraska nieder und heiratete.*

slow **down** ...... *langsamer werden*	All cars slowed down as they passed the accident. *Alle Autos wurden langsamer, als sie den Unfall passierten.*
▸ take **after** sb. ...... *nach jdm. kommen*	He takes after his father. *Er kommt nach seinem Vater.*
take **off** sth. ...... *etw. ausziehen*	She took off her coat. *Sie zog ihren Mantel aus.*
tear sth. **down** ...... *etw. abreißen/niederreißen*	The old building was torn down last year. *Das alte Gebäude wurde letztes Jahr abgerissen.*
tear sth. **up** ...... *etw. zerreißen*	He tore up the bill immediately. *Er zerriss die Rechnung sofort.*
think sth. **over** ...... *etw. überdenken*	She didn't give me an answer but said she would first have to think it over. *Sie gab mir keine Antwort, sondern sagte, sie müsse es erst überdenken.*
turn **out** to be sb. ...... *sich als jd. herausstellen*	He turned out to be a nice guy. *Er stellte sich als netter Kerl heraus.*
turn sb./sth. **down** ...... *jdn./etw. ablehnen*	She turned down his marriage proposal. *Sie lehnte seinen Heiratsantrag ab.*

Alphabetische Verbliste Englisch – Deutsch

Hier haben wir für Sie die wichtigsten englischen Verben mit ihren entsprechenden deutschen Übersetzungen alphabetisch aufgelistet. Die rechts angeführten Nummern stellen Konjugationsnummern dar. Auf den Seiten der einzelnen Konjugationstabellen finden Sie diese Nummern wieder. Jene Verben, die hier im Folgenden den jeweiligen Konjugationsnummern zugewiesen sind, werden nach genau diesem Muster konjugiert. Manchen Verben sind auch zwei Konjugationsnummern zugeteilt. Die hervorgehobenen Verben sind als vollständige Konjugationstabellen, also als Muster, vorne im Buch abgedruckt. Der Hinweis (HV) zeigt Ihnen an, dass es sich bei dem jeweiligen Verb um ein Hilfsverb handelt.

A

accomplish *schaffen/erreichen* 5
acquire *erwerben* 5
add *hinzufügen* 5
admire *bewundern* 5
adore *verehren* 5
amble *bummeln* 5
appoint *ernennen* 5
approach *sich nähern* 5
arise *sich erheben* 20
arrest *verhaften* 5
arrive *ankommen* 5
ask *fragen/bitten* 5
assume *annehmen* 5
awake *aufwachen* 10

B

babble *plappern/schwatzen* 5
be *sein* 2
beam *(an)strahlen* 5
bear *tragen/ertragen* 67
become *werden* 6
beg *bitten* 5
begin *beginnen* 7
believe *glauben* 8/5
belong *gehören* 5
bend *biegen/krümmen* 39
bet *wetten* 55
bid *bieten* 33/9
bind *binden* 24
bite *beißen* 9
blab *plappern* 5
bleed *bluten* 50
blow *blasen* 30
borrow *ausleihen* 5
break *brechen/kaputt machen* 10
breed *brüten* 50
bring *mitbringen* 11
broadcast *übertragen* 18
browse *durchblättern* 5
build *bauen* 39
burn *(ver)brennen* 38/5
burst *platzen* 38
buy *kaufen* 12

C

call *rufen* 5
can *können* 13/HV
capture *gefangen nehmen* 5
carry *tragen (Last)* 5
carve *schnitzen* 5
cast *werfen* 18
catch *fangen* 14
cause *verursachen* 5
cease *beenden* 5
censure *zensieren* 5
chat *plaudern* 5
cherish *wertschätzen* 5
chew *kauen* 5
choose *wählen* 15
chop *klein schneiden* 5
climb *klettern* 5
cling *festhalten* 68
coach *coachen* 5
come *kommen* 16
commence *anfangen* 5
compensate *entschädigen* 5
compliment *Komplimente machen* 5
conclude *schlussfolgern* 5
consult *um Rat fragen* 5
contain *enthalten* 5
contemplate *nachdenken* 5
continue *weitermachen* 5
contribute *beisteuern* 5
converse *sich unterhalten* 5
copy *kopieren* 5
cost *kosten* 17
crave *sich sehnen* 5
creep *kriechen* 50

criticize *kritisieren* (5)
crunch *knirschend zerkauen* (5)
cultivate *züchten/ziehen* (5)
cut *schneiden/reduzieren* (18)

D

dangle *herunterhängen* (5)
dare *wagen* (5)
deal *handeln/dealen* (50)
decide *sich entscheiden* (5)
decline *nachlassen/zurückgehen* (5)
decorate *tapezieren* (5)
decrease *abnehmen* (5)
demand *fordern* (5)
demonstrate *zeigen/beweisen* (5)
desire *begehren* (5)
despise *verachten* (5)
destroy *zerstören* (5)
detect *entdecken* (5)
detest *verabscheuen* (5)
develop *sich entwickeln* (5)
devour *verschlingen* (5)
dig *graben* (68)
diminish *verringern* (5)
disbelieve *nicht glauben* (5)
discover *entdecken/finden* (5)
dislike *nicht mögen* (5)
display *auslegen/ausstellen* (5)
dive *tauchen* (5)
do *tun/machen* (3)
doubt *bezweifeln* (5)
draft *entwerfen* (5)
draw *zeichnen/ziehen* (19)
dream *träumen* (50)/(5)
drill *drillen* (5)
drink *trinken* (7)
drive *fahren* (20)
drop *fallen/sinken* (5)
dwell *wohnen* (5)/(39)
dwindle *schwinden/schrumpfen* (5)

E

eat *essen* (21)
end *beenden* (5)
enjoy *genießen* (5)
enquire *sich erkundigen* (5)
exhibit *ausstellen* (5)
exist *existieren* (5)
express *ausdrücken* (5)

F

fall *fallen* (22)
fancy *Lust haben* (5)
feed *füttern* (50)
feel *fühlen* (23)
fetch *holen* (5)
fight *kämpfen* (12)
find *finden* (24)
finish *beenden* (5)
fit *passen* (5)
flee *fliehen* (50)
fling *schleudern/werfen* (68)
flutter *flattern* (5)
fly *fliegen* (25)
forbid *verbieten* (28)
forecast *vorhersagen* (18)
for(e)go *verzichten* (29)
foresee *vorhersehen* (2)
forget *vergessen* (26)
forgive *vergeben* (28)
found *gründen* (5)
freeze *frieren* (61)
function *funktionieren* (5)

G

get *bekommen/besorgen/werden* (27)
give *geben* (28)
glare *grell scheinen* (5)
gleam *glänzen/leuchten* (5)
glide *gleiten* (5)
glimmer *glimmen/schimmern* (5)
glitter *glitzern* (5)
glow *glühen* (5)
go *gehen/fahren* (29)
gossip *schwätzen* (5)
grab *(hastig) ergreifen* (5)
grant *gewähren/billigen* (5)
grasp *begreifen* (5)
graze *grasen* (5)
grind *zermahlen* (24)
grow *wachsen/anbauen* (30)
guess *denken/meinen* (5)
gulp *herunterschlingen* (5)
guzzle *hineinkippen* (5)

H

hang *hängen/hinhängen* (31)
happen *sich ereignen* (5)
hasten *sich beeilen* (5)
hate *hassen* (5)
have *haben* (4)
hear *hören* (32)
help *helfen* (5)
hide *(sich) verstecken* (9)
hike *wandern* (5)
hit *schlagen* (33)
hold *halten* (34)
honour *ehren* (5)
hope *hoffen* (5)
hug *umarmen* (5)
hurl *schleudern* (5)
hurt *wehtun* (38)

Alphabetische Verbliste

I

- idle *faulenzen* 5
- improve *sich verbessern* 5
- increase *zunehmen/ansteigen* 5
- indicate *andeuten/aufweisen* 5
- inform *informieren* 5
- instruct *beibringen* 5

J

- jog *joggen* 5

K

- **keep** *halten* 35
- kiss *küssen* 5
- kneel *sich hinknien* 50
- **know** *kennen/wissen* 36

L

- lack *fehlen* 5
- last *dauern* 5
- launch *lancieren/starten* 5
- **lay** *legen* 37
- lead *führen* 50
- lean *lehnen/sich neigen* 50/5
- leap *springen* 50/5
- **learn** *lernen* 38/5
- leave *weggehen* 50
- **lend** *(ver)leihen* 39
- let *lassen* 55
- **lie** *liegen* 40
- light *erhellen* 33/5
- like *mögen* 5
- loan *verleihen* 5
- loathe *verabscheuen* 5
- **look** *aussehen* 41/5
- **lose** *verlieren* 42
- **love** *lieben* 43/5

M

- maintain *beibehalten* 5
- **make** *machen/tun* 44
- manifest *manifestieren* 5
- march *marschieren* 5
- may *dürfen* HV
- mean *meinen* 50
- **meet** *(sich) treffen* 45
- memorize *einprägen* 5
- mention *erwähnen* 5
- mislay *verlegen* 37
- mistake *falsch verstehen* 63
- move *sich bewegen* 5
- mow *mähen* 58
- **must** *müssen* 46/HV
- **must not** *nicht dürfen* 46/HV

N

- **need** *brauchen* 47/5
- nibble *knabbern* 5
- nominate *berufen* 5
- note *notieren* 5
- notice *bemerken* 5

O

- observe *beobachten* 5
- obtain *erhalten* 5
- occur *sich ereignen/vorkommen* 5
- omit *versäumen* 5
- ought *sollen* HV
- overcome *überwinden/bewältigen* 16
- overlook *übersehen* 41/5
- oversleep *verschlafen* 50
- overtake *überholen* 63
- own *besitzen* 5

P

- paint *malen* 5
- pass *passieren* 5
- **pay** *(be)zahlen* 48
- peck *picken* 5
- perch *sich setzen* 5
- peruse *sorgfältig durchlesen* 5
- pick *auswählen* 5
- pitch *schlagen (Ball)* 5
- place *hinstellen* 5
- plant *anpflanzen* 5
- plod *sich dahinschleppen* 5
- plunge *dramatisch fallen* 5
- ponder *nachdenken* 5
- position *positionieren* 5
- possess *besitzen* 5
- **praise** *loben* 1/5
- prefer *vorziehen* 5
- present *präsentieren* 5
- prove *beweisen* 5
- provide *bereitstellen/zur Verfügung stellen* 5
- punch *schlagen (Faust)* 5
- purchase *käuflich erwerben* 5
- **put** *setzen/stellen/legen* 49

Q

- question *bezweifeln* 5
- query *infrage stellen/bezweifeln* 5
- quit *aufgeben/aufhören* 33

R

- race *rennen* 5
- radiate *strahlen* 5
- reach *erreichen* 5
- **read** *lesen* 50
- realize *sich bewusst werden* 5

recall *sich erinnern* 5
recite *vortragen* 5
reckon *meinen* 5
recognize *wiedererkennen* 5
recollect *sich besinnen* 5
redo *nochmals tun* 3
reduce *verringern* 5
reek *übel riechen* 5
reflect *reflektieren* 5
regard *(aufmerksam) betrachten* 5
regret *bedauern* 5
reimburse *entschädigen* 5
relax *sich entspannen* 5
remain *bleiben* 5
remark *bemerken* 5
remember *sich erinnern* 51/5
repay *zurückzahlen* 48
repose *ausruhen* 5
request *bitten* 5
require *brauchen* 5
resemble *ähneln* 5
rest *ruhen* 5
return *zurückbringen* 5
reveal *zeigen/sehen lassen* 5
rewrite *umschreiben* 70
ride *reiten/fahren* 20
ring *klingeln/anrufen* 7
rise *steigen* 20
run *rennen/laufen* 52
rush *eilen/hetzen* 5

S

saw *sägen* 58/5
say *sagen* 53
scan *kritisch prüfen* 5
scent *wittern* 5
scribble *kritzeln* 5
search *suchen* 5
see *sehen* 2
seek *suchen* 11
seem *scheinen* 54/5
seize *ergreifen* 5
select *auswählen* 5
sell *verkaufen* 64
send *senden/schicken* 39
set *(fest)setzen/stellen* 55
settle *ausgleichen* 5
sew *nähen* 58/5
shake *schütteln* 63
shall *sollen* 56/HV
shatter *zerstören* 5
shimmer *schimmern* 5
shine *scheinen* 57/5
shoot *schießen* 42
shop *einkaufen* 5
show *zeigen* 58/5
shrink *schrumpfen/einlaufen* 7/68
shut *schließen* 18
sign *unterschreiben* 5
sing *singen* 7
sink *sinken* 7/68
sit *sitzen/sich setzen* 59
sketch *skizzieren* 5
slap *einen Klaps geben* 5
sleep *schlafen* 50
slice *in Scheiben schneiden* 5
sling *schleudern* 68
slip *ausrutschen* 5
slit *aufschlitzen* 33
smash *zerschlagen* 5
smell *riechen* 60/5
smile *lächeln* 5
soar *hochfliegen* 5
sound *klingen* 5
sow *säen* 58/5
sparkle *funkeln* 5
speak *sprechen* 61
spell *buchstabieren* 39/5
spend *ausgeben* 39
spill *verschütten* 33/5
spin *spinnen/drehen* 7/68
spit *spucken* 59
split *spalten* 33
spoil *verderben* 5
spread *ausbreiten* 55
spring *springen* 7/68
sprint *sprinten* 5
squat *in der Hocke sitzen* 5
stagger *torkeln/wanken* 5
start *starten/anfangen* 5
stay *bleiben* 5
steal *stehlen* 61
stick *kleben/hängen* 68
sting *stechen* 68
stink *stinken* 7/68
stop *anhalten* 5
stretch *strecken* 5
stride *schreiten* 70
strike *schlagen* 62
strive *streben* 70/5
stroll *schlendern* 5
study *studieren* 5
stumble *straucheln* 5
suit *stehen* 5
suppose *annehmen* 5
surrender *ergeben* 5
suspect *anzweifeln* 5
swallow *schlucken* 5
swear *schwören* 67
sweep *kehren/fegen* 50
swim *schwimmen* 7
swing *schwingen* 68

T

take *nehmen/bringen* 63
talk *sich unterhalten* 5
taste *schmecken* 5
teach *unterrichten* 11
tear *(zer)reißen* 67

tell *erzählen* 64
think *denken* 65
throw *werfen* 66
thrust *stoßen* 18
tiptoe *auf Zehenspitzen gehen* 5
toil *schuften* 5
toss *werfen/schleudern* 5
touch *berühren* 5
track *aufspüren* 5
train *trainieren* 5
traspass *unbefugt betreten* 5
travel *reisen* 5
trip *stolpern* 5
trudge *sich schleppen* 5
trust *vertrauen* 5
twinkle *blitzen* 5

U

undergo *durchmachen/erdulden* 29
underwrite *zustimmen/Zustimmung geben* 70
undo *rückgängig machen* 3

V

vomit *sich übergeben* 5

W

wade *(durch Wasser) waten* 5
wait *warten* 5
wake *aufwachen* 10
walk *gehen* 5
wander *bummeln* 5
want *wollen* 5
watch *schauen* 5
wear *tragen (Kleidung)* 67
weave *weben* 61
weep *weinen* 50
will *werden/wollen* HV
win *gewinnen* 68
wind *wickeln/spulen* 24
wish *wünschen* 5
withdraw *abheben (Geld)* 19
work *arbeiten* 69/5
wring *auswringen* 68
write *schreiben* 70

Alphabetische Verbliste Deutsch – Englisch

Hier haben wir für Sie die wichtigsten deutschen Verben mit den entsprechenden englischen Übersetzungen alphabetisch aufgelistet. Auch hier steht die rechts angeführte Nummer für die Konjugationsnummer, also das Muster, nach dem das entsprechende englische Verb konjugiert wird. Die englischen Entsprechungen der hervorgehobenen deutschen Verben sind als vollständige Konjugationstabellen vorne im Buch abgedruckt.

A

abheben (Geld) withdraw 19
abnehmen decrease 5
ähneln resemble 5
andeuten/aufweisen indicate 5
anfangen commence 5
anhalten stop 5
ankommen arrive 5
annehmen assume 5
annehmen suppose 5
anpflanzen plant 5
(an)strahlen beam 5
anzweifeln suspect 5
arbeiten work 69/5
auf Zehenspitzen gehen tiptoe 5
aufgeben/aufhören quit 33
aufschlitzen slit 33
aufspüren track 5
aufwachen wake 10
aufwachen awake 10
ausbreiten spread 55
ausdrücken express 5
ausgeben spend 39
ausgleichen settle 5
auslegen/ausstellen display 5
ausleihen borrow 5
ausruhen repose 5
ausrutschen slip 5
aussehen look 41
ausstellen exhibit 5
auswählen pick 5
auswählen select 5
auswringen wring 68

B

bauen build 39

bedauern regret 5
sich beeilen hasten 5
beenden cease 5
beenden end 5
beenden finish 5
begehren desire 5
beginnen begin 7
begreifen grasp 5
beibehalten maintain 5
beibringen instruct 5
beißen bite 9
beisteuern contribute 5
bekommen/besorgen/ werden get 27
bemerken notice 5
bemerken remark 5
beobachten observe 5
bereitstellen/zur Verfügung stellen provide 5
berufen nominate 5
berühren touch 5
sich besinnen recollect 5
besitzen own 5
besitzen possess 5
(aufmerksam) betrachten regard 5
sich bewegen move 5
beweisen prove 5
bewundern admire 5
sich bewusst werden realize 5
(be)zahlen pay 48
bezweifeln doubt 5
bezweifeln question 5
biegen/krümmen bend 39
bieten bid 33/9
binden bind 24
bitten beg 5
bitten request 5
blasen blow 30
bleiben remain 5
bleiben stay 5
blitzen twinkle 5
bluten bleed 50
brauchen need 47/5
brauchen require 5
brechen/kaputt machen break 10
brüten breed 50
buchstabieren spell 39/5
bummeln amble 5
bummeln wander 5

C

coachen coach 5

D

sich dahinschleppen plod 5
dauern last 5
denken think 65
denken/meinen guess 5
dramatisch fallen plunge 5
drillen drill 5
durchblättern browse 5
durchmachen/erdulden undergo 29
dürfen may HV
nicht dürfen must not 46/HV

E

ehren honour 5
eilen/hetzen rush 5
einkaufen shop 5
einprägen memorize 5
entdecken detect 5
entdecken/finden discover 5
enthalten contain 5
entschädigen compensate 5
entschädigen reimburse 5
sich entscheiden decide 5
sich entspannen relax 5
entwerfen draft 5
sich entwickeln develop 5
sich ereignen happen 5
sich ereignen/vorkommen occur 5
ergeben surrender 5
ergreifen seize 5
(hastig) ergreifen grab 5
erhalten obtain 5
sich erheben arise 20
erhellen light 33/5
sich erinnern recall 5
sich erinnern remember 51/5
sich erkundigen enquire 5
ernennen appoint 5
erreichen reach 5
erwähnen mention 5
erwerben acquire 5
erzählen tell 64
essen eat 21
existieren exist 5

F

fahren drive 20
fallen fall 22
fallen/sinken drop 5
falsch verstehen mistake 63
fangen catch 14
faulenzen idle 5
fehlen lack 5
festhalten cling 68
(fest)setzen/stellen set 55
finden find 24
flattern flutter 5
fliegen fly 25
fliehen flee 50
fordern demand 5
fragen/bitten ask 5
frieren freeze 61
fühlen feel 23

führen lead (50)
funkeln sparkle (5)
funktionieren function (5)
füttern feed (50)

G

geben give (28)
gefangen nehmen capture (7)
gehen walk (5)
gehen/fahren go (29)
gehören belong (5)
genießen enjoy (5)
gewähren/billigen grant (5)
gewinnen win (68)
glänzen/leuchten gleam (5)
glauben believe (8)/(5)
nicht glauben disbelieve (5)
gleiten glide (5)
glimmen/schimmern glimmer (5)
glitzern glitter (5)
glühen glow (5)
graben dig (68)
grasen graze (5)
grell scheinen glare (5)
gründen found (5)

H

haben have (4)
halten hold (34)
halten keep (35)
handeln/dealen deal (50)
hängen/hinhängen hang (31)
hassen hate (5)
helfen help (5)
herunterhängen dangle (5)
herunterschlingen gulp (5)
hineinkippen guzzle (5)
sich hinknien kneel (50)
hinstellen place (5)
hinzufügen add (5)
hochfliegen soar (5)
hoffen hope (5)
holen fetch (5)
hören hear (32)

I

in der Hocke sitzen squat (5)
infrage stellen/bezweifeln query (5)
In Scheiben schneiden slice (5)
informieren inform (5)

J

joggen jog (5)

K

kämpfen fight (12)
kauen chew (5)
kaufen buy (12)
käuflich erwerben purchase (5)
kehren sweep (50)
kennen/wissen know (36)
Klaps geben slap (5)
kleben/hängen stick (68)
klein schneiden chop (5)
klettern climb (5)
klingeln/anrufen ring (7)
klingen sound (5)
knabbern nibble (5)
knirschend zerkauen crunch (5)
kommen come (16)
Komplimente machen compliment (5)
können can (13)/(HV)
kopieren copy (5)
kosten cost (17)
kriechen creep (50)
kritisieren criticize (5)
kritisch prüfen scan (5)
kritzeln scribble (5)
küssen kiss (5)

L

lächeln smile (5)
lancieren/starten launch (5)
lassen let (55)
legen lay (37)
lehnen/sich neigen lean (50)/(5)
lernen learn (38)
lesen read (50)
lieben love (43)/(5)
liegen lie (40)
loben praise (1)/(5)
Lust haben fancy (5)

M

machen/tun make (44)
mähen mow (58)
malen paint (5)
manifestieren manifest (5)
marschieren march (5)
meinen mean (50)
meinen reckon (5)
mitbringen bring (11)
mögen like (5)
nicht mögen dislike (5)
müssen must (46)/(HV)
nicht müssen do not have to (46)/(4)

N

nachdenken contemplate (5)
nachdenken ponder (5)
nachlassen/zurückgehen decline (5)
nähen sew (58)/(5)
sich nähern approach (5)
nehmen/bringen take (63)
nochmals tun redo (3)
notieren note (5)

P

- *passen* fit 5
- *passieren* pass 5
- *picken* peck 5
- *platzen* burst 38
- *plappern* blab 5
- *plappern/schwatzen* blabber 5
- *plaudern* chat 5
- *positionieren* position 5
- *präsentieren* present 5

R

- *reflektieren* reflect 5
- *reisen* travel 5
- *reiten/fahren* ride 20
- *rennen* race 5
- ***rennen/laufen*** run 52
- ***riechen*** smell 60
- *rückgängig machen* undo 3
- *rufen* call 5
- *ruhen* rest 5

S

- *säen* sow 58/5
- ***sagen*** say 53
- *sägen* saw 58/5
- *schaffen/erreichen* accomplish 5
- *schauen* watch 5
- ***scheinen*** seem 54/5
- ***scheinen*** shine 57/5
- *schießen* shoot 42
- *schimmern* shimmer 5
- *schlafen* sleep 50
- ***schlagen*** hit 33
- ***schlagen*** strike 62
- *schlagen (Ball)* pitch 5
- *schlagen (Faust)* punch 5
- *schlendern* stroll 5
- *sich schleppen* trudge 5
- *schleudern* hurl 5
- *schleudern* sling 68
- *schleudern/werfen* fling 68
- *schließen* shut 18
- *schlucken* swallow 5
- *schlussfolgern* conclude 5
- *schmecken* taste 5
- ***schneiden/reduzieren*** cut 18
- *schnitzen* carve 5
- ***schreiben*** write 70
- *schreiten* stride 70
- *schrumpfen* shrink 7/68
- *schuften* toil 5
- *schütteln* shake 63
- *schwätzen* gossip 5
- *schwimmen* swim 7
- *schwinden/schrumpfen* dwindle 5
- *schwingen* swing 68
- *schwören* swear 67
- *sehen* see 2
- *sich sehnen* crave 5
- ***sein*** be 2
- *senden/schicken* send 39
- *sich setzen* perch 5
- ***setzen/stellen/legen*** put 49
- *singen* sing 7
- *sinken* sink 7/68
- ***sitzen/sich setzen*** sit 59
- *skizzieren* sketch 5
- *sollen* ought HV
- ***sollen*** shall 56/HV
- *sorgfältig durchlesen* peruse 5
- *spalten* split 33
- *spinnen/drehen* spin 7/68
- ***sprechen*** speak 61
- *springen* leap 50/5
- *springen* spring 7/68
- *sprinten* sprint 5
- *spucken* spit 59
- *starten/anfangen* start 5
- *stechen* sting 68
- *stehen* suit 5
- *stehlen* steal 61
- *steigen* rise 20
- *stinken* stink 7/68
- *stolpern* trip 5
- *stoßen* thrust 18
- *strahlen* radiate 5
- *straucheln* stumble 5
- *streben* strive 5/70
- *strecken* stretch 5
- *studieren* study 5
- *suchen* search 5
- *suchen* seek 11

T

- *tapezieren* decorate 5
- *tauchen* dive 5
- *torkeln/wanken* stagger 5
- *tragen/ertragen* bear 67
- *tragen (Last)* carry 5
- ***tragen*** *(Kleidung)* wear 67
- *trainieren* train 5
- *träumen* dream 50/5
- ***(sich) treffen*** meet 45
- *trinken* drink 7
- ***tun/machen*** do 3

U

- *übel riechen* reek 5
- *sich übergeben* vomit 5
- *überholen* overtake 63
- *übersehen* overlook 41/5
- *übertragen* broadcast 18
- *überwinden/bewältigen* overcome 16
- *um Rat fragen* consult 5
- *umarmen* hug 5
- *umschreiben* rewrite 70
- *unbefugt betreten* traspass 5

sich unterhalten talk (5)
sich unterhalten converse (5)
unterrichten teach (11)
unterschreiben sign (5)

V

verabscheuen detest (5)
verabscheuen loathe (5)
verachten despise (5)
sich verbessern improve (5)
verbieten forbid (28)
(ver)brennen burn (38)/(5)
verderben spoil (5)
verehren adore (5)
vergeben forgive (28)
vergessen forget (26)
verhaften arrest (5)
verkaufen sell (64)
verlegen mislay (37)
(ver)leihen lend (39)
verleihen loan (5)
verlieren lose (42)
verringern diminish (5)
verringern reduce (5)
versäumen omit (5)
verschlafen oversleep (50)
verschlingen devour (5)
verschütten spill (33)/(5)
sich verstecken hide (9)
vertrauen trust (5)
verursachen cause (5)
verzichten for(e)go (29)
vorhersagen forecast (18)
vorhersehen foresee (2)
vortragen recite (5)
vorziehen prefer (5)

W

wachsen/anbauen grow (30)
wagen dare (5)
wählen choose (15)
wandern hike (5)
warten wait (5)
(durch Wasser) waten wade (5)
weben weave (61)
weggehen leave (50)
wehtun hurt (38)
weinen weep (50)
weitermachen continue (5)
werden become (6)
werden/wollen will (HV)
werfen cast (18)
werfen throw (66)
werfen/schleudern toss (5)
wertschätzen cherish (5)
wetten bet (55)
wickeln wind (24)
wiedererkennen recognize (5)
wittern scent (5)
wohnen dwell (5)/(39)
wollen want (5)
wünschen wish (5)

Z

zeichnen/ziehen draw (19)
zeigen show (58)/(5)
zeigen/beweisen demonstrate (5)
zeigen/sehen lassen reveal (5)
zensieren censure (5)
zermahlen grind (24)
(zer)reißen tear (67)
zerschlagen smash (5)
zerstören destroy (5)
zerstören shatter (5)
züchten/ziehen cultivate (5)
zunehmen/ansteigen increase (5)
zurückbringen return (5)
zurückzahlen repay (48)
zustimmen/Zustimmung geben underwrite (70)